JENA - AUERSTAEDT

The Triumph of the Eagle

F.-G. Hourtoulle

(Translated from the French by Alan McKay)

Uniform plates by André Jouineau
Maps by Morgan Gillard

Histoire & Collections - Paris

ACKNOWLEDGEMENTS
    The Author wishes to thank his friends collectors who have helped
him in illustrating this book, particularly Christian Blondieau,
Pierre Brétégnier, Jacques Garnier and Jacques Meyniel..

CONTENTS

A WORD ON FRENCH MILITARY TERMINOLOGY

In the many biographical notices to be found in this book (especially pp. 55 to 82 and pp. 101 to 111), special rules have been adopted. See p. 119. for details.

Frederic-William III, King of Prussia 1770-1840, from a miniature by Henri Plötz.

Louise, Queen of Prussia, 1776-1810, from a miniature by the Chevalier de Châteaubourg.

INTRODUCTION

There were not one, but two quite different battles, at Jena. Napoleon fought Hohenlohe's army at Jena. Davout fought the main army of the King of Prussia at Auerstaedt on his own, accomplishing the amazing feat of routing the elite of this arrogant army which had thought itself the best in the world.

The Emperor's skills were quite remarkable during the deployment phase of his strategy: how he organised his army and how he positioned his reserves at quite some distance from the theatre of operations. He managed to think of everything, of Italy, of Holland, of Boulogne, etc. He directed the movements of his army corps in the most admirable way, compared with his opponent who was caught up in discussions and hesitations. Napoleon thought quickly, acted quickly and could only succeed.

He had however dreamt of fighting a single decisive battle. This, he thought, would take place on the 16th October. But the enemy managed to slip away; instead of the whole of the King of Prussia's army, he found only Hohenlohe.

Unlike Austerlitz, where the adversaries had been drawn up the day before in front of each other ready for battle, Jena was the scene of two separate battles which took place spontaneously between armies in full strategic movement.

Napoleon was accompanied only by his grenadiers and his chasseurs à pied of the Guard; the rest joined him on the 18th; his other corps were still on the march. At the beginning of the battle he was only able to commit four divisions, but reinforcements were on their way. A part of the cavalry reserve, consisting of Klein's division and two of d'Hautpoul's regiments of cuirassiers, arrived for the final phase of the battle. Five divisions arrived eventually onto the battlefield in support and the last were used to chase the defeated enemy.

Davout was all by himself at Auerstaedt and had to deal with the King of Prussia's main force in front of him. Sahuc and his dragoons – as well as the light cavalry from the cavalry reserve – were impeded by Bernadotte's remaining inactive in Domburg and not coming to the help of either Davout or Napoleon.

On both sites, on the 14th October 1806, the Prussian army took a beating. It fled and was annihilated soon afterwards. None of Napoleon's other victories had been, or would be, as effective or as complete.

Lannes became the heros of Saalfeld and Jena. Davout was victorious at Auerstaedt and his title of Duke was well-deserved, as would be that of Prince some time later. Out of these soldiers, now at the best of their form, would be drawn the cadres of the Grande Armée.

THE REASONS FOR GOING TO WAR

PRUSSIA, hesitating and very much sought after, had finally decided to join the Coalition at the end of 1805. But it was too late: the victory at Austerlitz put paid to this move. King Frederick-William III had become 'friendly' towards Napoleon.

The Schönbrunn Convention was negotiated with the Emperor on 15th December 1805. In this convention, Hannover, still theoretically English was ceded to Prussia in exchange for the Principalities of Cleves and Neufchatel, the Grand Duchy of Berg, which was to be given to Murat and the Marquisate of Anspach, which returned to Bavaria.

Quite unjustifiably, the King tried to get more but Napoleon wouldn't have it, and the text was signed on 15th February 1806.

Prussia was getting more and more hostile towards France, rather like Tsar Alexander who had not got over his defeat. Queen Louise of Prussia, who worshipped the Tsar, was the head of the war-party which included Prince Louis-Ferdinand, the Prince of Hohenlohe and Generals Rüchel and Blücher. The King, like Pfühl, his weathercock of a counsellor, was still hesitating; the

Duke of Brunswick, together with Kalckreuth and Scharnhorst, headed the peace party.

Napoleon had meanwhile completed the annexation of Italy. Since Masséna had conquered Naples, the Kingdom of the Two Sicilies was given to Joseph on 31st March and Prince Eugene was made Viceroy of Italy. Marmont was keeping an eye on things in Dalmatia.

In Holland, Louis was made King on 24th May. Things were going well for the Bonapartes.

The Rhine Confederation, protected by France, was set up on 12th July 1806. For the moment, only Hesse remained outside it.

The secret Russo-Prussian agreement was reinforced the same day in the form of a pact.

*Queen Louise with her own 5th Queen's Dragoons Regiment.
Illustration by Richard Knötel in the book 'Königin Luise':
'...She was taken in the evening of the 13th October to Stettin
to join her husband after the defeat at Custrin'.*

THE GERMAN STATES
IN 1806
(Treaty of Presburg 1805)

RHINE CONFEDERATION
Confederation borders
A - *Principality of Aremberg*
F - *Principality of Frankfurt*
I - *Principality of Isenburg*

Napoleon believed in peace and negotiated with the Tsar. An agreement whereby Russia recognised the Kingdom of the Two Sicilies and the independence of the Ionian Islands, and removed its troops from Cattaro whose occupation had been seen as a provocation, was signed on July 20th with Ambassador Oubril. In compensation, French troops were to be evacuated from Germany within three months of the ratification of this agreement.

Austria and Prussia recognised the Rhine Confederation, which left only England where Fox was in power. Napoleon started negotiations and was prepared to hand back Hannover, in exchange for some suitable compensation for Prussia... Russia too, as usual, was playing its own little game with England; as soon as they learnt that Hannover might become English again, the Prussian war party went on the rampage.

Napoleon was thinking about the 15th August, his birthday. It had been conceived in the grand manner in order to comme-morate his victories. He would also have liked to get his soldiers back: they had deserved this homecoming. At the beginning of this month of August, he still thought that everything would work out. In a letter on 17th August, he even told Berthier, commanding six army groups spread over Germany, to organise the return of the troops.

The despatches coming from Ambassador Laforest in Berlin were getting more and more alarming however. Troops were mobilising and forming up everywhere and there were more and more provocations. On the 26th, the columns began marching westwards. On the 3rd September, the Tsar threw out the conventions which had been proposed earlier. Napoleon halted the armies which were on their way back to France and although the Emperor had promised to protect her, Saxony started to mobilise.

On the 5th September, the veil was lifted and war seemed inevitable.

Troopers of the Prussian Guard: Gardes du corps regiment, n° 13 (left) and Gendarmes regiment, n° 10 (right).
These horsemen were to sharpen their sabres on the steps of the French Embassy in Berlin as a provocation.
(Brunon Collection)

A MODEL OF PLANNING

The Napoleon computer now got going with its accustomed efficiency.

The orders which were sent off in every direction during this month of September 1806 make impressive reading. These precise and detailed orders are a marvel of territorial and military organisation.

In Holland there was an opening for Louis and General Michaud on the Wesel. Along the Rhine a reserve army was made up, with Kellermann forming the national guard into legions. Mortier was in the process of forming his 8th Corps which would be stationed in the Frankfurt area.

Brune was at Boulogne, Junot was in command in Paris, and Italy and Dalmatia were covered.

The new allies in the Rhine Confederation mobilised their reserve corps. Bavaria provided 10,000 men under the supervision of Jérôme Bonaparte.

Regiments' third battalions or fourth squadrons were detached to the reserves which were then spread out along the Rhine in order to receive conscripts: majors were put in command only if the colonels were absent.

All details were studied. The Breidt company would transport only the flour. This company was in the end deemed insufficient and was eventually replaced in 1807 by the Train des Équipages (French Army Service Corps). The Emperor thought of everything that had to be ordered: horses, carriages, tools, ambulances, and even the dixies – the German model like the water-bottles.

One important point: shoes. Each man needed three pairs, one on his feet, two in his haversack, and a fourth pair provided for in reserve. Greatcoats supplied from Augsburg were also needed; the 21st Light was to pick them up on the way.

Wurzburg and Forcheim were designated as the two strong points and an arsenal, good artillery defence, ammunition works and ten ovens for bread-making – each oven guaranteed bread for 3,000 men – were set up there. There was also a hospital for 500 sick or wounded…

Troops were concentrating and marching everywhere. Mobility was the key factor for Napoleon. It was one of his principal strengths. But you had to know how to organise all this, bear in mind that war fed on war and that an army was trained for just that. He ordered a reduction in the number of carriages in the main pool, no more than 400 reserved for ammunition. This was in order to prevent any congestion. It was always a question of mobility!

Napoleon's strategy was quite simple: it was a line straight to the enemy's capital by forcing a passage through on his left, this time near the Austrian border, which at the moment seemed to be quiet.

It was a three-pronged march by the corps; each group was within easy reach of its neighbours so as to have concentrated striking power at the right moment, should a battle need to be fought. For such an objective, having the right tools was essential: these were the soldiers and their leaders. And Napoleon at this time had the best army in the world; it had been formed in the Revolutionary mould by men who knew that their future depended on their merit. The regiments were full of veterans and the officers, the generals and the marshalls had once been grenadiers or hussars, in their early days.

THE TIME FOR INTELLIGENCE

The time has come to review intelligence gathering, an area controlled by Savary.

At headquarters, Berthier asked for money to pay his agents; but he also had a group of officers, taken principally from the Engineers, who made up a sort of 'MI5' of the day. As the war was not yet official, they were entrusted with missions on Saxon and Prussian territory. They knew how to be discreet. Here are the principal characters who operated during this month of September.

- Colonel *Blein*, from the Ponts et Chaussées School, colonel of Engineers in 1805, LH [1], OLH in 1807. Baron, Russian Campaign, General in 1813, CtLH in 1814. Wounded during the Fieschi outrage in 1835, GdOLH in 1837, died in 1847. He went to Leipzig, to the Fair, ostensibly to buy maps.

- Battalion commander *Guilleminot* who came through the historical and geographical service. This officer became a General in 1808, Baron, on the staff of Eugène de Beauharnais in Russia, wounded at Borodino, Major General in 1813, at Waterloo in front of Hougoumont. CrSL in 1821, fought in Spain in 1823, GdCxLH, GdCxSL, GdCx of Saint Ferdinand, Pair de France.

- Battalion commander *Huart*, from the Metz School, wounded at Montebello, present at Marengo, LH. Major and OLH in 1814, Strasbourg in 1815, Colonel in 1828, retired in 1834.

- Battalion commander *Legrand*, from Mézières, histographer with Moreau, LH, Colonel in 1808, Chevalier and OLH in1809, wounded. Mentioned at Berg-op-Zoom in 1814, retired in 1815, honorary Maréchal de camp in 1822.

- Captain *Rémond*, from the Engineers, Battalion commander in January 1807, wounded at Heilsberg, with Soult in Spain. General in 1811, wounded and Baron in 1813, retired in 1848, then a reservist.

There were also Captains *Conche* and *Beaulieu*.

Reports from these officers were very precious because they were drawn up by technical experts who not only judged troop

___
1. Please refer to p.119 for the meaning of all abbreviations connected to orders and decorations.

movements, their morale, and their behaviour, but were also capable of analysing routes, terrain, resources, etc.

As well as the intelligence officers, there were also the various other agents who had to be paid, such as the famous Schulmeister; the front line army corps sent agents too. For example, the 5th Corps put in claims for money for precisely this purpose. They needed 3,000 francs. On 1st October, Murat sent two students off on one such mission. Several of these agents were shot by the Prussians.

INTELLIGENCE ANALYSIS

On 25th September, it was already known that the King of Prussia had slept at Naumburgand, that he was heading for Weimar and that Rüchel was at Erfurt. Arrogant officers talked of heading for Wurzburg. On the other hand a number of deserters had been caught and Napoleon had already taken measures to regroup them at Landau under the command of General Zajonchek.

On 29th September, Huart reached Coburg and Fulda but was turned back.

Guilleminot said that a camp should be prepared at Hof and that the Saale was fordable up-river. Other watercourses were fordable, the bridges were of stone, the country was rich. Hohenlohe had gone to Hof and was supervising the Saxon troops who had been mixed with the Prussians. Hohenlohe, together with Prince Louis, would have 62,000 men at his disposal and would form the left wing. The main army was known to be 75,000 men strong and

Saxon horsemen. Left, a NCO of von Clemens' light horse regiment. Right, a trooper of the carabiniers regiment in full dress. (Brunon Collection).

Saxon generals (left) and Saxon infantry (right). (Brunon Collection).

Rüchel's right wing was estimated at 40,000. As for the Russians, they were known to be reforming an army on the Bug.

The Prussians were very irritated, the Saxons were not happy at having been dispersed and the young were bellicose. Although theoretically at war with the Prussians, the English nevertheless maintained envoys with the Prussian generals and many were in Dresden with the Saxons. Prince Louis, who was a very debauched person and brought back home every night drunk, nonetheless had spirit. The Duke of Brunswick however, slow and undecided like the older generals, did not want war.

Rémond announced the presence of Tauentzien at Hof with 8,000 men.

THE ORGANISATION OF THE OFFENSIVE

The positions were firming up and the Emperor began regrouping his army corps. A base for the vanguard was established in the town of Kronach, on the principal axis. Davout sent in Battalion commander Breuille [1] to get the position ready for defence.

Supervising the Commissariat, Napoleon replaced Villemanzy, considered as '*a grumbler and a formalist*', with Daru. The French machine got under way whilst the Prussians were still hesitating, still discussing, and still being inefficient.

At Bamberg, the Emperor drew up his famous proclamation, worthy of Victor Hugo. Here are some extracts:

'*Soldiers, the order for your return to France had been given… A triumphal return was awaiting you… War cries in Berlin could be heard. For two months, we have been provoked every day, more and more.*

They want us to evacuate Germany even though they are brandishing their arms… Soldiers, there isn't one of you who wants to return to France by any other way than that of honour. We must only return through the arches of triumph…'

THE 7th OF OCTOBER

An ultimatum came from the King of Prussia. It announced the beginning of hostilities from the 8th. Things were now clear.

The army corps were reviewed and their routes defined. Napoleon adopted the following disposition:

- the left wing would be made up of Lannes' 5th Corps, with Augereau's 7th following. They would march up the road which went through Cobourg, towards Saalfeld and Jena;

- Murat would be in the centre with Lasalle's cavalry and Milhaud, who would scout for Bernadotte's 1st Corps. He was to be followed by Davout's 3rd Corps. The Emperor, the Guard and the cavalry reserve would follow on the Bamberg road at Schleiz and Gera;

- the right wing would include Soult's 4th Corps followed by Ney's 6th Corps. They were to pass through Bayreuth and head for Hof.

There were therefore three parallel lines moving forwards. They were not very far apart; this would enable them to be manoeuvered and regrouped quickly into a single army in the case of a bigger battle. Facing them, or rather to the left of these columns, were the immobile Prussians, whose General Staff was still hesitating. They didn't want to wait for the Russians, as they considered they were easily capable of defeating the French all by themselves. They had to hold the road to Berlin; no doubt they should have attacked Napoleon. But in order to attack him, wouldn't it have been better to head for Neustadt?

More discussions and palaver. The old generals were for defending, the war-mongers for attacking.

Napoleon didn't hesitate at all; he gave orders and was obeyed. If all went well, he'd be able to turn the Prussian left and cut the road to Berlin, by which the Russians were supposed to be coming some day… Apparently they hadn't set out yet.

---

1. From the Engineers, LH, Colonel in 1809, OLH, retired in 1821, honorary Maréchal de camp.

POSITIONS
8th OCTOBER 1806

French troops

Prussian and Saxon troops

(French and German identifications of units have been retained)

0 25 50 km

MAGDEBURG

Würtemberg

Brunswick

Halberstadt

Elbe

KINGDOM
OF
PRUSSIA

Halle

Merseburg

LEIPZIG

Laucha

Freyburg

Weissenfels

Dresden

Eckartsberg

Naumburg

Camburg

Zeitz

Rüchel

Eisenach

Friedrich Wilhelm III

Dresden

Gotha

Erfurt

Weimar

Dornburg

Weimar

Iéna

Gera

Hohenlohe

Saxons

KINGDOM
OF
SAXONY

Kahla

Roda

Rudolstadt

Tauentzien

Neustadt

Auma

Prinz
Lüdwig

Saalfeld

Schleiz

Dresden

Milhaud

Grafenthal

Watier

Saalburg

Ebersdorf

Lasalle

Plauen

1er Corps
Bernadotte

Hof

Coburg

4e Don
dragons

Kronach

Beaumont

Sahuc

3e Don dragons

Lichtenfels

Scheinfurth

5e Corps

Davout

3e Corps

Lannes

4e Corps

Soult

Baireuth

AUSTRIAN
EMPIRE

Klein

Augereau

Bamberg

7e Corps

Cuirassiers
& carabiniers
D'Hautpoul
& Nansouty

1re Don
dragons

Garde

Ney

6e Corps

Wurzburg

Saxon grenadiers in the field. (Brunon Collection).

THE OPPOSING FORCES

THE PRUSSIANS AND THE SAXONS

The forces of the King of Prussia were split up as follows:

THE PRUSSIAN ARMY OF THE KING, THE PRINCIPAL ARMY

First this included a vanguard division entrusted to the Duke of Saxony-Weimar which was sent on to Erfurt, towards the Weser. This unit, 11,000 strong, was not able to join up and did not therefore take part in the battle of Jena on the 14th October. It was counted amongst Rüchel's troops.

The other divisions confronted Davout at Auerstadt. The King and Queen Louise accompanied this army, which included the elite of the Prussian troops. Here is its composition, which we will consider in more detail when discussing the battle of Auerstaedt.

✣ THE PRINCE OF ORANGE'S DIVISION

Two brigades of infantry, one of cavalry and two light battalions. For artillery, two 12-pounder batteries, one horse battery and the regimental pieces. A total of 11 battalions, 15 squadrons and three batteries of which one horse artillery.

✣ VON WARTENSLEBEN'S DIVISION

Same composition, but with an extra battery of 12-pounder.

✣ VON SCHMETTAU'S DIVISION

This had one extra battalion.

RESERVE (VON KALCKREUTH)

✣ VON KUNHEIM'S DIVISION

It included the Prussian Guard and had eight battalions, 15 squadrons and three batteries of which one horse artillery.

✣ VON ARNIM'S DIVISION

With 10 battalions, 10 squadrons and three batteries of which one horse artillery.

Blücher joined up with this army for the battle.

✣ THE PRINCE OF WURTEMBURG'S CORPS

This corps, whose total strength was estimated at 15,000 men was the reserve corps, quartered at Magdeburg. It advanced along the Halle road, too late to do anything.

PRO GLORIA ET PATRIA

Officer in full dress

Officer in service dress

Musketeer in field dress

NCO of the Grenadiers in service dress

NCO of the Grenadiers in field dress

Grenadier in field dress

Officer in field dress

Rifleman in full dress

Fife player in full dress

Drummer in full dress

Horn player in full dress

Sapper

Guard IR n° 15

Grenadiers

Leib Coy

Company of Musketeers

André Jouineau © Histoire & Collections 1998

Saxon troops 1806-1807. From left to right, Price Albrecht's Light Horse, Niesemenschel Fusilier Regiment, Kochitzski Cuirassiers, Bevilaqua Grenadier Regiment (Plate taken from 'Les Saxons dans nos rangs').

PRINCE HOHENLOHE'S ARMY

This was the army which confronted Napoleon at Jena. Towards the end of the battle it was helped by Rüchel's Corps. It included:

✜ PRINCE LOUIS-FERDINAND'S VANGUARD

Nine and a half battalions, 18 squadrons and three batteries of which one horse artillery. It will be reviewed with Saalfeld.

✜ VON ZEZSCHWITZ'S (SAXON) DIVISION

12 battalions, 16 squadrons and four and a half batteries of which one and a half horse artillery.

✜ VON GRAWERT'S DIVISION

11 battalions, 25 squadrons and three and a half batteries.

✜ TAUENTZIEN'S CORPS

This formed the vanguard, covering the left of the army. This corps had nine battalions, nine squadrons and a mortar battery at its disposal.

✜ VON PRITTWITZ'S RESERVE DIVISION

This had eight and a half battalions, nine squadrons and three batteries of which one horse artillery.

This mass represented therefore 33,400 infantrymen, 11,800 horsemen and 15 batteries, with about 2,000 artillerymen. To this has to be added Rüchel's Corps which although it arrived late, did actually take part in the end of the battle.

✜ RÜCHEL'S CORPS

Some elements of this corps were far away and could not get there in time. Without them, it consisted of 15 battalions, 13 squadrons and 3 batteries.

There was also the Duke of Weimar's Corps which was more to the west.

If one takes into account the losses which these corps suffered in the preliminary fighting and from desertions, Hohenlohe's army had a total strength of 52,000 combatants with 15 batteries, including Rüchel's troops. They were present at the battle of Jena, facing Napoleon, but they were dispersed and arrived one after the other.

THE SAXON TROOPS

These troops were mainly integrated into Hohenlohe's army and they have been counted as such. This dispersal didn't meet with the approval of the Saxons, who would have rather remained a single autonomous national force. A lot of them anyway had only reluctantly taken up the Prussian cause.

Their Grand Elector only sent the following regiments:

- two cuirassiers regiments (with four squadrons each): Kochitsky and Kurfürst;

- four light horse or dragoons regiments (four squadrons each): Clemens, von Polenz, Prince John and Prince Albrecht;

- the eight squadrons of Saxon hussars;

- nine infantry regiments (two battalions each): Elector, Clemens, Rechten, Bevilaqua, Low, Thümmel, Niesemenschel, Prince Maximilian and Prince Frederick-Augustus, together with the corresponding grenadier battalions.

The grenadiers of the Guard and two regiments of infantry remained at Dresden.

For the artillery, there was the Kotsch battery with mortars, the Hausmann and Ernst batteries of 8-pounders, the Bonniot battery of 12-pounders, the de Hoyer battery of 4-pounders and the Grossmann and Studnitz horse artillery batteries. In all, the Saxon artillery consisted of 16 foot batteries and two horse, but the origins of the batteries which served at Jena are not always well enough documented.

GENERAL POINTS ON THE STRUCTURE OF THE PRUSSIAN ARMY IN 1806

It consisted of:

THE LINE INFANTRY

This consisted of regiments comprising two field battalions and one ordnance battalion.

Each battalion consisted of five companies of musketeers (120 men each) and a company of grenadiers (maximum strength 145 men). The two companies of grenadiers left over from the regiment were brought together with two other companies

Prussian Army

Fusiliers

Officer in full dress

NCO in field dress

Fusilier in field dress

Fusilier in full dress

NCO in full dress

Horn-player in full dress

Jägers

Officer in full dress

NCO in field dress

Private in field dress

Private in full dress

The fusiliers made up eight brigades of three battalions each.

In each brigade the 1st battalion had red pompoms and dragonnes, the 2nd had white ones and the 3rd had yellow ones. Four brigades had silver buttons and four had gold ones. There were four colours for the brigades: red, green, blue and black. Therefore two brigades had the same colours and the distinction was made by the colour of the buttons. Thus there was a black brigade with white buttons and one with gold ones, etc.

Gunner in full dress

Gunner in field dress

Artillery

The Prussian artillery used 6-pounder guns with long or short tubes. There were also 12-pounder guns and 7-pounder howitzers.

6-pounder gun

André Jouineau © Histoire & Collections 1998

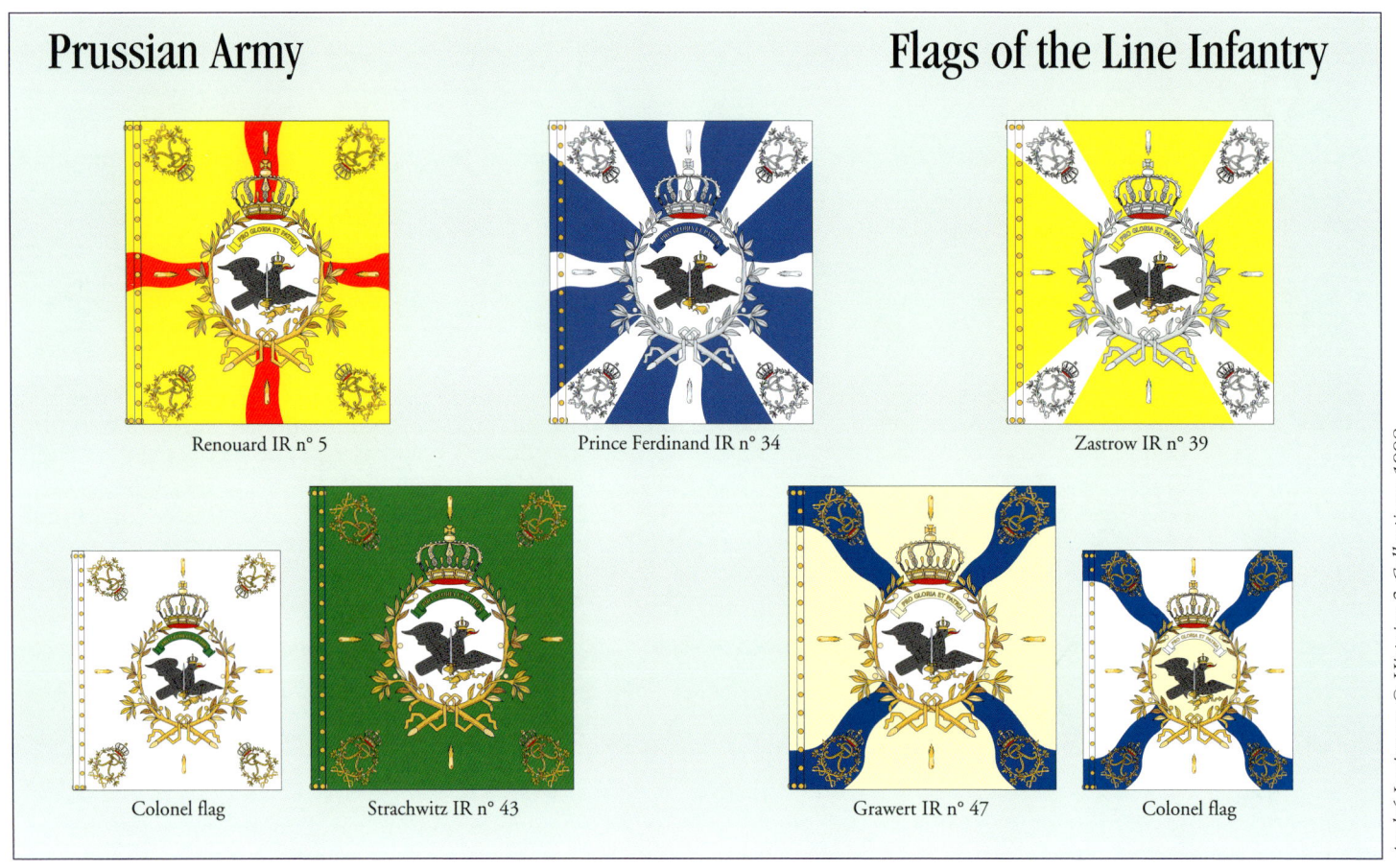

Renouard IR n° 5

Prince Ferdinand IR n° 34

Zastrow IR n° 39

Colonel flag

Strachwitz IR n° 43

Grawert IR n° 47

Colonel flag

André Jouineau © Histoire & Collections 1998

from another regiment to make an separate grenadier battalion bearing the name of its leader.

The regiment was thus made up of ten companies of musketeers, making a total of 1,200 men. But this figure does not include many other people have to be added in each battalion: the officers, the drummers (three per company including one drummer-major affected to the 2nd battalion), 8 sappers and 40 extra men to replace those put out of action, an armourer, surgeons, etc. There were also two artillery pieces per battalion. They were 6-pounder guns as a rule, served by 17 regimental gunners commanded by an NCO.

At regimental headquarters, in addition to the officers, there was a band consisting of 8 oboes, fifes, plus a cornet for the tirailleurs. Normally ten men selected from each company were used as sharpshooters and armed with rifled carbines with a fork. These skirmishers could be detached as flankers or scouts; the Prussians however, when in the line, prefered to fight in close order, unlike the French.

To all these must be added the officers' servants (280 per regiment) and a large quantity of luggage in carriages or on pack horses, and the ammunition and ordnance wagons. All this weighed a regiment down.

THE UNIFORMS OF THE INFANTRY REGIMENTS

All the infantry wore a hat with a black cockade.

In the field, the musketeers did not have white plumes on their hats, but a simple pompom in the regimental colours. They also wore trousers with buttons at the bottom of the legs. These trousers were grey-beige, grey-yellow or white. The colour of the sabre's strap was different for each company. In the field, the tirailleurs or the carabiniers did not wear their usual plume with

three black stripes, but a black pompom with a black top like the NCO's, who themselves did not wear their black-topped plume or their esponton, which was left with the ordnance. Certain regimental coats had different side braids. The cravates were different too.

Sappers wore a black plume like the regimental gunners and the drummers had swallows' nests and various braids.

When in the field, officers didn't wear the white black based plume, nor their esponton, nor their hausse col. Instead they maintained their silver-coloured scarf, which was common to all Prussian officers. They wore trousers or overtrousers which were blue or grey with side buttonnings. Their hats were sometimes covered with waxed cloth and they wore blue cloth coats, including sometimes a rotonda. Their saddle cover was dark blue wlth a border the same colour as the button, i.e. silver or gold according to the regiment; this followed the custom, as with the uniform.

THE FLAGS OF THE INFANTRY REGIMENTS

Normally there were two for each battalion, though some only had one. Three of these four regimental flags bore the colours of the regiment; the fourth was the *Leib Fahne* or the colonel flag, predominantly white. The embroidery was the same as on the button, gold or silver.

The colonel flag was carried in the front rank of the 1st battalion which carried its second flag, known as the retreat flag, in the third row.

In each regiment ten young aristocrats were appointed 'ensigns' and the most senior carried the flags.

The flags were of different types and bore, most frequently, the Maltese Cross (Iron Cross) separating eight cantons or some-

Prussian Army

Hussars

Officer
von Bila n° 11
in full dress

Hussar
Blücher n° 8
in full dress

Hussar
Würtemberg n° 4
in field dress

Trumpeter
von Bila n° 11
in full dress

PRO GLORIA ET PATRIA

Standard of
von Prittwitz
Dragoon
Regiment n° 2

Dragoons

Officer
von Katte n° 4
in full dress

NCO
Queen Louise n° 5
in full dress

Trumpeter
Queen Louise n° 5
in full dress

Dragoons in full dress

von Irwing n° 3 (front)
von Krafft n° 11 (back)

André Jouineau © Histoire & Collections 1998

times a flaming cross. We have used the Brauer reproductions inspired by Kling's work, which is our reference work. Certain modern documents show different types of flaming crosses with rounded edges but which are symetrical in relation to the axis. Some, however, did not bear any cross at all.

UNIFORMS OF THE GRENADIER BATTALIONS

The grenadiers did not have a flag, but a characteristic plumed hat. They kept the distinctive of their original regiment. The battalions also included carabiniers and two cannons. They did not have a flag either.

LIGHT INFANTRY

FUSILIERS
In 1806 the Prussian army had in all 24 battalions of fusiliers (about 600 men per battalion). They had neither flag nor artillery. The 3-pounders with which they had been equipped, had been taken away from them.

Except for their officers who wore a hat, the fusiliers' headgear was a black cylindrical shako edged on the top with white braid. In the field they wore a pair of beige or grey trousers over their shoes and gaiters. The battalions could be differentiated by the distinctive on their clothes, by the pompom of their headgear, by the colour of their straps and by the colour of their buttons.

They did not have grenadiers but sharpshooters for support.

JÄGERS
They were formed into 12 companies of 200 men each, equipped with rifled carbines. They didn't have a flag. Their plume was green like their jacket. They wore boots but also over-trousers.

CAVALRY

This was the pride of the Prussian army and was made up of:

HUSSARS
The cavalry was based on the same principle as the battalion, each battalion having five squadrons of two companies each.

The majority of hussar regiments had two battalions, or ten squadrons. A squadron was 150 horsemen including 24 carabiniers. There were 12 men in reserve per squadron and one trumpeter per company.

In 1806, the hussars' headgear was in the process of being completely changed, and the new shako hadn't yet been taken up by everybody.

Thus many regiments at Jena were still wearing the mirliton with or without a visor; it was not uncommon however for some officers and carabiniers to be wearing the new shako. The Bila Regiment wore the new headpiece. At the front of these shakos, there was a cockade rosette; its centre was the same colour as the pelisse and its edging was the same colour as the braid. The raquettes bore the squadron colour.

The buttoning of the overtrousers, which not everybody wore, was edged with piping of the same colour as the squadron.

The hussars rode small tough Polish horses. They were armed with a musketoon, hanging from its strap.

They did not carry a standard.

DRAGOONS
These regiments carried a standard when in the field and nearly all consisted of five squadrons except the famous regiment of the Queen's Dragoons, which was ten squadrons strong at Auerstaedt.

The coat of the dragoons was blue with a distinctive for each regiment. The NCO's had a stripe the same colour as the button on the collar, on the facings and on the two lists of the musketoon's banderole.

The officers had gold or silver ornaments or braid on the lapels.

The trumpeters wore a red stripe on their hat with a white red-topped plume, special regimental stripes and swallows' nests. The stripe lined the edge of the lapels and the banderole. They rode Polish horses like the hussars, but theirs were bigger.

CUIRASSIERS

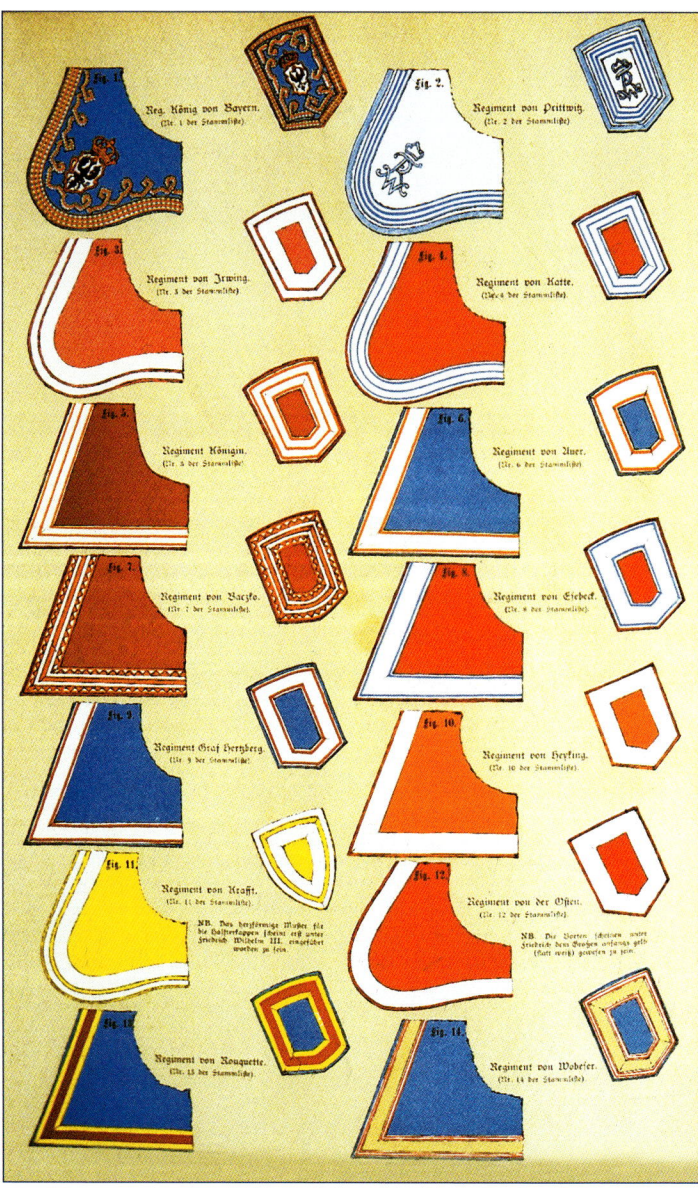

Prussian dragoons saddlecovers. (Kling, coll. Brunon).

Officer von Beeren n° 2 in full dress	NCO Graf von Henckel n° 1 in full dress	Trooper Reitzenstein n° 7 in full dress	Trooper von Beeren n° 2 in full dress	Trumpeter von Bünting n° 12 in full dress

André Jouineau © Histoire & Collections 1998

The regiments consisted of five squadrons. They included carabiniers, armed with rifled carbines who were used as flankers.

The hats and the plumes they wore were both very tall. The cuirassiers – who had abandoned their breastplates in 1798 – wore a white coat with a distinctive colour on the collar, on the facings and on the edge of the retroussis. Each regiment had its own short double stripe on the front of the coat and on the edges of the waistcoat, whose tips stuck out from under the lower edges of the coat. The waistcoat was blue, or the appropriate colour for the regiment.

As well as the straight sabre, the cuirassiers were armed with two pistols and a smooth bore rifle.

These regiments rode large Prussian horses.

ARTILLERY

The uniform of the artillerymen had a black distinctive. They wore grey-greenish or white trousers in the field. The uniform was identical for the foot and for the horse artillery. The artillery pieces were black and the equipment was painted in medium blue.

The 6-pounders (whose tube-length varied) together with the 7-pounder howitzers were the standard equipment. There were also short 12-pounders which were difficult to move around; this would be criticised after the defeat at Jena.

GENERALS

They wore a simple dark blue uniform with grey or blue overtrousers. The braid on the collar and the facings denoted the rank.

The particular distintives of the Prussian Guard will be considered in the chapter about Auerstaedt (see pp. 84-87), because they fought there.

Prussian cuirassiers saddlecovers. (Kling, coll. Brunon).

Saxon Army

Line Infantry

Officer
IR von Thümmel
in full dress

NCO
IR Prince Frederick-Augustus
in full dress

Musketeer
IR Prince Xavier
in full dress

Drummer
IR Prince Xavier
in full dress

Grenadier
IR Prince Elector
in full dress

André Jouineau © Histoire & Collections 1998

GENERALITIES ON THE STRUCTURE OF THE SAXON ARMY IN 1806

As was explained on page 12, the Grenadier guards, the Life-guards and two infantry regiments (Prince Anthony and von Saenger) remained in their garrison. The other units were committed, dispersed amongst Hohenlohe's Prussians.

LINE INFANTRY

The organisation of this army was modelled on the Prussian army. Each infantry regiment numbered therefore two musketeer battalions, and tirailleurs. The grenadiers were drawn up in independent regiments, each battalion consisting of two companies from one regiment and two companies from another.

LINE INFANTRY UNIFORMS

The Saxon infantry cockade was white.

The musketeers wore a French-style coat. The facings, the collar and the lapels were of the distinctive colour; the cravate was red. They wore white trousers, with tall gaiters even in the field. They wore their hair knotted in a tail with a black ribbon. Their sabre was attached to a white belt. The hat was bordered in white and had a white tassel whose top bore the colour of the distinctive.

The tirailleurs wore a green plume.

The grenadiers had the right to wear a moustache. The hat was the bearskin with a leather visor without a chinstrap. The base was in the distinctive colour, with a plait the same colour as the button. Their sabre was attached to a shoulder belt passing over the right shoulder, over the cartridge box strap.

NCOs hats were edged in gold or silver like the buttons. In full dress the plume was short and white with a black top.

The drummers had swallow's nests whose distinctive colour

Saxon flags

Obverse of IR Prince Xavier's flag

Cavalry standard

Reverse of IR Prince Xavier's flag

André Jouineau © Histoire & Collections 1998

Saxon Army

Light Horse

Prince Clemens Regiment

Trumpeter   Trooper

Von Polenz Regiment

Trumpeter

Prince John Regiment

Trooper   NCO   Trumpeter (Prince John)

Prince Albert Regiment

Cuirassiers

Kurfürst Regiment

Trroper   Trumpeter

Kochitzky Regiment

Trumpeter

André Jouineau © Histoire & Collections 1998

was the same as the feathers of the hat. The drums were chec-kered with the distinctive colour and white.

INFANTRY REGIMENT FLAGS

Each battalion had one. The colonel flag had a white back-ground and accompanied the 1st battalion. The regimental flag bearing the distinctive was carried by the 2nd battalion. Each regiment had different edging stripes.

CAVALRY

HUSSARS

There was only one regiment of eight squadrons; they did not carry a standard. The hussars wore a mirliton with blue and whi-te cordons, and a white plume. The fur-lined pelisse was worn in the field and they wore white over-trousers.

The trumpeters were distinguished by a blue and yellow plume.

LIGHT HORSE

There were four regiments. Each regiment consisted of four squadrons and numbered 650 horsemen.

They wore a white-plumed black hat, a red coat, a red crava-te, and the facings, lapels, collar, retroussis all bore the distinc-tive. The buttons were yellow. The officer's hat had a gold stri-pe; he wore gold epaulettes and a white cravate.

Depending on the regiment, the distinctives were light green (Prince Clemens), blue (von Polenz), black (Prince John) or dark green (Prince Albert).

The colonel of the 11th Chasseurs à cheval (French 4th Corps) noticed that the Saxon light horse had little chains sewn into their sleeves and as a result gave the order not to sabre them on the arm.

CUIRASSIERS

Like the light horse, the cuirassiers regiments had four squa-drons with a total of 650 horsemen. Their uniform was of the Prussian type but without the sabretache. They wore a straw yel-low coat with lining, retroussis, collar and facings with the dis-tinctive colour. The cravate was red for the men and black for the officers. The collar which descended down the front of the coat was edged with a special regimental stripe. This stripe also ador-ned the facings and the retroussis as well as the saddle cover. The scabbard of the sabre was covered with blackened leather. The distinctive colour was scarlet (Kurfürst) or yellow (Kochitsky, later known as Zastrow).

The trumpeters wore their colours the other way around with a red plume. The facings, the collar and the retroussis were whi-te with the regimental stripe. The cordons for the trumpets were red and yellow for Kurfürst, and yellow and black for Kochitsky. Each squadron had its own standard.

ARTILLERY

They wore a green coat with red collar, facings and retrous-sis. The buttons were yellow and the leather equipment was fawn-coloured. The hat was striped with white, with a plume in a black and white tuft. The saddle cover was bordered with dents de loup, threaded with yellow. They used 6-, 4-, and 12-pounders, and howitzers.

GENERALS

They wore a blue coat with red trousers and waistcoat, a sil-ver scarf-belt threaded with gold and crimson. The numerous braidings were an indication of rank. Their aides de camp wore a white armband and golden shoulder knots.

Saxon Army

Hussars

Officer in field dress

Trumpeter in field dress

Trooper in field dress

André Jouineau © Histoire & Collections 1998

French troops entering Prussia, by Richard Knötel, in 'Konigin Luise'.

THE FRENCH

I T IS QUITE AMAZING the mistakes that are still made nowadays about the French army of 1806 present at the battle of Jena, particularly where uniforms and units are concerned. The first obvious point is that this infantry was the same as at Austerlitz: the regiments had been quartered in Germany and were unable to return to Paris before the Prussian campaign started. They were thus still soldiers wearing hats. Napoleon's only preoccupation was supplying them with a fourth pair of shoes, shoes being at this period the same for each foot. One pair was worn, two were carried in the haversack and a fourth was held in reserve. The Emperor's soldiers knew that they won battles by marching better, faster and longer than the others. Greatcoats had also been handed out because the cold season was closing in.

As for the rest, war had to feed war… The enemy's clothing depots and any clothes recovered would be a extraordinary source of supplies for the men. The same could be said for food, and in a country as rich as Germany, this would be easy to find. The less the ordnance weighed down the convoys, the more the army was mobile; ammunition transportation took priority over the rest.

The infantry regiments were most often made up of two battalions (1,000 men each) with a third being formed at the advance depot along the Rhine. Some had three battalions on the road and a fourth at the depot.

Flags were of one type only and the light infantry regiments did not carry any. These regiments wore the cylindrical shako with the plume on the left; the carabiniers wore bearskins.

The light cavalry regiments consisted of three squadrons on the march and a fourth at the advance depot. A regiment numbered 500 horsemen.

Light cavalry regiments did not carry any standards in the field; each corps had a few of these regiments at its disposal. The remainder of the cavalry was regrouped in the cavalry reserve, under the command of Murat, with his light brigades and the mass of the dragoon and cuirassier divisions.

In general the artillery had 8-pounders with a few batteries of 12-pounders. However, certain corps like the 4th had 42 Austrian guns out of 48. The 4-pounders mentioned were Austrian.

The Emperor was in command of seven army corps, Murat's cavalry reserve, a part of the Imperial Guard on foot, and the artillery pool. Each army corps was an autonomous unit with its maréchal, its own infantry, its cavalry and its artillery.

BERNADOTTE'S 1st CORPS

18,500 men strong, 1,500 cavalry and 34 cannon.

Only two regiments of cavalry and infantry elements were used by Murat in the first confrontation at Schleiz on 8th October; but during the battle of Jena, Bernadotte was strangely inactive. Napoleon found this suspicious and had him watched thereafter.

DAVOUT'S 3rd CORPS

24,000 infantrymen, 1,200 cavalry and 44 cannon.

They became the heroes of Auerstaedt, the victors of this historic day; it was an exceptional feat of arms.

SOULT'S 4th CORPS

25,000 men, 1,200 cavalry and 44 cannon.

Only Saint-Hilaire's Division and the cavalry were engaged, together with some lighter elements, mentioned in the march towards the battlefield. The other divisions got there towards the end of the fight and occupied the conquered terrain with the mass of their numbers.

LANNES' 5th CORPS

19,000 men, 1,500 cavalry and 28 cannon.

They were the heroes of the battle in the main sector: they won at Saalfeld; they took Iena and started the offensive which permitted the other corps to deploy. The 17th Light in particular were to be found everywhere in the heart of the action and distinguished themselves especially.

NEY'S 6th CORPS

18,500 infantrymen, 1,000 cavalry and 24 cannon.

From this corps only the 25th Line, two battalions of elite troops and the cavalry reached the battle in time. In the manner of their leader, they charged straight into the fray, but in rather a haphanded way. The two divisions arrived at the end and occupied the terrain directly behind the troops which were fighting. They took part in the march on Weimar, during the chase.

AUGEREAU'S 7th CORPS

15,500 men, 1,000 cavalry and 36 cannon.

This came up behind Lannes 5th, acting brilliantly on the left using Desjardin's Division and the cavalry. Only the front part of Heudelet's Division was finally engaged.

MURAT'S CAVALRY RESERVE

Murat had 13,600 horsemen of which 5,000 were cuirassiers or carabiniers. They only arrived for the end of the battle, to take part in the kill. Only Klein's dragoons and two of d'Hautpoul's regiments of cuirassiers were able to arrive in time for this finale.

THE IMPERIAL GUARD

At this date it had not yet been completed. There were 4,000 men of the Vieille Garde (the two grenadier and the two chasseur regiments) and 2,000 foot dragoons seconded to the Guard. The 2,400 cavalry didn't arrive until the 18th October. It is surprising to see nowadays so many later paintings showing cavalry of the Guard or even worse, fusiliers of the Guard cheering the Emperor at Jena when these regiments were not even present.

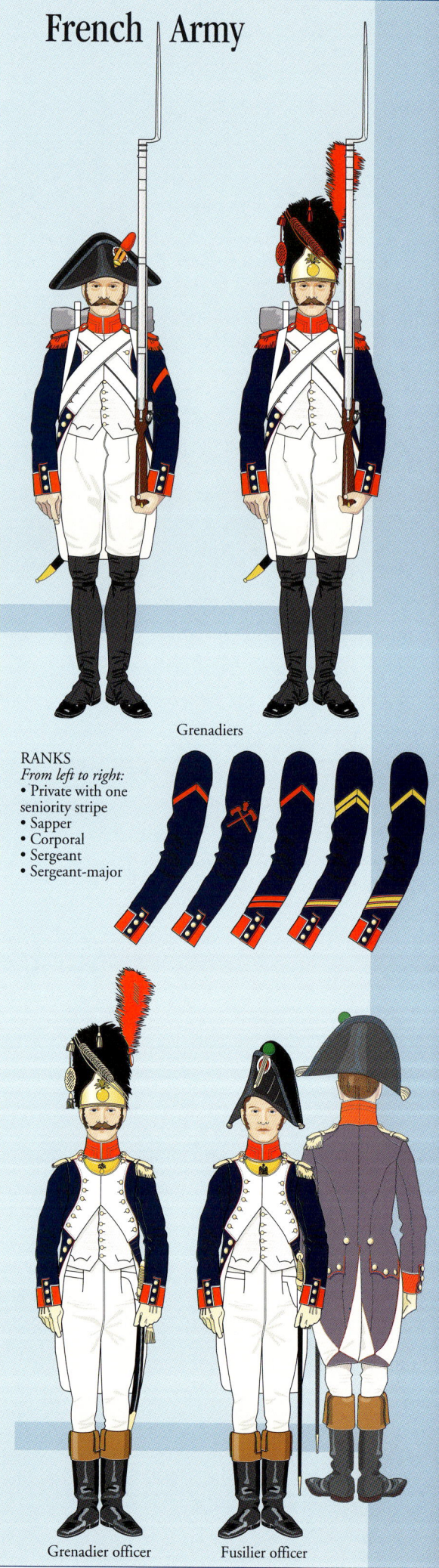

French Army

Grenadiers

RANKS
From left to right:
• Private with one seniority stripe
• Sapper
• Corporal
• Sergeant
• Sergeant-major

Grenadier officer   Fusilier officer

Line Infantry

Fusilier

Voltigeur

Grenadier
sergeant

Fusilier
in marching dress

Fusilier
wearing greatcoat

Grenadier
wearing greatcoat

Warrant
Officer

Lieutenant

Battalion
Commander

Colonel

Second
Lieutenant

Captain

Major

Sapper in full dress

Voltigeur officer in overcoat

Senior officer

Colonel

Obverse of the
44th Line's flag,
'Challiot' pattern.

L'EMPEREUR
DES FRANCAIS
AU 44.ME RÉGIMENT
D'INFANTERIE
DE LIGNE.

André Jouineau © Histoire & Collections 1998

French Army

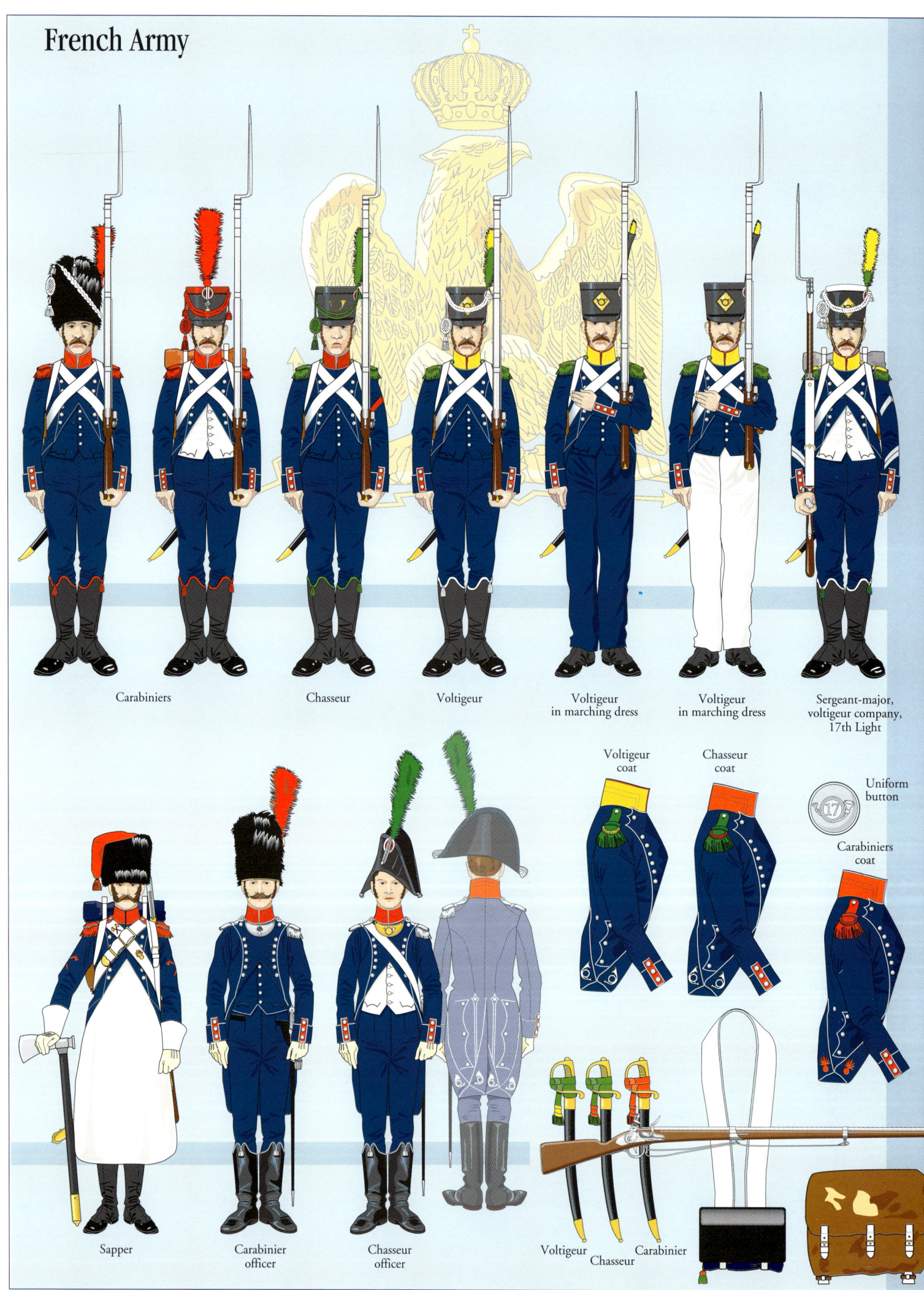

Carabiniers

Chasseur

Voltigeur

Voltigeur
in marching dress

Voltigeur
in marching dress

Sergeant-major,
voltigeur company,
17th Light

Voltigeur
coat

Chasseur
coat

Uniform
button

Carabiniers
coat

Sapper

Carabinier
officer

Chasseur
officer

Voltigeur
Chasseur
Carabinier

24

Light Infantry

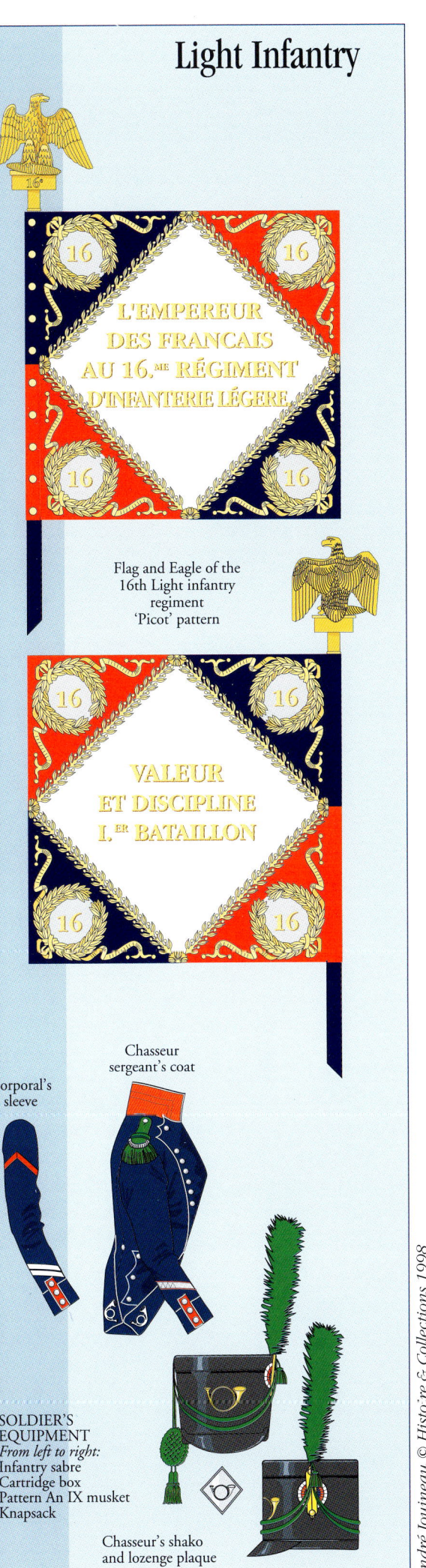

Flag and Eagle of the
16th Light infantry
regiment
'Picot' pattern

L'EMPEREUR
DES FRANCAIS
AU 16.ᵐᵉ RÉGIMENT
D'INFANTERIE LÉGERE

16 16 16 16

VALEUR
ET DISCIPLINE
I.ᵉʳ BATAILLON

16 16 16 16

Corporal's
sleeve

Chasseur
sergeant's coat

SOLDIER'S
EQUIPMENT
From left to right:
Infantry sabre
Cartridge box
Pattern An IX musket
Knapsack

Chasseur's shako
and lozenge plaque

André Jouineau © Histoïre & Collections 1998

As for the Guard artillery, it consisted of a variety of weapons picked up en route. Eight of the pieces were taken from Oudinot; General Songis gave them 12 and six others came from Mainz. Of these 26 pieces, 12 arrived late. On the 13th October, they were still at Auma with the 2nd regiment of foot dragoons and joined up on the 14th. At the time when Napoleon set up his big central battery in front of Jena, he had only 14 of the 26 pieces so he commandeered seven cannon from the 7th Corps and four from the 5th.

Thus the Emperor had at his disposal near Jena or joining the battlefield by forced march, a mass of over 100,000 men. Neither Davout's Corps, totally isolated to the north, on the point of fighting the battle of Auerstadt, nor Bernadotte's Corps which remained passive between the two battlefields, was on the move towards Jena.

The superiority of the French at Jena became quite clear because, towards the end of the day, the divisions which were coming up in reinforcement, were able to lend a hand pursuing Prussians and Saxons in full flight. On the other hand Davout couldn't count on anybody. Bernadotte, who was within reach, left him to his fate.

We can quote the famous sentences:

'At Jena Napoleon won a battle he could not lose. At Auerstaedt, Davout won a battle he could not win.'

Details concerning French regiments will be dealt with later.

French light infantry in action inside the woods on the Army's right wing, battle of Jena, 14th October 1806.

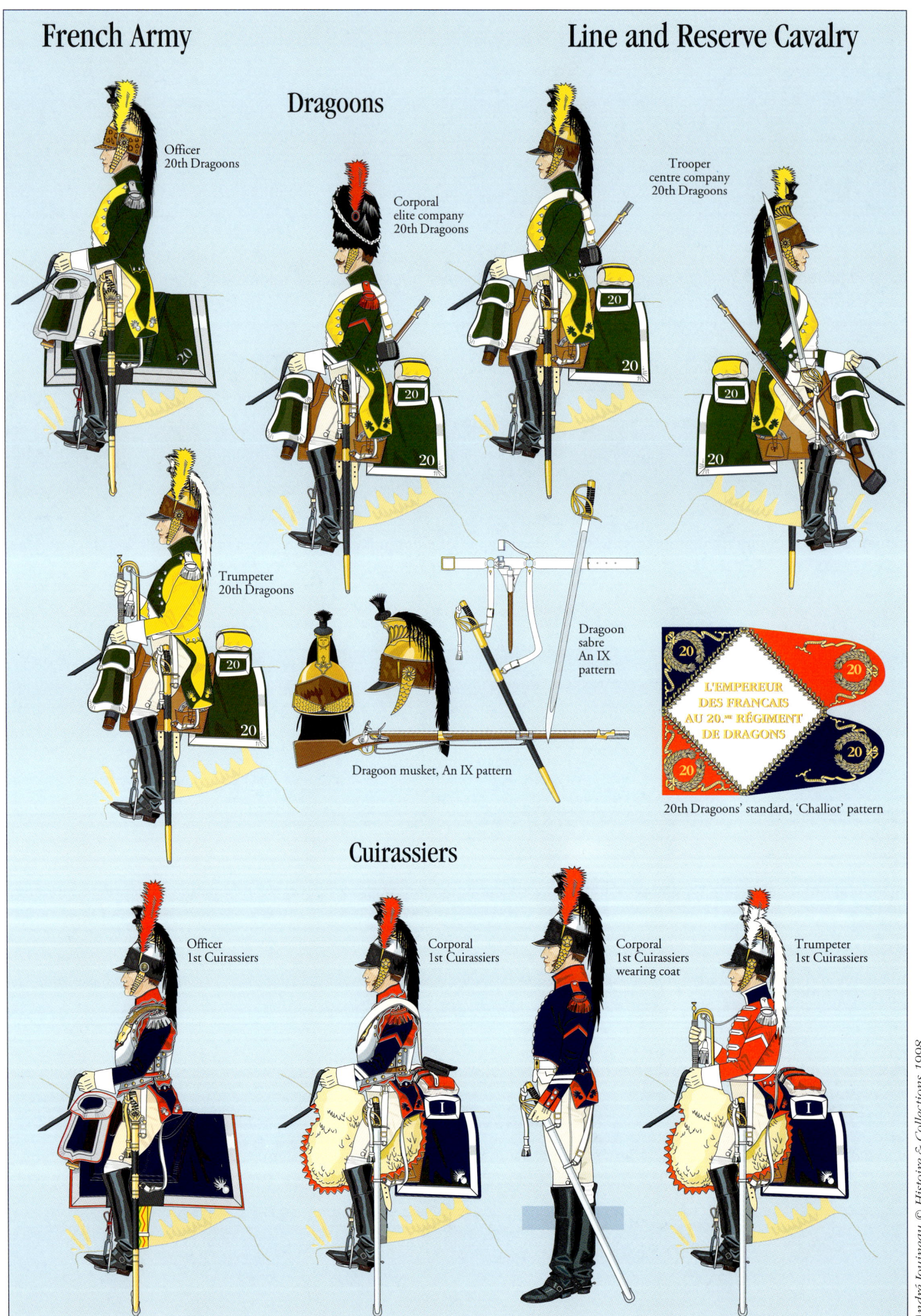

Dragoons

Officer
20th Dragoons

Corporal
elite company
20th Dragoons

Trooper
centre company
20th Dragoons

Trumpeter
20th Dragoons

Dragoon musket, An IX pattern

Dragoon
sabre
An IX
pattern

L'EMPEREUR
DES FRANCAIS
AU 20.ME RÉGIMENT
DE DRAGONS

20th Dragoons' standard, 'Challiot' pattern

Cuirassiers

Officer
1st Cuirassiers

Corporal
1st Cuirassiers

Corporal
1st Cuirassiers
wearing coat

Trumpeter
1st Cuirassiers

André Jouineau © Histoire & Collections 1998

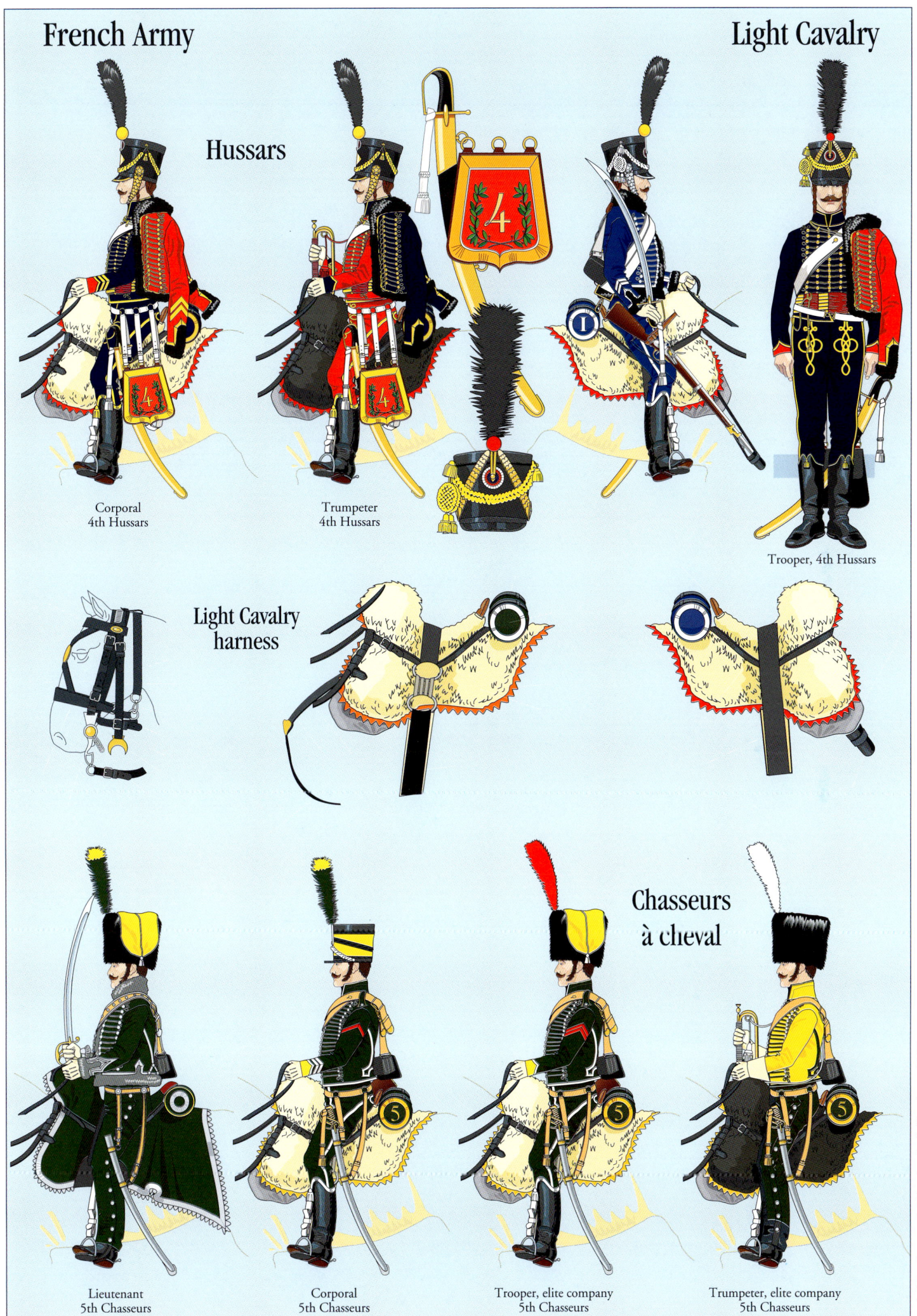

French Army

Hussars

Corporal
4th Hussars

Trumpeter
4th Hussars

Trooper, 4th Hussars

Light Cavalry

Light Cavalry
harness

Chasseurs
à cheval

Lieutenant
5th Chasseurs

Corporal
5th Chasseurs

Trooper, elite company
5th Chasseurs

Trumpeter, elite company
5th Chasseurs

André Joutineau © Histoire & Collections 1998

THE FIRST CONTACTS

URAT WAS IN THE VANGUARD with the light cavalry. He was marching on the Gera road with Wattier's cavalry belonging to Bernadotte's 1st Corps, whose infantry was spread out behind. The 27th Light was at the head of this infantry and if needed, could support the cavalry. The rest of Drouet's Division was following.

Lasalle's (5th and 7th Hussars) and Milhaud's (13th Chasseurs by itself because the 1st Hussars had been detached to the Emperor's Headquarters) Brigades were scouting on either side of the principal road.

On the 8th October, Murat found Saalburg occupied by the enemy. He ordered the bridge on the Saale which had had some beams removed to be attacked by the elite companies of the 27th Light. But the enemy fell back on Schleiz without firing. They were elements from Tauentzien's Corps who were rejoining Hohenlohe's Army at Jena.

**THE FIGHT AT SCHLEIZ
9th OCTOBER 1806**

■ French troops
■ Prussian and Saxon troops

*(French and German identifications
of units have been retained)*

Morgan Gillard © Histoire & Collections 1998

9th OCTOBER: SCHLEIZ

This was more of a scuffle than a proper fight and was the first confrontation of the campaign.

Murat loved charging, especially in Napoleon's presence. The Emperor had just arrived and gave the order to attack. The 27th Light was in front, the 94th and 95th Line following behind. The Prussians and the Saxons had evacuated Schleiz but nevertheless were in position in front of Ottersdorf. Murat had only the 4th Hussars with him but he didn't wait for the arrival of the 5th Chasseurs to charge. He ran straight into the Bila Regiment of Prussian hussars and the Prince John Regiment of Saxon Light

Horse. The French hussars were held off three times. It took the 27th Light and of the 94th Line, as well as a charge by the 5th Chasseurs, to get the enemy to fall back. Tauentzien continued on his way towards Jena, leaving the road to Leipzig open.

10th OCTOBER, SAALFELD

This was a real battle giving Maréchal Lannes an opportunity to show his real qualities. Leaving Grafenthal at six in the morning, he started off on the road to Saalfeld. Having received more precise information and fearing that a large force might have been placed in his way by Hohenlohe, Napoleon warned Lannes to expect to meet a force of 10,000 to 15,000 men. If he thought he could attack, then he would have to attack.

This Prusso-Saxon corps was the vanguard commanded by Prince Louis-Ferdinand whose headquarters were in Rudolstadt. The prince set out his troops as follows:

- at Blankenburg where the bridge must be held: General von Pelet with his own fusilier battalion, the Masars company of Prussian light cavalry, three squadrons of Saxon hussars and half (four 6-pounders) of Gause horse artillery battery. This made a total of 850 infantry, 320 cavalry and a hundred or so artillerymen. These men only took part at the end of the battle to protect the retreat. Masars company advanced to Unterwirbach;

- towards Pösneck and Oppurg: General Schimmelpfennig with five squadrons to cover the left and ensure the meeting up with Tauentzien. His five other squadrons of hussars were behind Saalfeld (780 cavalry).

- in Saalfeld: colonel Rabenau commanding his own Fusilier battalion as well as the Rühle Fusilier battalion, the Valentini Jäger company, and the Riemann battery of twelve 6-pounders, making a total of about 1,400 combatants.

Learning of the approach of the French and having received orders suggesting an attack, Prince Louis-Ferdinand left Rudolstadt with General Bevilaqua and the main part of his forces: this consisted of General Trützschler with five squadrons of Saxon hussars, tirailleurs regrouped from the Saxon battalions and the 1st battalion of the Elector Regiment followed by the 2nd battalion, and the Prince Xavier Regiment who left a company guarding the bridge at Rudolstadt. The Saxon Hoyer battery with twelve 6-pounders and the Saxon Clemens Regiment brought up the rear. The Prussian Müffling Regiment came last.

This group represented about 5,700 men and 550 cavalry. The battalions had their usual two cannon, which with the Saxons were 4-pounders.

Prince Louis-Ferdinand therefore had a little more than 7,000 men and 1,300 cavalry, bearing in mind that the Schimmelpfennig Hussars were not really used effectively.

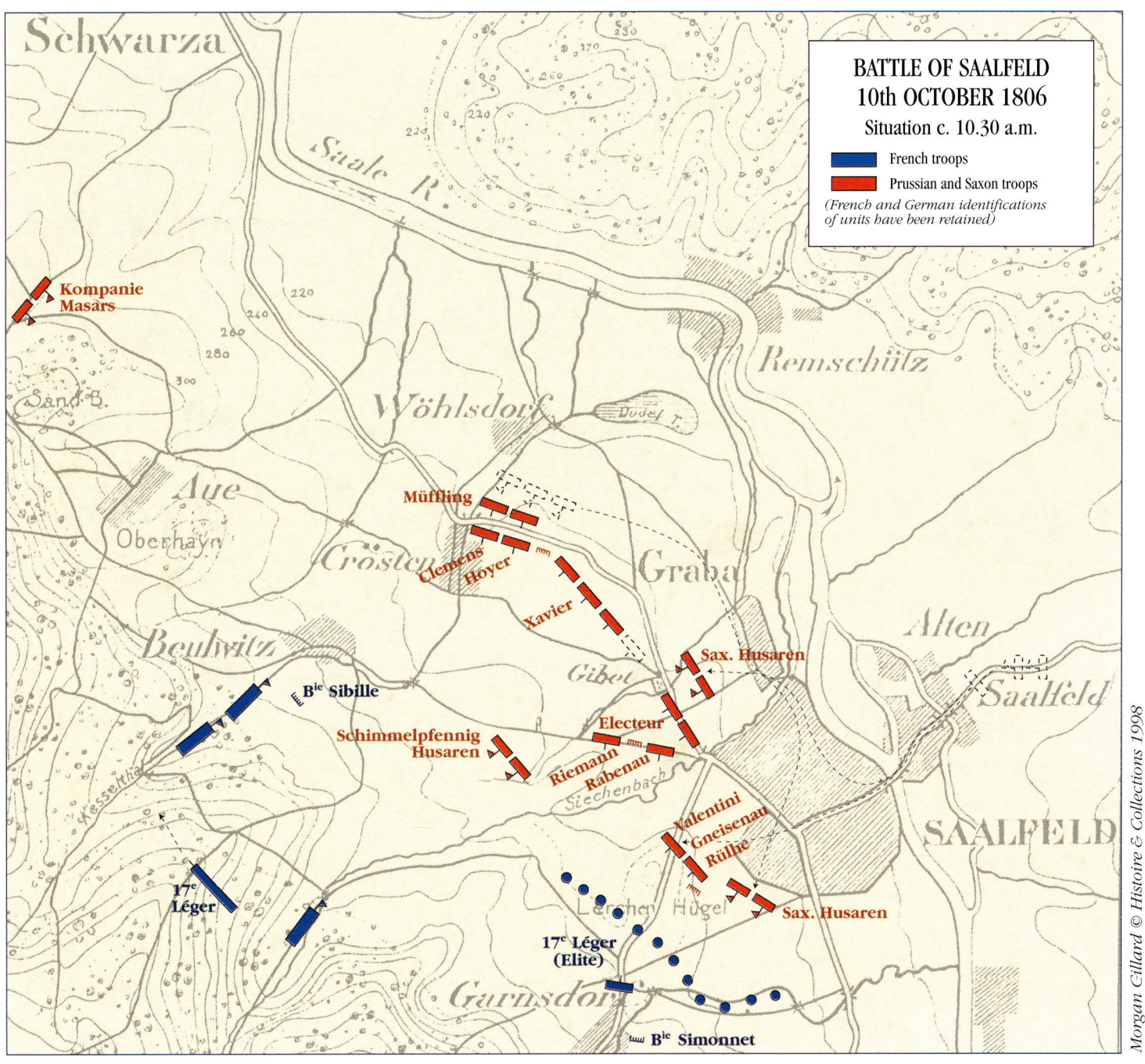

Morgan Gillard © Histoire & Collections 1998

Maréchal Lannes emerged onto the Grafenthal road with the 17th Light in the lead. This regiment was commanded by General Claparède and consisted of two battalions, plus the elite companies of the third battalion. The rest of Suchet's Division was following with Reille's Brigade (34th and 40th Line) and Vedel's Brigade (64th and 88th Line).

General Treillard's cavalry was also present with the 9th and 10th Hussars as well as the 21st Chasseurs.

No other troops were engaged by Lannes but as his Chief of Staff at the time was General Victor, three future Maréchals de France were therefore on the battlefield and they were about to distinguish themselves.

The French arrived in Garnsdorf where Prussian Jägers halted them. Colonel Rabenau sent the Valentini Jäger company and a fusilier company from his own battalion to a position in front of Saalfeld. The fusilier company was commanded by a future famous soldier: Gneisenau. They were on the Lerchen Hügel. The Rabenau battalion and Riemann battery had been placed behind the little valley of the Sichenbach. The Schimmelpfennig

Hussars and the Rühle battalion were in Saalfeld.

Bevilaqua's column arrived towards 9 a.m. and took up its position between Crösten and Saalfeld with the Saxon hussars in the second line and Müffling Regiment on the right. Before ten o'clock, having had Napoleon's proclamation read to his soldiers, Lannes got the Jägers out of Garnsdorf and placed the little elite battalion there supported by Lieutenant Simmonet's two 4-pounders on the far right. Skirmishers of the 17th Light followed by the cavalry approached the plain but most of the regiment moved along the woods in the direction of Beulwitz; this was in order to threaten the enemy's line of retreat.

Prince Louis reinforced his left wing by having the Rühle battalion and two squadrons of Schimmelpfennig hussars intervene together with the other half-battery of Gause horse artillery. The fight settled down at this point.

Lannes ordered his troops to advance through the woods towards the Prussian right, leaving the skirmishers of the 17th Light to occupy the enemy. The cavalry followed on the edge of the wood, hiding as best it could. Artillery Captain Sibille got his

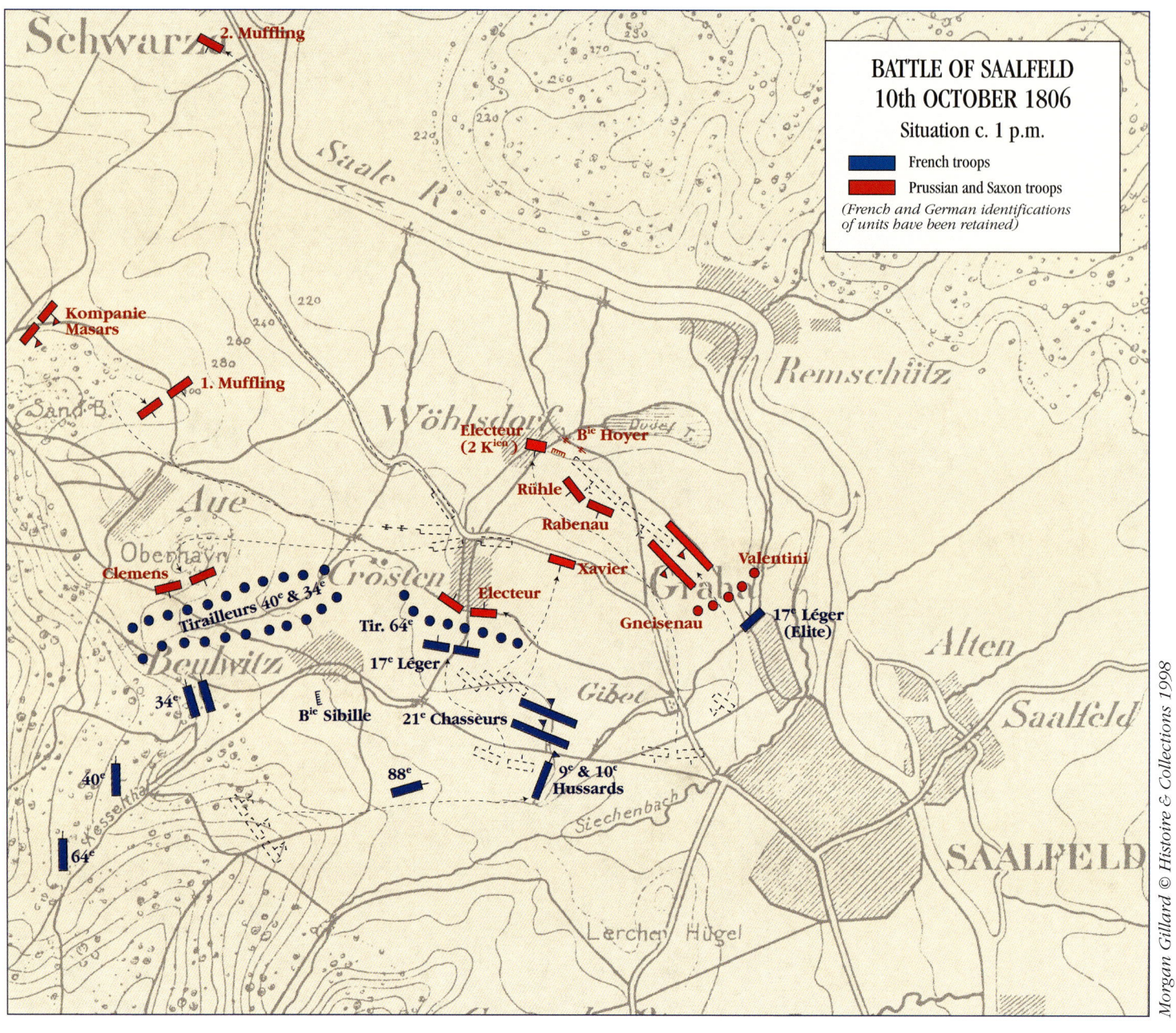

Morgan Gillard © Histoire & Collections 1998

three 4-pounder cannon into place in front of Beulwitz, supporting the skirmishers.

Prince Louis ordered his cavalry on the left to come back to the centre because they were too exposed to the French skirmishers. At this moment he received new orders to hold Rudolstadt and not to attack any more. The Prince decided to get his troops to fall back towards the town and sent a battalion of the Müffling Regiment off to hold the Schwarza bridge. His other battalion moved towards Aue. It was now 11 o'clock.

The Hoyer battery and two companies of the Clemens Regiment took up their positions on the Sandberg hill. The remainder of the regiment set up in Oberhayn. Reinforcements were requested but didn't arrive.

The Prince Xavier and Elector (leaving two companies near the Riemann battery) Regiments were lined up to attack towards Beulitz, with the cavalry in the second line in support.

The skirmishers of the 17th Light had already infiltrated Beulwitz where they sniped on advancing Saxons. Sibille fired at them from an angle with his cannon. At this moment, the first two battalions of the 34th emerged the woods, drums beating and entered Beulwitz then attacked the Prince Xavier Regiment which

fled towards Crösten. The 17th penetrated the village. With a lot of difficulty, Prince Louis rallied his fleeing Saxons then got the Elector Regiment, which was still intact, to attack and retake Crösten where he set himself up. It was midday.

Before continuing his offensive, Lannes waited for the other regiments to come out of the woods. This pause in the troop movements lasted an hour. Prince Louis got his troops back between Aue and the Saale, protected in front by the assembled cavalry. But the furthest troops, who were fighting in front of Saalfeld, had already been pushed back by the elite battalion and the 17th Light skirmishers under General Victor. Lieutenant Simmonet continued firing his two guns, which in all fired 264 times.

The Riemann battery met with resistance in a hollow before Wöhlsdorf. The fusiliers followed up and together they ended up entering Wöhlsdorf. Crösten was still held by the Elector Regiment.

It was one o'clock; having gathered together all his troops, Lannes launched his attack.

First objective

Crösten, held by the Elector Regiment and behind this the Prince Xavier Regiment around Wöhlsdorf, the Riemann battery, the

Prussian and Saxon combatants at Saalfeld

Prussian troops

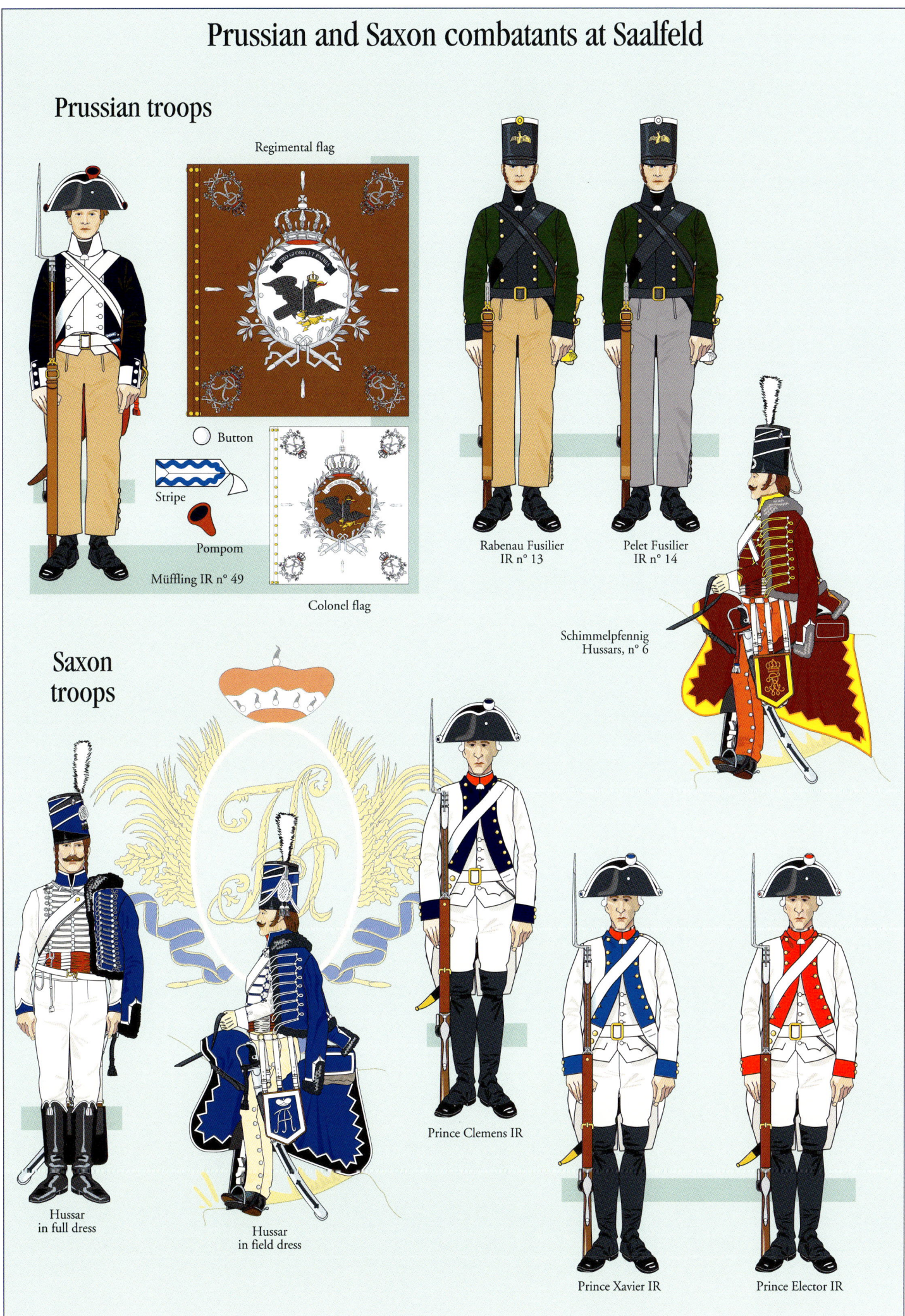

Regimental flag

○ Button

Stripe

Pompom

Müffling IR n° 49

Colonel flag

Rabenau Fusilier
IR n° 13

Pelet Fusilier
IR n° 14

Schimmelpfennig
Hussars, n° 6

Saxon troops

Hussar
in full dress

Hussar
in field dress

Prince Clemens IR

Prince Xavier IR

Prince Elector IR

André Jouineau © Histoire & Collections 1998

Rabenau and Rühle battalions covered on the Graba side by the Valentini and Gneisenau companies. And behind them by the Prussian and Saxon light cavalry.

The 64th Line and the 17th Light attacked, and took Crösten. Then they fell upon the Prince Xavier Regiment which retreated in disorder. The troops which had reassembled in Wöhlsdorf fell back also; this was because the French cavalry had just drawn up ready to charge, to be followed by the 88th. A charge by the 21st Chasseurs was driven off by two companies of the Elector Regiment who were there in support of the Riemann battery and were, as yet, intact. Wishing to profit from this failure, Prince Louis charged with the five squadrons that made up the front line of his cavalry. He was overwhelmed by the 9 and 10th Hussars thrown in at top speed.

The Saxon hussars were routed; on top of this, the Schimmelpfennig hussars who wanted to intervene were drawn into the fray and then could only pull out by falling back. The cavalry crossed the Saale as best it could. Enemy troops in Wöhlsdorf were cut off and attacked from all sides; they tried to cross the river but a lot were taken prisoner by the French. All the cannon were captured except one. Colonels Rabenau and Rühle were taken prisoner.

Prince Louis tried in vain to rally his fleeing troops. He had to get to Schwarza as quickly as possible. Sergeant Guindey, from the 10th Hussars, caught up with him and after a brief struggle, killed him.

The elite companies and those from the 17th Light who were with Victor, crossed the Saale and started the pursuit.

Second objective

The Sandberg held by the Hoyer battery which was supported by the Müffling battalion and two companies of the Clemens Regiment; the rest of this regiment was placed towards Ober-Hayn. The 34th and 40th Line led the attack, but on that side progress was harder because the enemy was standing up well to their attacks; but the advance party of the Clemens Regiment ended up by falling back on the Sandberg.

At this point the 21st Chasseurs, now well re-grouped, came up to support the attack. Faced with the disaster at Wohlsdorf, General Bevilaqua gave the order to fall back on Schwarza. The Müffling battalion succeeded in doing so, but the Hoyer battery was captured and the Clemens Regiment, charged by the 21st Chasseurs, was put to flight. General Bevilaqua was captured by the light cavalrymen. The only troops remaining intact were Pelet's forces, the Masars company of light cavalry, the Gause

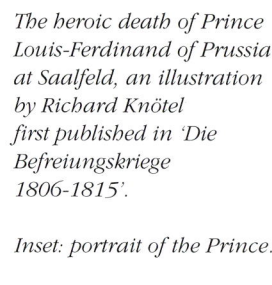

The heroic death of Prince Louis-Ferdinand of Prussia at Saalfeld, an illustration by Richard Knötel first published in 'Die Befreiungskriege 1806-1815'.

Inset: portrait of the Prince.

*Portrait of Sergeant Guindey - see biographical notice p. 69.
(Miniature from the Christian Blondieau Collection).*

half-battery and three squadrons of Saxon hussars. The skirmishers of the 40th Line first pushed back the Masars company which had moved up towards Unter-Wirbach, then marched on to Blankenburg. Here Pelet was trying to set up a line of defence but seeing the general rout, he fell back beyond the bridges. He got back to Hohenlohe on the 12th.

The retreat continued beyond Rudolstadt and it was there that the French gave up the chase.

That day the French seized four flags, 34 cannon with more than 1,700 Saxons and Prussians dead, wounded or captured. Wagons and baggage were captured together with the rich shops in Rudolstadt and Saalfeld.

Lannes announced that he had lost 172 men out of action. It was therefore a marvellous victory. At Jena, Suchet's Division would continue giving invaluable service, with the 17th Light always in the forefront.

Lannes' Corps would became the heroes of Jena.

MARCHING TO JENA

11th OCTOBER

Lasalle was at Langenberg and his hussars captured a convoy of 300 wagons containing an absolute fortune and piles of equipment. The hundred men who were escorting it, were captured. Beaumont's dragoons were just behind them.

Napoleon moved towards Auma and sent Davout, Bernadotte and Soult on towards Gera. Lannes reached Neustadt with Augereau behind him.

12th OCTOBER

Davout had to move to Naumburg with Sahuc's dragoons. His light cavalry got there at 3.30 p.m. and captured a convoy and 12 copper pontoons still harnessed up.

Bernadotte and Murat also headed for Naumburg but by way of Zeitz. Napoleon reached Gera and had Ney and Soult join him there.

Lannes marched on Jena, still followed by Augereau. He pushed the Erichsen Fusiliers and the Werner Jägers together with the Studnitz half-battery out of Winzerla. The 17th Light lost 30 men in this action and Lannes set up camp for the night in the area. A little detachment managed to get through to Burgau which had been deserted by the enemy.

Lannes put scouts out as far as Leipzig.

13th OCTOBER

Klein, d'Hautpoul and Nansouty were summoned to Gera. Ney had to march towards Jena. So did Soult.

Word came that the Prussians had probably begun their march towards Magdeburg. The Prussians who were in front of, and in Jena received the order to fall back to the Closewitz-Lützeroda line. Three columns were concerned:
- a half battalion of Herwath Grenadiers, the Zweiffel first battalion and two cannon moved to Closewitz;
- the Zweiffel second battalion with the Werner and Valentini Jägers also moved to Closewitz;
- the Rosen and Erichsen Fusilier battalions moved towards Lützeroda.

This retreat was protected by the Rechten battalion (which had been set up on the slopes of the Landgrafenberg), and by the Bila hussars, together with the Masars light cavalry and Colonel Boguslawski's remaining forces.

In the mist of the early morning, Claparède with the untiring 17th Light set off towards Jena. The Prussians, as foreseen, fell back in front of the French skirmishers on the Weimar road. In Jena, Prussian skirmishers were driven back and 30 of them were taken prisoner. Lannes' Corps spread out on the Weimar road towards Cospeda which they bypassed. Napoleon arrived at about 4 p.m., took a look at the Prussian lines and ordered the occupation of the Landgrafenberg, which was the next day's starting point. The enemy front line was very close.

Hohenlohe hurriedly reinforced Tauentzien. He was thinking about attacking the French, when his Chief of Staff, who had gone to the King's headquarters, returned with new orders. The main army was to leave for Auerstaedt and on the 14th, he was to send a division to Kösen. The majority of the army would then cross the Unstrutt at Freyburg and General Kalckreuth's reserve would move through Laucha. Hohenlohe had to maintain his position and cover Dornburg in particular, in order to protect the planned retreat on the right…

THE TROOPS FACING EACH OTHER ON 14th OCTOBER

HOHENLOHE'S ARMY

This army included:

✤ THOSE WHO ESCAPED SAALFELD

They comprised the very much depleted Saxon regiments, the Schimmelpfennig Hussars, which hadn't been used very much, Pelet's men and the Müffling Fusiliers and Jägers.

Almost all the artillery had been lost.

Infantry of von Grawert's Division

Fürst Hohenlohe IR n° 32

Sanitz IR n° 50

Grawert IR n° 47

Zastrow IR n° 39

✢ VON GRAWERT'S DIVISION

VON MÜFFLING'S BRIGADE

Hohenlohe and Sanitz Regiments, Hahn Grenadiers and Glasenapp battery of 12-pounders.

VON SCHIMONSKI'S BRIGADE

Grawert and Zastrow Regiments, Sack Grenadiers and Wolframsdorf battery of 12-pounders.

VON HOLTZENDORFF'S CAVALRY

Henckel and Holtzendorff Cuirassier regiments, Krafft Dragoon regiment and Steinwehr horse artillery battery.

LIGHT TROOPS

Erichsen Fusiliers, Gettkandt Hussars and Studnitz half-battery of horse artillery.

A total of 11 battalions, 25 squadrons and three and a half batteries.

✢ VON ZEZSCHWITZ I'S SAXON DIVISION with General von Niesemenschel

VON BURGSDORF'S BRIGADE

Thümmel, Prince Xavier (sent in reinforcement to Saalfeld before the fight and thus much weakened) and Prince Frederic-Augustus Regiments together with Haussmann and Ernst batteries of 8-pounders.

VON DYHERN'S BRIGADE

Bevilaqua (one battalion), Low and Niesemenschel Regiments, Bonniot battery of 12-pounders.

VON ZEZSCHWITZ II'S AND VON KOCHITZKY'S CAVALRY

Albrecht Light Horse, Kochitzky Carabiniers and Cuirassiers (the three regiments were four squadrons strong each), together with the Grossmann battery of horse artillery.

COLONEL BOGUSLAWSKI'S LIGHT TROOPS

Boguslawski Fusiliers, Polenz Light Horse (four squadrons) and Studnitz half battery of horse artillery.

A total of 12 battalions, 16 squadrons and four and a half batteries.

Infantry of Von Zezschwitz I's Saxon Division

IR Thümmel

IR Niesemenchel

IR Prince Frederick-Augustus

IR Bevilaqua

André Jouineau © Histoire & Collections 1998

VON ZWEIFFEL'S BRIGADE

Herwath half battalion of grenadiers and von Zweiffel Regiment.

VON SCHÖNBERG'S BRIGADE

Rechten and Prince Maximilian Regiments, Winkel Grenadiers and Koch mortar battery.

VON BILA'S LIGHT TROOPS

Bila Hussars (five squadrons), Prince John Light Horse (four squadrons), Rosen Fusiliers and two Jäger companies.

Tauentzien's Corps amounted to a total of nine battalions, nine squadrons and one battery.

✤ VON PRITTWITZ'S RESERVE DIVISION

VON SANITZ'S BRIGADE

Losthin, Borcke and Dohna Grenadiers with Kollin half battalion plus Schülenburg battery of 12-pounders.

VON CERRINI'S BRIGADE

Thiollaz, Lecoq, Lichtenhayn, Metzsch, Hundt Grenadiers and Tullmann mortar battery.

VON KRAFFT'S CAVALRY

Clemens Light Horse (four squadrons), Prittwitz Dragoons (five squadrons) and Hahn battery of horse artillery.

A total of eight and a half battalions, nine squadrons and three batteries.

After the initial fighting and their losses, Hohenlohe's forces were estimated at 40,000 men.

Rüchel's Corps arriving in reinforcement was too late and rather incomplete. Its composition will be given later.

Von Zezschwitz I's Division *(continued)*   Infantry   Tauentzien's Corps

IR Low

Zweiffel IR nº 45

IR Rechten

IR Prince Maximillien

André Jouineau © Histoire & Collections 1998

THE TROOPS COMMITTED BY NAPOLEON AT JENA

All Napoleon's corps were making forced marches to reach the battlefield, which had been imposed upon the Emperor a little earlier than expected. They included:

LANNES' 5th CORPS

On top of Suchet's Division and the cavalry, who had been fighting since Saalfeld, the Marshal committed also his second division, Gazan's.

This corps represented 19,000 infantrymen, 1,500 cavalry and at least 28 cannon.

AUGEREAU'S 7th CORPS

He committed first Desjardin's Division with Lapisse's Brigade (the 16th Light and the 14th Line), followed by Conroux's Brigade (the 44th and the 105th). Augereau also used the division's artillery and the corps' cavalry (regrouping the 7th and the 20th Chasseurs) under the command of General Durosnel.

Heudelet's Division arrived towards the end of the battle and the 7th Light of General Amey participated in the final clashes. Sarut's brigade, consisting of the 24th and 63rd Line, was used for the chase. It was estimated that out of the 15,500 infantrymen in the corps, some 9,000 took part in the battle supported by the 1,000 cavalry and the main part of the artillery.

SOULT'S 4th CORPS

It served first with Saint-Hilaire's Division, including Cambras'

(continued on p. 40)

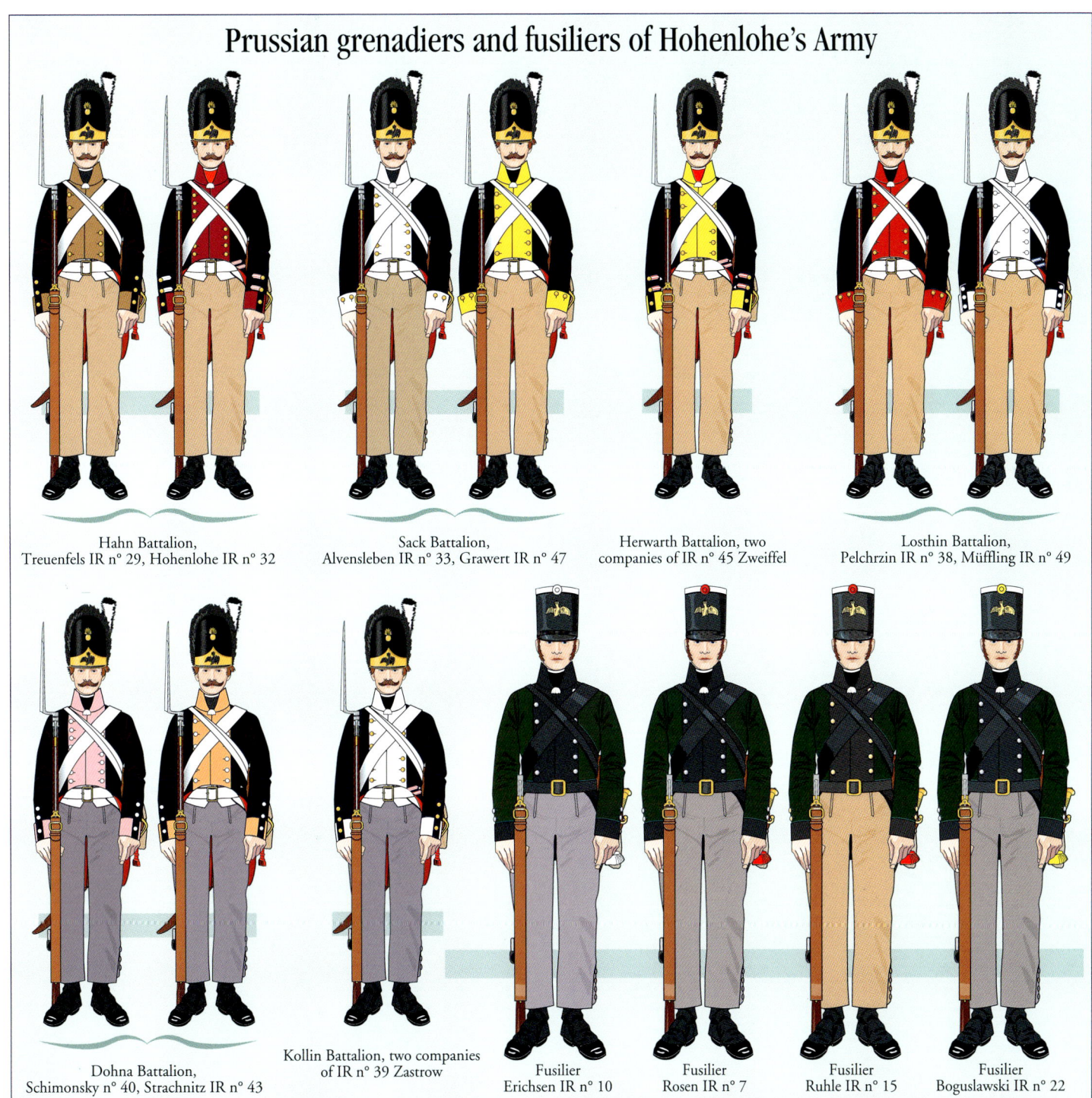

Prussian grenadiers and fusiliers of Hohenlohe's Army

Hahn Battalion,
Treuenfels IR n° 29, Hohenlohe IR n° 32

Sack Battalion,
Alvensleben IR n° 33, Grawert IR n° 47

Herwarth Battalion, two
companies of IR n° 45 Zweiffel

Losthin Battalion,
Pelchrzin IR n° 38, Müffling IR n° 49

Dohna Battalion,
Schimonsky n° 40, Strachnitz IR n° 43

Kollin Battalion, two companies
of IR n° 39 Zastrow

Fusilier
Erichsen IR n° 10

Fusilier
Rosen IR n° 7

Fusilier
Ruhle IR n° 15

Fusilier
Boguslawski IR n° 22

André Jouineau © Histaire & Collections 1998

Prussian Cavalry of Hohenlohe's Army

Hussars

Gettkandt
Hussars, n° 1

Von Bila
Hussars, n° 11

Dragoons

Von Prittwitz
Dragoons, n° 2

Von Katte
Dragoons, n° 4

Cuirassiers

Krafft
Dragoons, n° 11

Graf Henckel
Cuirassiers,
n° 1

Holtzendorff
Cuirassiers
n° 9

Coat stripes

NCO's stripes

Saxon Cavalry of Hohenlohe's Army

Light Horse

Prince Albert
Light Horse

Prince Clemens
Light Horse

Von Polenz
Light Horse

Prince John
Light Horse

Prince
Elector
Cuirassiers

Kochitsky
Cuirassiers

Hussars

Cuirassiers

Hussars

André Jouineau © Histoire & Collections 1998

Napoleon and Murat in front of the foot grenadiers of the Old Guard, at Jena.
(Painting by Horace Vernet, Château de Versailles, © Réunion des Musées nationaux photograb).

(continued from p. 37)
Brigade (10th Light and 36th Line) and Varé's Brigade (43rd and 55th Line). The cavalry also intervened with General Margaron commanding the 11th and 16th Chasseurs and General Guyot only the 8th Hussars.

There were 48 artillery pieces of which 42 had been captured from the Austrians.

The other divisions arrived towards the end, taking up the terrain.

In all there were 25,700 infantrymen of which 9,000 were actually committed, together with 1,400 cavalry and 48 cannon.

NEY'S 6th CORPS

Only General Auguste de Colbert's cavalry from this corps was engaged (3rd Hussars and 10th Chasseurs), together with some elements of infantry reduced to the 25th Light from Marcognet's division, operating with two battalions (one of grenadiers, one of voltigeurs) gathering the elite companies. The rest of the corps arrived at the end of the fighting and took part in the pursuit. In total about only 4,000 infantrymen were really committed with 1,100 cavalry.

THE GUARD

It was on the battlefield but only the artillerymen with their 14 guns, making up the large central battery required by the Emperor, participated directly in the battle.

MURAT'S CAVALRY RESERVE

Only the dragoons from Klein's Division were present for the final phase with two of d'Hautpouls' regiments (1st and 10th Cuirassiers). This represented about 3,500 cavalry.

———

Thus Napoleon engaged gradually only a little more than 40,000 men, 8,500 cavalry and 110 cannon. Large reinforcements were arriving from the rear; from the direction of Durnburg. Bernadotte was stationed with 18,500 infantry, 1,500 cavalry and 34 cannon. He advanced slowly towards Apolda and kept Sahuc's dragoon division and the cavalry reserve's light regiments including Lasalle's Brigade nearby.

In the afternoon of 13th October 1806, the artillery of Lannes' 5th Corps begins to climb up and take position on top of Landgrafenberg. (Work by Benjamin Zix, Château de Versailles, © Réunion des Musées nationaux-Arnaudet photograph).

THE BATTLE OF JENA

NEEDING TO DEPLOY his closely-packed troops, Napoleon got Lannes' 5th Corps going at a little after 6 a.m., in spite of the thick fog which covered the terrain. Suchet's Division opened the march.

Naturally Claparède again led off with the 17th Light, accompanied by the elite battalion, in the general direction of the village of Closewitz. He had two cannon with him and advanced in total fog.

He was followed by Reille's Brigade, the 34th Line deployed on the left and the 40th on the right in columns. Vedel's Brigade followed with the 64th on the right of the 88th.

Gazan's Division strengthened Suchet on his left wing.

Further to the left, Desjardin's Division from Augereau's Corps, positioned on the Weimar road, in turn advanced towards Lützeroda.

THE FIGHT FOR CLOSEWITZ
AND LÜTZERODA

Tauentzien placed his troops in the following manner:

- in Clozewitz: the Pelet battalion and the Valentini Jäger;

- on the left of the village: the Metzsch and Hundt battalions of Saxon grenadiers, supported by three squadrons of Gettkandt Hussars;

The vanquished general, Hohenlohe, commanding the Prussian and Saxon troops at Jena. (Deutsche Helden).

- on the right of Closewitz lined up facing Lützeroda: the Zweiffel Regiment, the half-battalion of Herwath grenadiers, the Rechten battalion and Studnitz half-battery. The Frederick-Augustus battalion was drawn up behind them. The Saxon grenadiers from the Lichtenhayn, Thiolay and Lecoq battalions completed the line towards Lüzeroda.

- in Lützeroda itself: the Erichsen battalion and the Werner Jägers and beside them a battery made up of six battalion cannon under Lieutenant Bose. Three squadrons of Gettkandt Hussars were in support and the Rosen battalion was in the second line, in front of the Isserstedter forest.

Acting on orders recieved, Hohenlohe dispersed his troops – in particular the detachments given to Holtzendorff to guard Dornburg – so much so that he left Tauentzien quite alone in the centre of the line and too far away to be reinforced easily.

The 17th Light was directed a bit too far to the right and when they heard the Prussians giving orders, they fired into the fog. This random firing lasted more than an hour causing a lot of casualties on both sides. Suchet's cannon made the enemy's situation worse and the Zweiffel Regiment with the Frederick-Augustus and Rechten battalions had to be brought back to the rear.

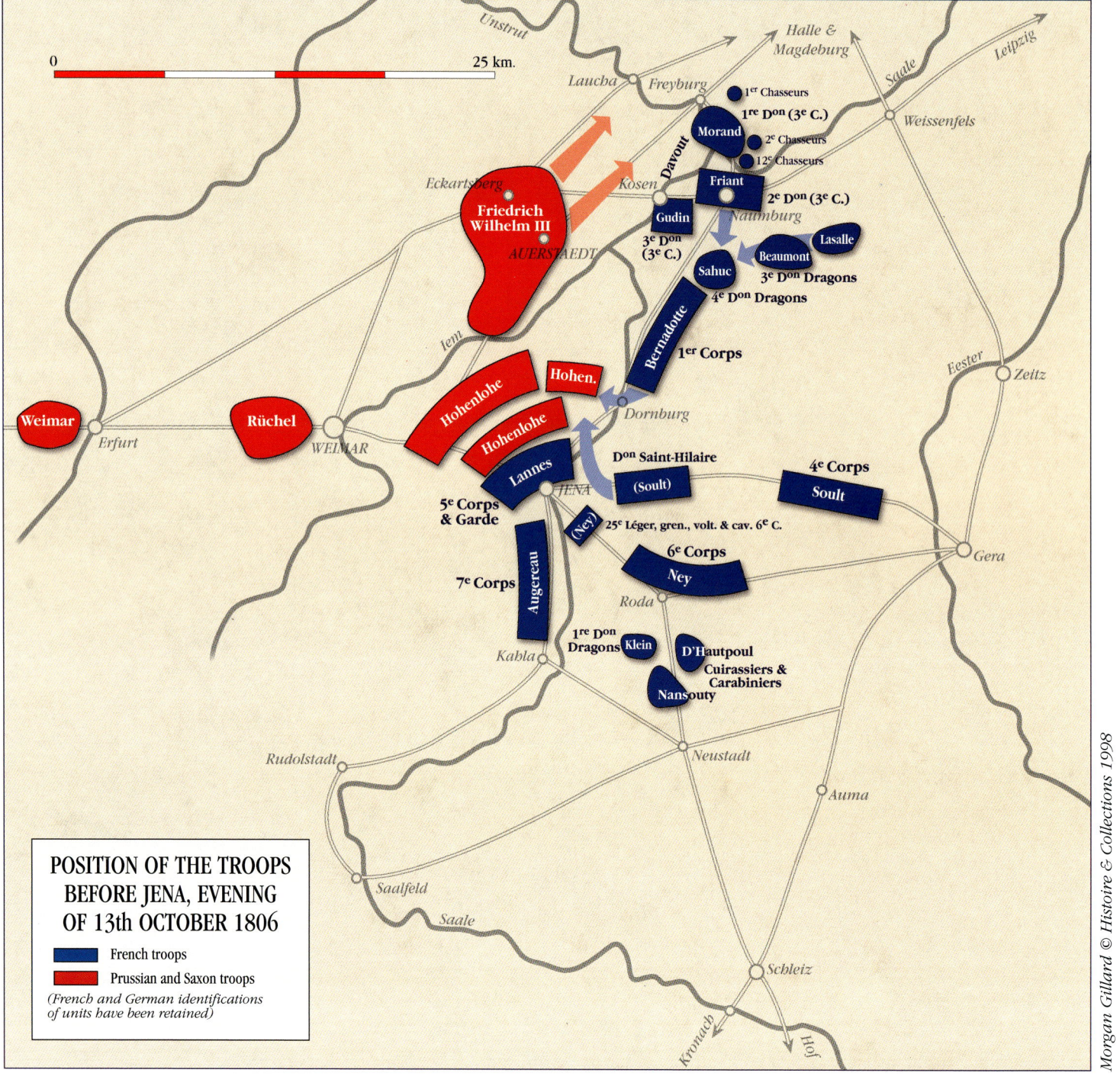

POSITION OF THE TROOPS BEFORE JENA, EVENING OF 13th OCTOBER 1806

■ French troops
■ Prussian and Saxon troops
(French and German identifications of units have been retained)

Morgan Gillard © Histoire & Collections 1998

The positions could then be seen and Claparède saw the little wood that covered Closewitz. Orders were recieved to take it. It was now 8.30.

The Herwath Grenadiers and the Pelet battalion were pushed out of the wood and rallied the left of the Zweiffel Regiment.

Further to the left, the 21st Light, which was at the front of Gazan's Division, took the Ziskau wood and after a fierce struggle, forced three Saxon battalions to retreat. These battalions had been setting themselves up on Tauentzien's new line to the west of the Rechten battalion. The Tüllmann battery of howitzers managed to get back the line. Losses were high and ammunition was running out. Having been warned of this situation, Hohenlohe allowed Tauentzien to fall back through the second line to Kleinromstedt in order to reform and resupply. He began his retreat using the Saxon grenadiers as rearguard.

On Suchet's side, the 17th Light was exhausted and was taken out of the fight. The 34th, still supported by the elite detachment,

took its place. The Saxon grenadiers trying to obstruct the French advance were attacked by the 34th, a battalion from the 88th, and the 21st Light which had seized Lützeroda by chasing out Erichsen's and Werner's infantry, who went and hid themselves in the Isserstedter forest. A lot of prisoners and artillery pieces were taken, in particular the Tüllmann battery, which had succeeded in falling back under the protection of the hussars only to get bogged down; the light cavalry abandoned it and it was completely overwhelmed by Lannes' skirmishers.

Thus Closewitz and Lützeroda were taken; the 5th Corps had opened the way for the Emperor to deploy his troops.

SOULT'S FIGHT AGAINST HOLTZENDORFF'S FORCES

Coming from the right along the Spital road, Soult went through Closewitz wood, then the Zwatzener wood. The Saint-Hilaire Division was at the front with Candras' Brigade which was made up of the 10th Light, in front of the 36th Line.

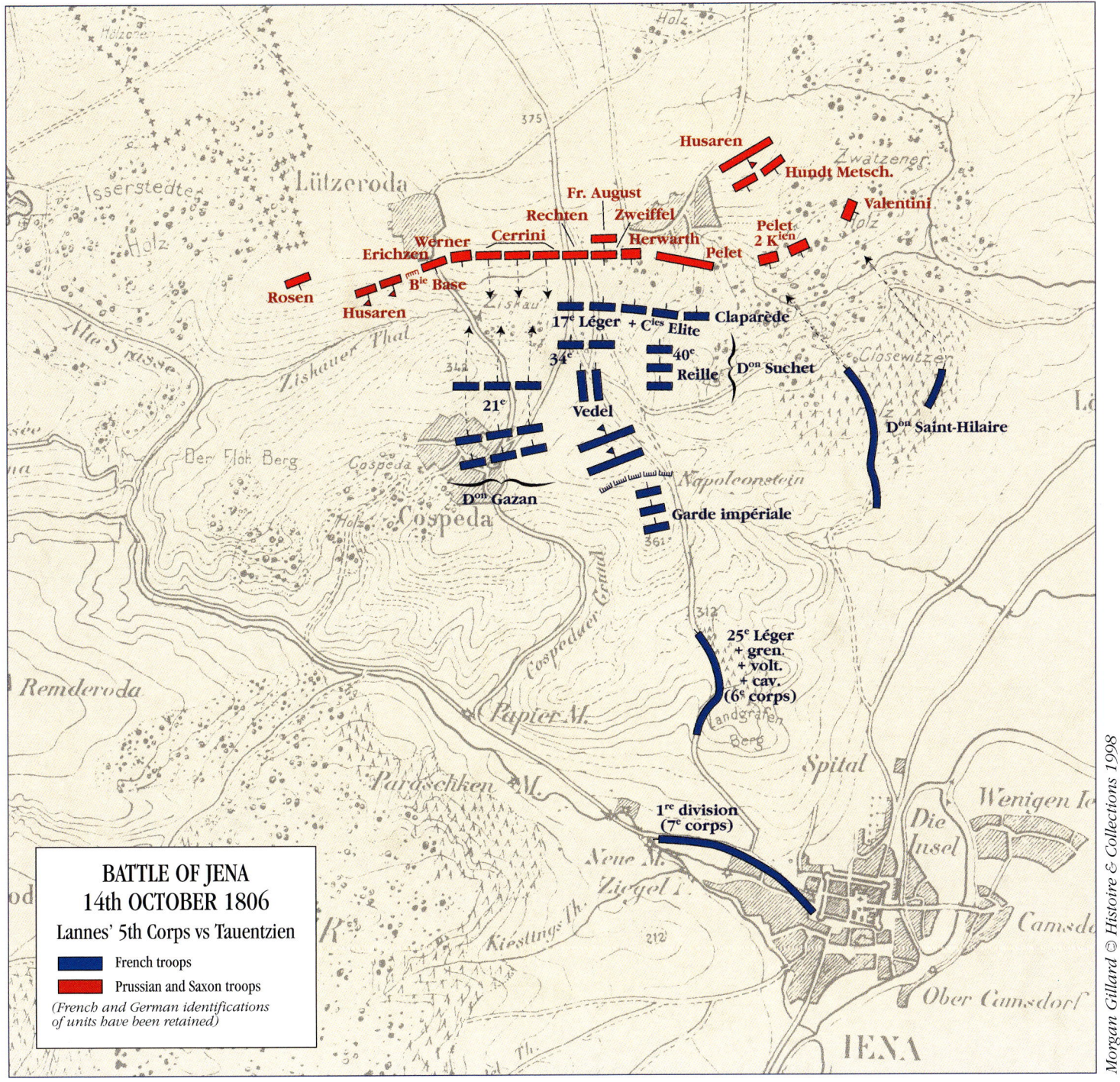

Varé's Brigade came next with the 43rd and the 55th Line. After having pushed what was left of Pelet's men and the Valentini Jägers out of the wood, they themselves came out of the wood and came across the Merzsh and Hundt battalions. The two Saxon battalions, which were in a line formation, were overwhelmed and fell back in the fog.

Soult was obliged to wait for his artillery and his cavalry which had been forced to go round the wood to the east. The Marshall finally joined these troops up with Saint-Hilaire's Division towards 9.30.

Totally isolated on the extreme left of the Prussian lines, Holtzendorff had at his disposal:

- the four squadrons of Holtzendorff Cuirassiers, the Hahn battery of horse artillery and General Senft's cavalry: the Prince John (two squadrons) and Clemens (four squadrons) Light Horse.

- General Sanitz's infantry with the Kollin, Borcke, Dohna and Losthin grenadiers and the Schulemburg 12-pounders battery plus Major Lessel's 400 volunteers.

- half of the Schimmelpfennig Hussars regiment.

The remainder of the Valentini Jägers coming out of the wood rallied this corps which had met up at Rodigen. Getting themselves completely lost, the Kollin half-battalion and Gause half-battery rallied on the left of Grawert's Division, some distance from this particular fight.

Towards 9.30 the fog began to lift. Holztendorff could now make out Soult's skirmishers setting out for Rodingen and Lehesten. They soon occupied the little wood on the Heiligenholz. Sanitz's infantry emerged, and Borcke battalion chased the French skirmishers from this wood and occupied it with their own skirmishers whilst the troops got themselves into line.

Between Rödigen and Lehesten, Holtzendorff set up the front line, from left to right: the Dohna and Losthin units, Lessel's 400 volunteers (taken the day before from Grawert's Division) and the main part of Borcke grenadiers. The Schulemburg battery

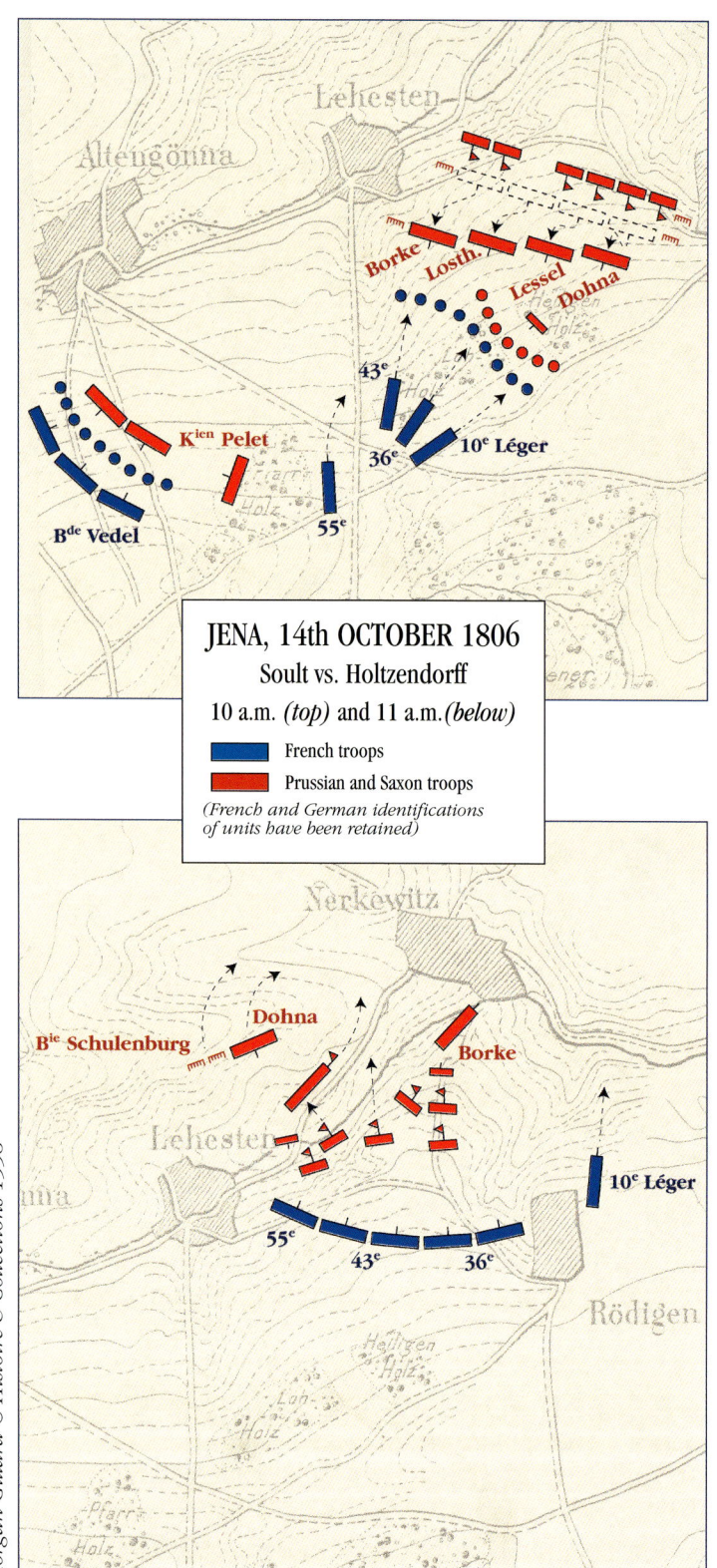

Morgan Gillard © Histoire & Collections 1998

JENA, 14th OCTOBER 1806

Soult vs. Holtzendorff

10 a.m. *(top)* and 11 a.m.*(below)*

🟦 French troops

🟥 Prussian and Saxon troops

(French and German identifications of units have been retained)

driven off. Three other Holtzendorff's battalions were on the march to the west when Soult's cavalry appeared and charged the retreating Saxon light horse. They charged three times before succeeding in putting the Saxons to flight.

In their flight, the Saxon cavalry got all caught up with the cuirassiers. It was the Borcke battalion which stopped the French rush and held them off. Thanks to this battalion, Holtzendorff's infantry was able to retreat through Nerkwitz, but General Sanitz and 20 officers were taken with 400 men. Two standards and six cannon were also captured.

Saint-Hilaire's Division continued to attack, penetrated Nerkwitz and attacked again. The 36th was at the front; its colonel was killed but the regiment still took the Schulemburg battery. Holtzendorff rallied the survivors from this group on Stobra and disappeared from the scene.

Soult now set off towards the left in the direction of Hermstedt to join the action.

THE INITIAL FIGHTING FOR VIERZEHNHEILIGEN

Tauentzien had finally pulled back in reasonably good order beyond the Dornberg. There he set up a line of defence between Krippendorf and Vierzehnheiligen, supported by four fresh battalion from his division: two of Rechten, one of Winkel and one of Maximilian from the von Schönberg's Brigade. He positioned them on his right, reinforcing them with the Bose battery which had managed to get out of Lützeroda. Further to the left, he deployed five and a half batteries which he had got out in good order.

Claparède, now leading the elite detachment and the 34th, took the village of Krippendorf, capturing four cannon in addition to the eighteen he had already taken since the beginning of the battle.

On its left, the main part of the 5th Corps was covered by a mass of skirmishers. Napoleon had joined Lannes and was marching with the first line behind the skirmishers. The Emperor sent the 40th to attack Vierzehnheiligen and set up a large battery of 14 pieces from the Guard with four 8-pounders from the 5th Corps. Cannon from the 7th Corps were brought in to reinforce this artillery line which now set its sights on the Bose battery.

Tauentzien counter-attacked and repulsed the 40th's attack, also pushing back the 34th which the cavalry from the 5th Corps had joined. The Gettkandt Hussars covering Tauentzien's left, took part in this attack. The 34th's first battalion held them off and, forming a square near the windmill at Krippendorf, managed to hold this position in spite of heavy losses.

It was ten o'clock and the fog had almost entirely lifted.

THE REACTION OF THE PRUSSIANS

Hohenlohe slept peacefully and when woken, was not convinced that he was seriously under attack. It was only towards eight o'clock that he reached Grawert's Division whose commander informed him of the impending danger. Hohenlohe warned Rüchel immediately and asked for his support. Tauentzien was permitted to fall back. The fog was still thick but Grawert's Division had to be moved towards Vierzehnheiligen.

General Zezschwitz's Saxon division was already dug in between Isserstedt and the little valley of the Schwabhauser Grund,

was placed on the right and the Hahn battery on the left. The cavalry was stationed behind, the Light Horse on the left (six squadrons), with the Holtzendorff Cuirassiers (four squadrons) and the Schimmelpfennig Hussars. This only represented 2,500 infantry, 2,500 cavalry and 20 cannon.

Seeing himself thus cut off from the rest of Hohenlohe's troops, the Prussian general tried to open up a passage through to Altengona to the west of Nerkwitz; he began his move towards 10 o'clock. The Schimmelpfennig Hussars and the Dohna battalion covered the Schulemberg battery which went back beyond Lehesten and got itself into position so that the rest of the troops' retreat would be protected.

Candras' Brigade attacked in the direction of Rödingen. The cuirassiers and the light horse tried to charge them but they were

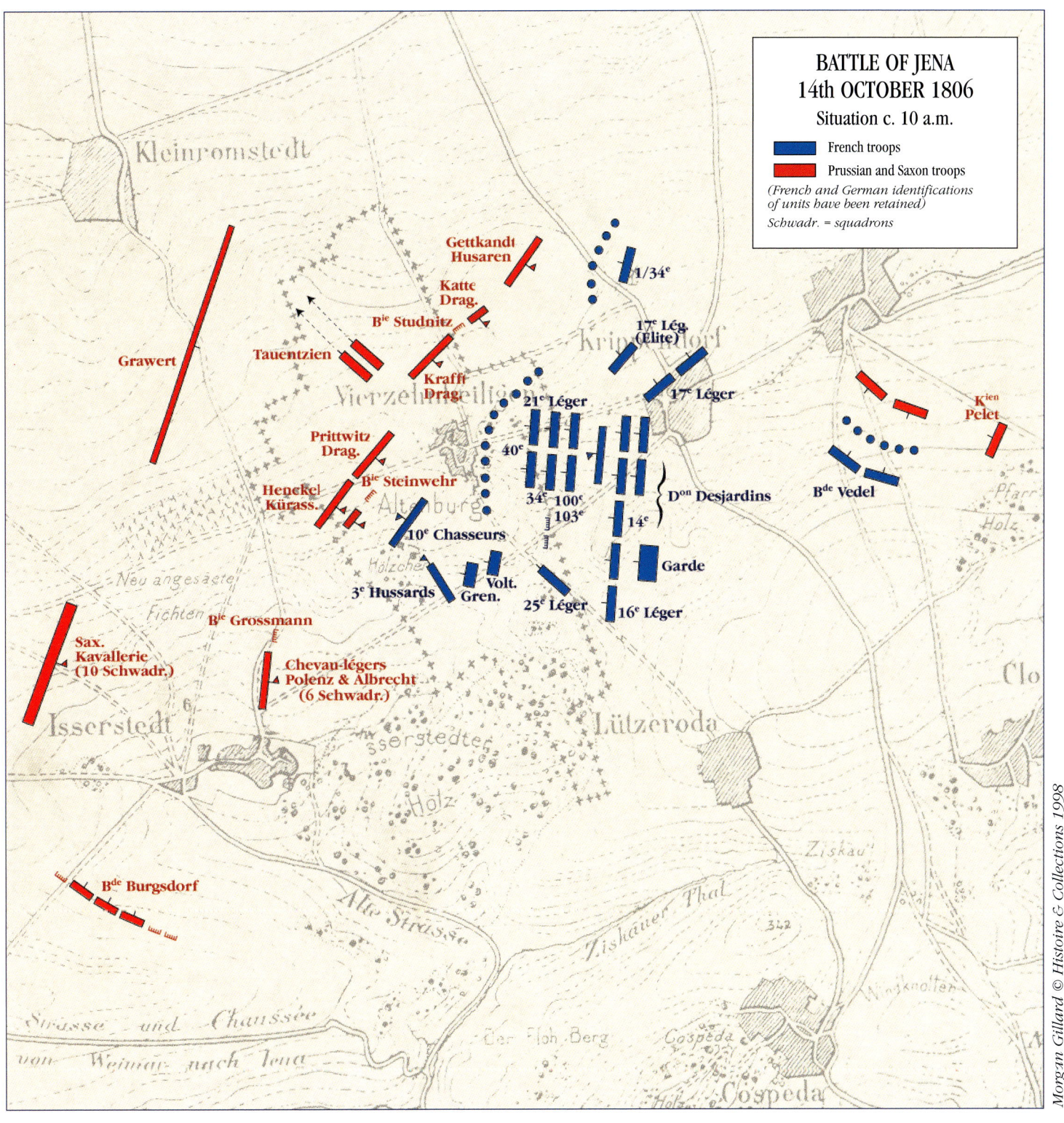

Morgan Gillard © Histoire & Collections 1998

where it remained inactive for along time. At about 10, Hohen-lohe came across Lannes' troops whose 40th had just been sent packing. He sent the cavalry off to the north of Vierzehnheiligen. This cavalry consisted of the Krafft Dragoons with the Stüdnitz battery, the Prittwit Dragoons, the Henckel Cuirassiers and finally Holtzendorff's 250 cuirassiers who had been left behind and had reinforced the Steinwehr battery.

These elements joined up with the Gettkandt Hussars who had been present from the beginning.

With the arrival of these reinforcements, Tauentzien got his troops to fall back towards Klein-Romstedt to get them re-orga-nised and re-supplied with ammunition. The village was left emp-ty and only the Steinwehr battery could be seen in action. All the cavalry was concealed.

Of Zezschwitz's Saxon division on the Schnecke, the cavalry was reaching Isserstedt together with the Polenz and Albrecht Light Horse; the Kochitzky Cuirassiers were in the rear, waiting for the infantry.

THE ARRIVAL OF NEY'S VANGUARD

Ney at first went off in the wrong direction and instead of pas-sing to the right of Lannes, he slipped through between Lannes and Augereau. His system was simplistic: he charged as soon as he saw the enemy. But this time he was only accompanied by Colbert's two regiments (3rd Hussars and 10th Chasseurs), fol-lowed by the 25th Light and the elite detachments (a battalion of grenadiers and one of voltigeurs).

So he charged the Steinwehr battery, but where his chasseurs

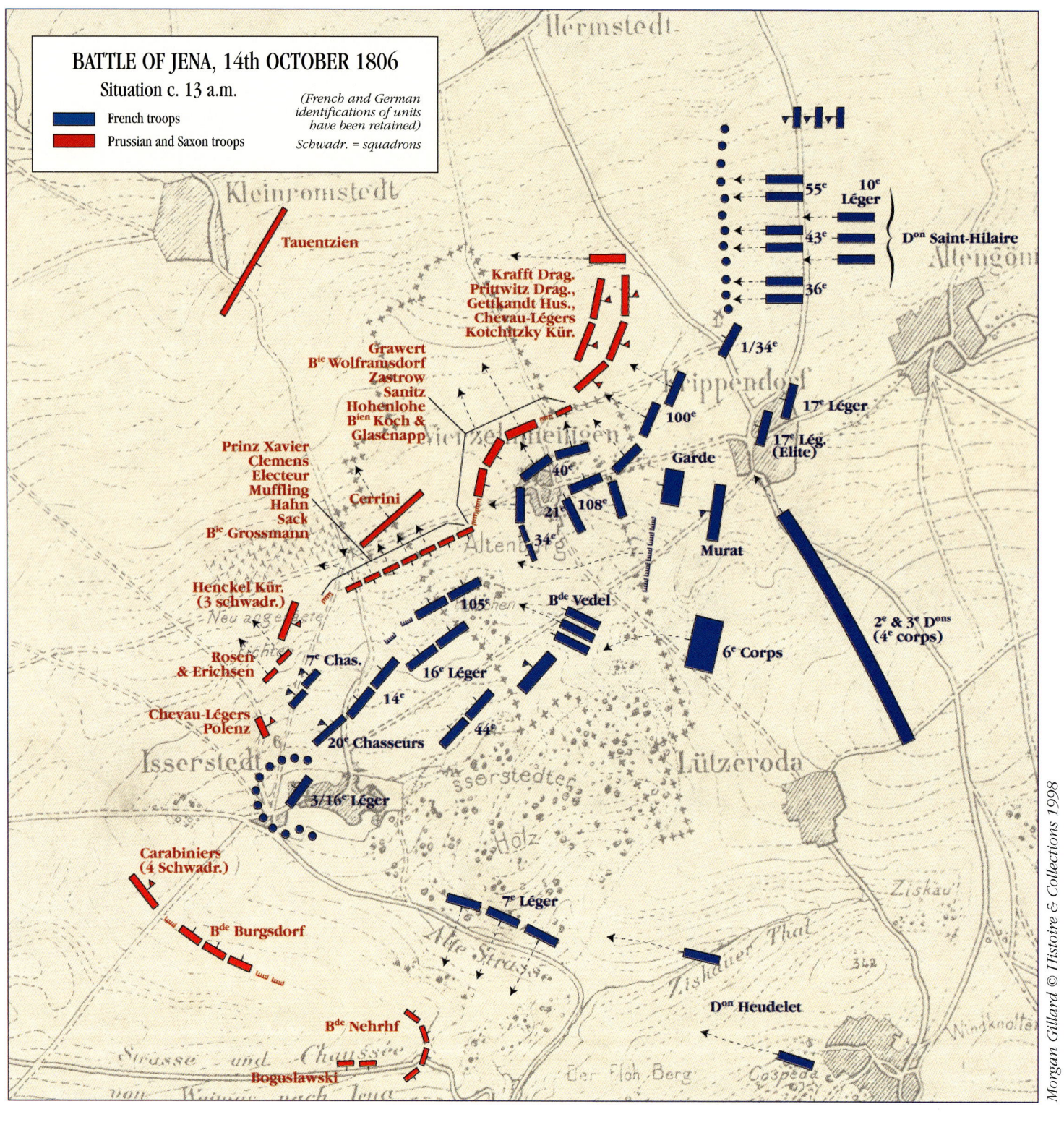

were able to get past the artillery, they were pushed back by the cavalry, right back onto the squares formed by the elite detachments. To stop this the 3rd Hussars had to intervene with the help of the 5th Corps' cavalry who were just arriving. Faced with this new threat, the Prittwitz Dragoons and the Henckel Cuirassiers fell back. Ney was put out and got his infantry to move towards the Isserstedter forest.

THE FIGHTING AROUND VIERZEHNHEILIGEN

Towards 10 o'clock, hearing Soult fighting on his right, Napoleon decided to detach Vedel's Brigade from Lannes' Corps and send it in that direction; Conroux's Brigade from Augereau's Corps came up to replace it.

Vedel hustled the Mertzsch and Hundt battalions who had

got lost. With greater difficulty they then forced Pelet back out of the Pfarr Holz, where his men were holding on with great determination.

At this precise moment the Emperor had Lannes on his right supported by Suchet's Division, with Campana's Brigade (which had replaced Vedel's) in support at the rear, and Gazan's Division. The main battery was spread out on the left, next to Desjardin's Division from the 7th Corps with the 21st Light, in front of Vierzehnheiligen village. The 5th Corps' cavalry was on the left with the 6th's. Ney's infantry was beginning to infiltrate the Isserstedter forest. The 40th and the 21st Line were thrown into the attack on the village. This was occupied without problem, because the Prussians were not interested in villages and prefered operating in open country.

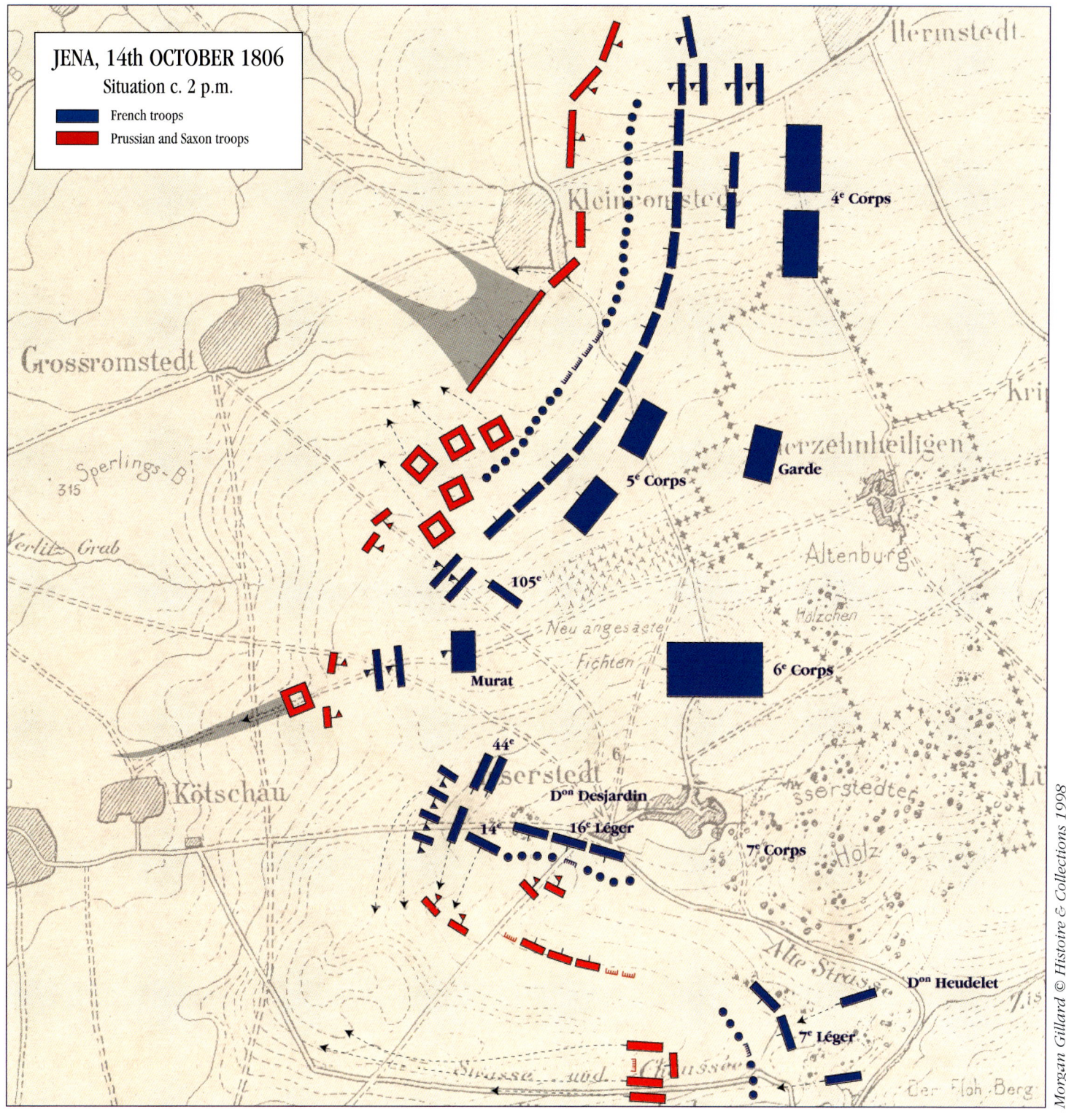

Morgan Gillard © Histoire & Collections 1998

At 10.30, Hohenlohe thought that it was the moment to attack and moved the Grawert Division forwards. The Grawert and Zastrow Regiments together with the Wolframsdorf battery, then emerged to the north, the Sanitz and Hohenlohe Regiments to the west, of the village occupied by the French. The Kollin half battalion and the Gause half battery, lost from Holtzendorff's group, covered their left.

Further to the right there were the Hahn and Sack battalions with the Glasenapp battery, then the Erichsen and Rosen battalions. With the help of the Werner Jägers, they managed to push the 25th Light back out of Isserstedt and the forest.

Behind this line, Hohenlohe had grouped his cavalry on the left, with 20 squadrons regrouping the Katte, Krafft and Prittwitz Dragoons and the Gettkandt Hussars present since the begin-

ning. In the middle, there were five squadrons of which four consisted of cuirassiers; and on the right, three squadrons of Henckel Cuirassiers.

On a level with Isserstedt, ten Saxon squadrons linked Grawert's right to the Saxon division which was on the Schneke.

As a reserve, Hohenlohe only had Dyhern's five battalions and Cerrini's four battalions in front of Klein-Romstedt.

The line gave way, and the six pieces that Ney had just set up were immediately badly mauled and obliged to fall back. Lapisse's Brigade from Desjardin's Division got the situation under control on the Isserstedt side, clearing the forest out with the 16th Light and the 14th Line. The village was retaken by about 11.30.

In front of Vierzehnheiligen, the situation was more critical and it took firing from both the large battery and from Reille's

Brigade to make the Prussian line hesitate and stop. A charge by the 9th Hussars was thrown back.

Lannes then tried an attack with Gazan's 100th and 103th Line, but the enemy cavalry, reinforced by Saxon squadrons, called in from the right, threw them back. To fill in the gap created on the right by this movement of the Saxon cavalry, Grawert slotted in the reserve battalions.

The Saxon division to the south decided to move and came closer to the three battalions in Isserstedt. For the moment it was still not being used for anything.

Hohenlohe hesitated. Then, learning that French columns were on the move towards the Dornberg, he decided to wait for Rüchel and merely burnt the village of Vierzehnheiligen.

NAPOLEON REGAINED THE INITIATIVE

Napoleon, informed of Soult's success, recalled Vedel's Brigade and returned the second brigade commanded by Conroux (10th and 44th) to Desjardin.

Now that his brigade was back in its place, Vedel was told to support Conroux because Desjardin's Division was starting its attack on Grawert's right wing, in order to separate it further from Zezschwitz's Division which was still to the south of Isserstedt.

It was 11.30 when Augereau began his offensive. The cavalry brigade from the 7th Corps had just joined up. Behind them the two divisions of the 6th Corps arrived on the battlefield together with the head of Klein's Dragoon Division, followed by the 1st and the 10th Cuirassiers from d'Hautpoul's Division. Heudelet's Division was not far away. Soult moved up on the right beyond Lannes.

The action of Desjardin's Division

Facing this division, there were the four Cerrini battalions, the Hahn and Sack battalions, the Glassnapp and Grossmann batteries and the survivors of the Erichsen and Rosen battalions chased out of Isserstedt by the 16th Light.

Dyhern's Brigade was behind with two squadrons of Polenz

Light Horse and three squadrons of cuirassiers. The French attack was led by the 16th Light, and the 14th and 105th Line. Captain Benoist's three guns were there to reinforce them and the 44th was behind with the cavalry of the 7th Corps (7th and 20th Chasseurs). Vedel's Brigade was following.

Cerrini's four battalions were the first to give way, throwing the cavalry into disorder; both had to retreat. The Grossmann battery was now exposed and a charge by the 7th Chasseurs cut through it. But the 7th did not have the support, as planned, of the 20th whose colonel's death confused orders. So they were pushed back by the enemy cavalry and actually had a lot of trouble regaining the French lines.

In the meantime the 16th Light and the 105th chased out the Hahn and Sack battalions, capturing the Glassenapp battery. In all 14 cannon were taken and turned against the enemy. Grossmann's last pieces were either captured or destroyed.

So Grawert's right fell back to the north with heavy casualties, regrouping with Dyhern's Brigade.

To the south, the Saxons of Burgdorf's Brigade, finally aware of what was happening, opened fire on the 44th, the left of Desjardin's Division. It was more than 12.30.

The action of Saint-Hilaire's Division supporting Lannes

This division continued its march towards Hohenlohe's left, joined up with Lannes' right. Their combined attack was able start at one p.m.

Lannes started the attack with the 100th and the 103rd supported by six artillery pieces. The Grawert, Sanitz and Zastrow Regiments were shaken.

The Saint-Hilaire Division goes into the attack. The French advanced to the sounding of the charge by the drums and the bands. Large numbers of skirmishers marched in front.

The church of Vierzehnheiligen today, with the battle's commemorative monument. (DR).

Hohenlohe's line buckled then retreated abandoning 15 cannon and a lot of prisoners. The remainder rallied towards Klein-Romstedt where Tauentzien, who was well organised, took them in and formed up a new line.

At the other end of the fight, Napoleon gave Desjardin's Division the order to turn round against the Saxons in the south, but at that moment the 105th was committed against Dyhern's battalions, the losers at Saalfeld. The 105th therefore continued with this action towards the north and Desjardins went on towards the south with his other three regiments.

The struggle was very fierce for the 105th, but it received support from the 5th Corps' cannon which had been part of the large central battery, now no longer of use. These cannon immediately helped the situation because Vedel's Brigade simultaneously rushed at the enemy's right wing. Dyhern's battalions were routed. It was nearly two o'clock in the afternoon.

THE DECISIVE ATTACK

The French army was in the following situation:
- on the right: Soult with Saint-Hilaire's Division and on his right the 4th Corps' cavalry and the first brigade of Klein's dragoons (1st and 14th). Soult's other two divisions arrived in support;
- in the centre: Lannes, keeping the 105th with him on the far left. Behind the skirmishers were the cavalry from the 5th and the 6th Corps. The divisions of the 6th Corps followed behind them on the left of the Guard. Murat covered the nearest regiments on Lannes' left with the rest of Klein's Division and the two cuirassier regiments.
- on the left: Desjardin's Division, reduced to three regiments attacking the Saxons in the south. Heudelet's Division had at last been able to reach the battlefield and rally his corps. His 7th Light marched up in front and engaged the Saxons from his side.

Faced with these increasingly impressive forces, Hohenlohe tried to reform a line with Tauentzien who took up Grawert on his right with Cerrini's battalions further to the right. The command of

General Ernst Wilhelm von Rüchel. (Deutsche Helden).

these residual troops was given to Tauentzien with Gross-Romstedt as his line of retreat.

The general held on as best he could, but he was overwhelmed on all sides and began to retreat.

On the main road to Weimar, the 105th and Vedel's Brigade pursued Dyhern's survivors. Grawert, wounded, tried to keep the Sack and Hundt battalions under control as long as possible.

Charged, attacked and pursued, the Prussian lines started to disintegrate towards 2.30 p.m. Only the survivors on the left wing maintained a semblance of good order in their retreat. This left Zezschwitz's Saxon divisions confronting Augereau.

THE FIGHT BETWEEN AUGEREAU AND THE SAXONS

Cut off from Grawert, Zezschwitz had the Bonniot, Ernst and Hausmann batteries driven up to towards Isserstedt supported by Burgsdorf's Brigade (the Thümmel and Prince Frederick-Augustus Regiments) and the four squadrons of carabiniers.

Behind there was Nehrhof's Brigade with one of the Bevilaqua battalion, and the Low and Niesemenschel Regiments, together with Boguslawski's light troops, i.e. his own battalion and the Masars light cavalrymen. Hussars from four Bila and two Gettkandt squadrons were set up as mounted sentries lower down.

The men of the 7th Light, heading first towards Isserstedter forest attacked Nehrhof's Saxons in support of the skirmishers.

Seeing his retreat threatened, Zezschwitz ordered the troops furthest south to fall back.

Meanwhile, Augereau attacked the Saxon batteries with the voltigeurs of the 14th who went ahead of their regiment. Behind and on the same line, were the 16th Light and the 44th Line; the horsemen of the 1st, 14th and 26th Dragoons took part in the attack. The 14th Line attempted to overrun the enemy's left.

The Saxon carabiniers charged the skirmishers three times without managing to stop them. The 16th Light captured six battalion cannon, the charging 26th Dragoons were pushed back towards Heudelet's 7th Light which was moving up to take part in the combat.

Surrounded and overwhelmed, Burgdorf's battalions finally surrendered. Zezschwitz, regrouping his carabiniers, forced his way through and reached the Weimar road where he met his brother, commanding the Saxon cavalry. The French dragoons progressively caught up with the batteries which had succeeded in getting out.

On the other hand, Nehrhof's Brigade succeeded in getting away hidden by the slope. Likewise, the six squadrons of hussars bustled their way through the dragoons who were trying to block their retreat, and fell back.

The French were advancing everywhere and it was at this moment that Rüchel decided to enter on stage, missing his queue completely.

GENERAL RÜCHEL'S HOPELESS STRUGGLE

Rüchel had taken a long time to get there; it was too late to hope. The only thing he was able to do was to make the retreat a bit easier for the other units. Forced to decide between

Schenck IR n° 9

Wedel IR n° 10

Winning IR n° 23

Alt-Larisch IR n° 26

André Jouineau © Histoire & Collections 1998

three choices – helping the Duke of Weimar's retreat, helping the King, or helping Hohenlohe – he chose to do the only thing he could still do: try to protect Hohenlohe's retreat. But it was already 2.30 p.m. Hohenlohe had installed himself in Kapellendorf with his remaining troops which now consisted of:

- the Bailliodz Cuirassiers, 250 Köhler hussars, three squadrons from Katte Dragoons and the Neander battery of horse artillery.
- the Alt-Larisch, Winning, Wedell, Strachwitz, Tschepe and Schenk Regiments. The 2nd battalion of the Treuenfels Regiment (the rest of the regiment was left at Weimar), the Sobbe Fusiliers, and the Borstell and Hallmann grenadier battalions.
- the Kirchfeld and Schäfer 12-pounder batteries.
In all about 12,000 men.

Hohenlohe, admitting himself defeated, gave the command to Rüchel, who tried to regroup the retreating units and reinforce his line. First he found the Rühle and Rabenau Fusiliers and the remains of the Pelet battalion.

He established his line in front of Kapellendorf. Tauentzien and Zweiffel regrouped what was left and recoverable of the troops on the left of this line. The Gettkandt Hussars were sent to the right. The Prittwitz Dragoons and the two squadrons of Katte Dragoons sent in reinforcement during the morning, were regrouped with the rest of the regiment on the right of the line. The Saxon cavalry joined them, and the whole thing now looked a little more respectable.

In front, the French cavalrymen and their light batteries appeared between Kötschau and Gross-Romstedt, and the cannon started firing with deadly accuracy. Rüchel was wounded but his line advanced.

Murat threw in his dragoons who were driven back and the French batteries who were then under threat, fell back, but the

Schimonsky IR n° 40

Zweiffel IR n° 45

Malschitzki IR n° 29

Tschepe IR n° 37

Strachwitz IR n° 43

Fusilier
Sobbe IR n° 18

Hallmann Battalion,
Wedel IR n° 10, Lettow IR n° 41

Borstell Battalion,
Wedel IR n° 9, Hagken IR n° 44

André Joutineau © Histoire & Collections 1998

Infantry of von Rüchel'Corps (II and III)

Arnim IR n° 13

Zenge IR n° 24

Pirch IR n° 22

Müffling IR n° 49

infantry columns, getting more and more numerous continued advancing. The cannon from the former large central battery took up position in front of the Prussian centre.

On the right, Saint-Hilaire threatened to overrun Rüchel's left. On the left it was Vedel's Brigade still with Augereau's 105th, which attacked, followed by the dragoons and finally by the cuirassiers. The 1st Cuirassiers finished off the Winning Regiment of which 400 men and the flag were captured. The Wedell Regiment, under attack by the 105th and the 4th, was charged three times by the 10th Cuirassiers. Most of the men were taken.

Nehrhof's Saxons who were falling back from the south with Boguslawski, were charged by cavalry from the 5th and the 7th Corps before they could set up squares. They were captured.

The enemy army was routed, the biggest part fleeing towards Weimar, but those who were further north tried to take the Apolda road. Soult guessed their intention and went off in this direction to cut off their route. It was 3.30.

Murat with his cavalry, helped by five pieces of light artillery detached from the 7th Corps, pursued these columns in full flight towards Weimar. A rearguard tried to protect the retreat through the congested town. This last link gave way and the Ernst battalion which was the last to try to fall back, was overrun and left behind 250 prisoners.

At 5.30 p.m. the French cavalry entered Weimar and all the elements of Hohenlohe's army who had been able to take the Erfürt road moved on even faster. The 105th, the battalion of the 88th commanded by Cambronne, the 44th and Ney's vanguard reached Weimar at about 6.30 p.m. and took up position there around Murat who was gradually joined by his cavalry from the reserve.

Hohenlohe, completely beaten, learned beyond Weimar of the King's army's defeat at the hands of Davout's Corps.

André Jouineau © Histoire & Collections 1998

Cavalry of von Rüchel'Corps

Bailliodz
Cuirassiers,
n° 5

Von Katte
Dragoons,
n° 4

Köhler
Hussars,
n° 7

The enemy losses at Jena were heavy and difficult to evaluate. Napoleon believed at the beginning that he had beaten the King's army and gave rough estimates in his 5th bulletin of 14th October. He announced 25 to 30 flags and 300 cannon captured and almost 20,000 enemy casualties together with a great number of prisoners whose tally grew all the time. This seems to be the truth as only Lestocq's little Corps succeeded in making it to the banks of the Vistula to rejoin the Russians. The Prussian army, once so proud, collapsed on these two battlefields this 14th October 1806.

We have now to study the battle of Auerstaedt which is probably one of the most remarkable feats of arms in all the history of France.

The day after the battle of Jena, on 15th October 1806, in front of Napoleon, the Saxon officers swear never again to raise arms against him.
(Work by Benjamin Zix, Château de Versailles, © Réunion des Musées nationaux-Arnaudet photograph).

A panoramic view of the battle of Jena, water-colour after a drawing by the Augsburger painter Johann Lorenz Rugendas. The scene shows the situation at 10.15 a.m. The windmill of Krippendorf can be seen on the right. (Author's Collection).

THE FRENCH COMBATANTS
AT JENA

W E WILL TRY IN THIS CHAPTER to classify the men who had an interesting career according to their regiment. It was they who fought with Napoleon against Hohenlohe at Jena on 14th October. We will consider those who were with Davout at Auerstaedt later.

NAPOLEON'S GENERAL STAFF

The Emperor had with him *Duroc*, the Master of the Horse *Caulaincourt*; Major General *Clarke*, Secretary to the Cabinet; *Corbineau*, Equerry to the Empress and *Gardane*, Master of the Pages.

His aides de camps were *Lemarois*, *Savary*, *Rapp*, *Bertrand* and *Mouton*.

His ordnance officers were:

- *Deponthon*, Engineer Captain, Egyptian campaign, Colonel and Baron in 1810. Made General in Hamburg by Davout in 1814. GdOLH in 1844. Pair de France

- *de Lamarche* (or *Drouot-Lamarche*), Captain in the 4th Hussars, Squadron commander of the 2nd Hussars on the 25th October.

- *Scherb*, Captain of the 10th Cuirassiers, Squadron commander at Berlin.

- *Castille*, Artillery Captain.

Duroc

Caulaincourt

Clarke

Bertrand

Gardane

Savary

Rapp

Mouton

Lemarois

- *de Montesquiou*, sent to the King of Prussia on the 13th October.

- *de Turenne*, Chamberlain in 1812, retired in 1815, Honorary Maréchal de camp in 1827.

BERTHIER'S STAFF

The Chief of Staff was Colonel *Blein*, replacing General *Lecamus* who was absent. The senior officer at Headquarters was General *Ménard*. They were assisted by:

- *Bailly de Monthion*, former aide de camp of Turreau in Vendée where he met Berthier. General in 1808, Count in 1809. Wounded at Waterloo, back in favour in 1830, Pair de France and GdCxLH. Retired in 1848.

- *René*, General, burnt alive in Spain on 29th June 1808.

- *Wolff*, Colonel, post-master.

His aides de camps were:

- *Bruyères*, General 30th December 1806. Major General in 1809, he married a daughter of César Berthier and was killed in 1813.

- *Girardin d'Ermenonville*, Squadron commander from Italy, Count in 1810. Russian Campaign, Major General in 1814. GdOLH in 1825. Died in 1855.

- *Edouard de Colbert*, Squadron commander. General and Baron in 1809, he commanded the Red Lancers of the Guard in 1811. Major General in 1813, wounded at Waterloo. Empriso-

French Army

General Staff (I)

General aide de camp of Napoleon

Aide de camp in hussar-style uniform

Armband of an aide de camp of a Maréchal

Adjudant-commandant in undress

Assistant adjudant-commandant in undress

Staff officer

War Commissaire in full dress

André Jouineau © Histoire & Collections 1998

ned in 1815, back in favour in 1826. In Constantine in 1836. GdCxLH in 1837, died in 1853.

- *Lagrange* (Count *Le Lièvre de*) Captain, General in 1812, Russian campaign. Lieutenant General in June 1814, not active in 1815, GdOLH in 1836, Senator in 1859, died 1864.

- *Montholon*, General, Count and chamberlain in 1811. Napoleon's aide de camp at Waterloo, he went to St-Helena with him.

Additional aides de camps:

- *Canouville*, Sergeant of the Palace in 1812, Russian campaign. Maréchal de camp in 1817, Count in 1832, Pair de France. His brother, Pauline Bonaparte's lover, was killed at Borodino as a Squadron commander of the 16th Chasseurs.

- *de Noailles*, killed at the Beresina.

His assistants were:

- *Lejeune*, Battalion commander in the Engineers, wounded at Saragossa, followed Berthier as colonel in 1809. Baron in 1810. Sent on a mission to Spain, he was captured by the guerillas near Toledo and escaped death by a miracle. Sent to England as a prisoner. He came back in 1811 and followed Berthier to Russia where he was promoted to the rank of general on 25th September 1812. Wounded at Hanau and retired, returned in 1817. GdOLH in 1841. A great military painter.

- *Simonin*, Captain in command of the interpreter-guides.

- *Marin*, Captain, aide de camp of Lecamus.

The private secretaries that followed Berthier everywhere were *Leduc* and *Guillabert*.

THE DEPARTMENTS OF THE GENERAL STAFF

The Adjudant commandant *d'Hastrel de Rivedoux*, General in 1810, Major General in 1811, GdOLH in 1835.

The Adjudants commandants *Petiet*, *Petit-Pressigny*, *Passinges* and *Romoeuf* (Davout's chief of staff in Russia, killed at Borodino).

Daru the Senior Commissariat Officer replaced *Villemanzy*, considered '*too formalistic and whimpering*'; *Dufresne* worked in accountancy and *Deniée*, *Duprat*, *Joinville* and *Lombart* helped to organise the administrative departments who were cruelly lacking in officers.

The topographical section was under General *Sanson* and the engineer *Bacler d'Albe* joined Napoleon.

THE ARTILLERY STAFF

This was commanded by *de Songis*, Grand-Aigle of the LH, Count in 1809, the date of his retirement.

The Chief of Staff was *Pernety*, Major General in 1807, Baron in 1810, Russian campaign, Viscount and State counsellor in 1817, Pair de France in 1835 and Senator in 1852.

(continued on page 60)

French Army

Imperial Guard

Colonel of Engineers, in charge of the topographical section, attached to Maréchal Berthier's staff.

Lieutenant of the 1st Hussars, attached to the Imperial Guard

Corporal, centre company, 4th Dragoons, attached to the Imperial Guard

Grenadiers à pied of the Imperial Guard

Drummer in full dress

Officer wearing coat

Officer wearing overcoat

Sapper in full dress

Sapper wearing overcoat

Drummer wearing overcoat

Sergeant in full dress

Grenadiers in full dress

wearing overcoat

André Jouineau © Histoire & Collections 1998

French Army

Imperial Guard

Chasseurs à pied of the Imperial Guard

Officer
wearing coat

Sapper
wearing overcoat

Drummer
in full dress

Sergeant
in full dress

Chasseur
in full dress

Chasseur
wearing overcoat

Foot Dragoons attached to the Imperial Guard

1st regiment

2nd Rgt   14th Rgt   20th Rgt   26th Rgt

6th Rgt   11th Rgt   13th Rgt   22nd Rgt

2nd regiment

8th Rgt   12th Rgt   16th Rgt   21st Rgt

17th Rgt   18th Rgt   25th Rgt   27th Rgt

André Jouineau © Histoire & Collections 1998

Daru

Berthier

Edouard de Colbert

Montholon

Bruyère

Lejeune

(continued from page 57) There was also *Sénarmont*, who had just been appointed General. Baron and Major General in 1808, sent to Spain and killed before Cadiz in 1810.
- *Bergé*, General in 1813, GdOLH in 1827, died in 1832.
- *Doguereau*.
- *Boulart*, transfered to the Guard. Wounded twice in 1809, Baron in 1810, Russia 1812, General in 1813, died in 1842.

THE GENERAL ARTILLERY POOL

Regrouping 48 guns, 318 limbers, 393 carriages and 11 forges.

THE ENGINEERS

Commanded by *Chasseloup-Laubat* with *Kirgener* as chief of staff.

THE PROTECTION OF THE STAFF

a. in Napoleon's service
In the absence of the cavalry of the Guard, it was the responsibility of the 1st Hussars detached from Bernadotte's Corps.
b. the Head-Quarters Guard
There was first of all an officer of the Gendarmerie with 97 gendarmes.
And there were especially the dragoons from the 4th regiment. Those of the elite company were attached to Berthier, but the rest of the regiment was also present. They came from Klein's division and were not committed in the battle of Jena.

THE IMPERIAL GUARD

This was commanded by General Lefebvre who had handed over the command of the 5th Corps to Lannes. He had only:
THE OLD FOOT GUARD
- the Grenadiers of the 1st and 2nd regiments: 2,000 men.
- the Chasseurs of the 1st and 2nd regiments: 2,000 men.
THE FOOT DRAGOONS
They formed two regiments and their companies were taken from several dragoon regiments. A total of 2,000 men.
THE ARTILLERY
This was picked up on the way at Mainz, from the reserve and among Oudinot's troops. This made a total of 26 cannon of which 12 were in reserve.

AUGEREAU'S 7th CORPS

- Chief of Staff: *Pannetier*, Count of Valdotte, wounded at Rivoli, General in 1803, CtLH, in Lyons in 1804. Lieutenant General in 1815, struck off and reinstated in 1831.
- *Rouyer*, baron de St Victor, wounded at Marengo, OLH, Adjudant Commandant, General in 1808, retired in 1815.
- *Picquet*, Squadron Commander, Colonel, Murat's aide de camp in 1807, Baron, General in 1813, mentioned and wounded at Rheims. GdOLH in 1815, Lieutenant General at Waterloo, wounded. Struck off, reinstated in 1831 with the Gendarmerie.
- *Gressot*, Battalion commander, General in Russia, OLH 1813, Waterloo. CrSL in 1823, retired in 1833.

Aide de camp
of a Major General
in regulation dress

Aide de camp
of a Brigadier General
in regulation dress

Aide de camp
of Maréchal Berthier

1st Hussars
servicing as
the Emperor's
horse guard at Jena

Lieutenant,
1st Hussars

Trumpeter,
1st Hussars

Corporal,
elite company,
1st Hussars

Corporal,
centre company,
1st Hussars

André Jouineau © Histoire & Collections 1998

Maréchal Augereau, Duke of Castiglione. (Painting by Robert Lefèvre, Château de Versailles, © Réunion des Musées nationaux photograph).

- *Simmer*, Baron, General at Moscow. CtLH in 1813, Major General in 1815 at Waterloo. Struck off, exiled to Le Mans then reinstated in 1831. Deputy till 1839.

- *La Gastine*, Engineer Colonel, mentioned at Jena, OLH, CtLH in 1807, then Baron, retired in 1812.

The aides de camp were:

- *Albert*, Adjudant commandant, General in 1807, Baron in 1810, Major General in Russia, wounded at the Beresina. Aide de camp to the Duke of Orleans. Died in 1822.

- *Augereau*, the General's half brother. General, CtLH, in reserve on 5th October 1807 after severe wounds. Taken back in 1808. Surrendered in Russia, prisoner, suspended in 1813, honorary Lieutenant General in 1815.

- *Noguès*, LH, Battalion commander, went through Holland in Nov. 1806, General in 1813, wounded at Waterloo, CrLH in 1832.

- *Marbot*, author of famous memoirs, Lieutenant, Pair de France in 1845.

- *Massy*, friend of Marbot, Colonel, died at Borodino.

- *Sicard*, Colonel, wounded at Eylau and killed at Heilsberg.

- *Nicolas*, Captain originally from the 1st Hussars, hero of Arcole, LH. Baron and Colonel of the 11th Chasseurs in Russia, CtLH in 1814, Waterloo, sacked in 1815. Maréchal de camp in 1823, GdOLH in 1834 and retired.

- *Mainvielle* and *Brô*, Lieutenants.

❖ DESJARDIN'S DIVISION

General *Desjardin*, CtLH, killed at Eylau.
- aide de camp: *Gauddart*, Battalion commander. General in 1813, Baron, OLH, inactive in 1816, retired in 1825.

LAPISSE'S BRIGADE

General *Lapisse*, Baron of Sainte-Hélène, CtLH, Major General 30th December 1806, Iron Crown. Killed at Talaveira in 1809.

16th Light

This was commanded by Colonel *Harispe*, wounded at Jena. CtLH, Major General in 1810, Count in 1813, wounded and captured at Toulouse, served in 1815, then inactive. Reinstated in 1830, Deputy, GdCxLH, Pair de France in 1835, Maréchal of France in 1851, Senator, died in 1855; lost his two brothers at Jena.
- *Jouardet*, Battalion commander, took command after the Colonel was wounded. CtLH in 1812, retired with rank of major in 1816.
- *Laborey*, Battalion commander died at Eylau.
- *Gheneser*, 'Frederic', Captain. Colonel in 1813, CtLH in 1814, wounded ten times, retired after Strasbourg in 1815, he had been with Rapp.
- *Raphin*, Captain, killed at Eylau.
- *Gauthier*, LH, killed in Spain in 1812.

Marbot, lieutenant in the 7th Corps' staff.

Harispe, commander of the 16th Light.

- *Lefebvre*, Captain adjutant-major, hero of Heilsberg, OLH, retired as Colonel.
- *Bidault*, Lieutenant, wounded at Austerlitz, LH, Captain in 1808, mentioned at Saragossa. Maire of Pontigny in 1835.
- *Deligny*, Second lieutenant. Hero of Spain, Captain in 1810.
- *Lombard*, sergeant, LH, mentioned in Spain, retired in 1814.
- *Dathy*, Musket of Honour, retired in 1808.
- *Gohin*, Musket of Honour, died at Eylau
- *Maitrot*, Musket of Honour, retired in 1807.
- *Mazan* or 'Masson', drummer, honoured in Italy. Amputated in 1813 and retired in 1814.
- *Parisot* and *Maillet*, voltigeurs, captured a flag at Jena.

This regiment known as the 'Brave', lost six killed and 49 wounded at Jena. It had detached two voltigeurs companies to help the 16th Light committed in front of it. At Eylau it was completely overrun, with its square; 28 officers and 590 men killed.

CONROUX'S BRIGADE

General *Conroux* wounded at Jena. CtLH in 1807, Baron, Major General in 1809, Spain. Killed at Ascain in November 1813.

This regiment was 2,606 men strong on 8th October 1806. Five of its officers and 31 of its soldiers were killed at Jena, plus 19 officers and 383 men wounded. It succeeded in capturing 17 cannon off the enemy.

14th Line

Commanded by Colonel *Savary*, killed 26th December 1806.
- *Dupuy de Saint-Florent*, Battalion commander, wounded 14 times at Ulm. Wounded at Jena then at Eylau. Colonel in Spain, Russia, General in 1814, non active in 1815.
- *Roulle*, Battalion commander, Major in 1807, retired in 1814.
- *Daussy*, Battalion commander, in command at Eylau and killed there.
- *Thuillier*, Captain, wounded at Austerlitz then at Jena where he captured 2 cannon; retired in 1808.
- *Arnaud*, Captain, captured two cannon and turned them against the enemy. Mentioned 24th December 1806. LH. Captured at Baylen, returned in 1811 and retired in 1814.
- *Barbanchon*, Captain, hero of Rivoli and Marengo. Received a Sabre of Honour. Died from wounds in 1807.
- *Stahl*, captain, heros of Heilsberg, wounded, OLH, Battalion commander. Killed 1809.
- *Brosset*, captain, OLH, Battalion commander in 1807, retired in 1814.

44th Line

Commanded by Colonel *Saudeur*, captured 29 cannon at Jena. Sabre of Honour, OLH, promoted General and retired after Jena.
- *Lafosse*, Major, Baron, OLH, General in 1811, retired in 1815.
- *Jacquemard*, Battalion commander, LH at Marengo, Colonel of the 5th Voltigeurs of the Guard in 1813. Baron, CrLH. Was with Ney at Waterloo. Arrested in 1815, retired in 1824.
- *Labat*, LH, hero of Switzerland, killed at Eylau.

This regiment had 7 killed and 36 wounded at Jena. On 8th October it numbered 1,728 men.

15th Line

The commander was Colonel *Habert*, Egyptian Campaign, hero of Heilsberg, General in 1808, hero of Spain, Major General, GdOLH, Commander of La Réunion. Wounded at Ligny, died in 1825.
- *Lescaudey*, battalion commander, OLH in 1809, died in Spain in 1812.
- *Imbeau*, Captain. LH, wounded and missing in action at Jena.
- *Jarot*, LH, Second lieutenant in 1810, Captain in 1813, retired in 1814.
- *Gobance*, Sergeant-major, LH, Lieutenant in 1811, retired in 1815.

- *Bontemps*, Corporal, LH, Wounded at Eylau, retired as Sergeant in 1811.

On the 8th October when it passed through Bamberg the regiment numbered 1,840 men. One officer and 23 men were killed, six officers and 160 men were wounded.

DESJARDIN'S DIVISIONAL ARTILLERY

It was commanded by General *Dorsner*, Baron, CtLH, retired 12th November 1806. In fact his request dated from 20th September and he was replaced by General *Sénarmont*, to whom Battalion commander Dubois' report was addressed on 28th October. However Dorsner must have been present at the battle because Sénarmont only arrived on the 21th November 1806.
- *Durand*, Baron d'Herville, Colonel, in command of the pool in 1814, CtLH, retired in 1814.
- *Dubois*, Battalion commander of the 1st division.

The pool of the 1st division, in Bamberg on the 8th October, included: four 8-pounders, two 4-pounders, a howitzer and eight 8-pounder limbers, two 4-pounders limbers, three howitzers limbers and nine infantry limbers, two ammunition waggons, three carriages with miscellaneous items, and a mobile campaign forge. In addition there were the regimental guns with their own supplies.

In his report of the battle, Battalion commander Dubois reported that the divisional cannon had been used in the following way:
- Captain *Chopin*, with four 8-pounders and a howitzer, served by the 5th company of the 6th Horse artillery regiment.
- Captain *Grosjean* had one 8-pounder and a howitzer served by the 2nd company of the 6th Horse artillery regiment.

These two officers brought their guns to join the large central battery organised by Napoleon, who put them with the 14 cannon of the Guard which had arrived on the field. Captain *Benoist* followed the division with one 4- and two 8-pounders (4th Coy of the 3rd Foot Artillery). Losses were limited to 5 men killed and 2 guns dismantled.

✣ HEUDELET'S DIVISION

It arrived at the end of the battle and only the 7th Light was actually engaged against the Saxons and in the chase towards Weimar.
- *Amet*, General (with the 7th Light), CtLH, wounded at Eylau, Baron, mentioned in Russia at Polotsk, Major General, wounded at Beresina. GdOLH in 1813, retired in 1815.
- *Boyer*, Colonel, OLH, General in 1807, garrison commander on account of his wounds, retired in 1815.

Castex, at the head of the 7th Chasseurs, was named Colonel on Jena's battlefield.

Sourd, a Lieutenant in the 7th Chasseurs.

- *Cartier*, Battalion commander, Toulon and Italy. LH. Colonel in 1813, seriously wounded. Retired in February 1815.
- *Lendy*, Battalion commander. LH. Colonel in 1809, retired in 1815.

SARRUT'S BRIGADE

General *Sarrut* was killed at Vittoria in 1813.

24th Line

Commanded by colonel *Semellé*, general in 1807, Baron, Major General in 1811. Inactive in 1815, Deputy in 1818, GdOLH in 1831.

63rd Line

Commanded by colonel *Lacuée*. Although the regiment only arrived at the end of the battle, Lacuée was mentioned as wounded at Jena. He was killed at Eylau. His brother, a former aide de camp of Napoleon's, was killed in 1815; he was colonel at the head of the 59th Line.

✣ 7th CORPS' CAVALRY (DUROSNEL)

General *Durosnel* was, after Jena, Napoleon's equerry and aide de camp. Count in 1809, then Master of the Pages, Major General and commanding officer in Moscow. Pair de France and inactive on 1815. Deputy in 1830, aide de camp of Louis-Philippe. GdCxOLH in 1832. Pair de France again in 1837, died in 1849.
- aide de camp: Lieutenant *Lafitte*, LH, Captain in 1807, Squadron commander and OLH in 1808. With the Chasseurs of the Guard in 1811. Baron, fought at Montereau, wounded at Waterloo, CrLH in 1831.

7th Chasseurs

Commanded by Colonel Marquis *de Lagrange et de Fourilles*. General in 1807, opposed Dupont at Baylen, Major General in 1809, Count in 1813, retired in 1815.

As Lagrange was ill at Jena, the officer in command during the battle was Major *Castex*. He led a memorable charge, upsetting two Prussian battalions and Grossmann's battery; but his charge wasn't followed up by the 20th whose colonel had just been killed. He had to extricate himself from Polentz's Saxon regiment. Castex was promoted to the rank of Colonel on the battlefield and OLH. General in 1809. Wounded at the Beresina, he was a major in the Horse Grenadiers of the Guard. Major General in 1813, served in the Jura in 1815. In Spain in 1823, GdOLH and GdCx de Saint-Ferdinand.
- *Blancheville*, major, probably absent at Jena. OLH. Adjudant commandant in 1807. Spain, CtLH, murdered by guerillas in 1810.
- *Barbe*, Squadron commander, LH, mentioned at Jena. Major in Spain, Chevalier, OLH, retired in 1813.

- *Simon*, Squadron commander, mentioned at Jena.

- *Latour-Foissac*, Captain, wounded twice in 1809. Colonel in 1813, General in 1814, Viscount in 1817. GdOLH and CrSL in 1823, retired in 1832.

- *Roger*, Captain, wounded and captured at Jena, escaped on 16th October. Captured in Spain in 1808.

- *Larderet*, Captain, wounded at Eylau. Challenged an Austrian Hussar officer at Essling, killed him but was himself wounded. Three horses killed under him at Wagram. Squadron commander in 1814.

- *Sourd*, Lieutenant, twice wounded at Jena. Colonel in 1814 with the 20th Chasseurs. On the 17th June 1815, while chasing the English, he received six sabre strokes on his arm. He was amputated by Larrey, and then got back on his horse and continued the chase. Maréchal de Camp in 1831, retired in 1848.

- *Chevallier*, corporal, received eight sabre strokes and had one horse killed under him. Wounded at Wagram, Second lieutenant in Russia, wounded at the Beresina, Lieutenant in 1813.

On the 8th October in Bamberg, the regiment numbered 536, of which 36 officers. Losses were heavy: one officer and 37 killed. 11 officers were wounded as well a large number of men. A lot of horses were killed.

20th Chasseurs

Commanded by Colonel *Marigny*, who was killed at the very moment that he was going to lead the charge in support of the 7th.

- *Watrin*, Squadron commander.

- *Lion*, Captain, in the Guard in 1809. General in 1813, Lieutenant General in 1815, Count, GdCxLH in 1825.

Two other battalions formed part of the 7th Corps: one from Hesse-Darmstadt and one from Nassau. They were not committed but were used to guard the towns and the prisoners.

Maréchal Lannes, Duke of Montebello. (Painting by Charles Percier for the 'Table of Austerlitz' or the 'Marshalls' Table', ordered in 1806 by Napoleon. Château de Malmaison, © Réunion des Musées nationaux photograph).

Victor, Chief of Staff of the 5th Corps.

Suchet, divisional commander in the 5th Corps.

LANNES' 5th CORPS

Lannes only arrived on the 5th october after having 'sulked' on his estate at Maisons (Maisons-Lafitte). His Corps played an essential part in the battle.

His Chief of Staff was General *Victor*, future Maréchal, wounded at Jena. His assistant-Chief of Staff was *Dembrowski*, general in 1809, died in 1812.

- *Borrelli*, Squadron commander, General in Russia, Baron then Lieutenant General in 1831, Pair de France, retired in 1848.

- *Clerget*, Captain in the sappers in 1806. Hero of Saragossa. Made Colonel during the Hundred-Days, but demoted and retired in 1812.

The aides de camp were:

- *Thomières*, General in 1807, killed at the Arapiles in 1812.

- *Guéhéneuc*, Captain, the Maréchal's brother in law. General and aide de camp to Napoleon in 1812. Retired on half pay, reinstated in 1830. Lieutenant General in 1836, military commander of Oran, then retired in 1848.

- *Huguet-Chataux*, Victor's aide de camp. Married his daughter in 1811, General in 1813, mortally wounded at Montereau.

✥ SUCHET'S DIVISION

The future Maréchal has *Humbert de Molard* as Chief of Staff, who became honorary Maréchal de camp in 1817.

- *Gauthrin*, Adjudant commandant, General and Baron in 1809. Captured wounded in Russia on 19th December 1812, he got back and served at Ligny. Reinstated in 1830 as Lieutenant General.

- *Mesclop*, Assistant captain, General in 1813.

- *Monnay*, Commissaire ordonnateur, OLH, at Hamburg in 1813.

The aides decamp were:

- *Saint-Cyr Nugues*, Captain. Baron and General in 1811, Pair de France in 1832 and GdCxLH in 1833.

- *Meyer de Schauensée*, Lieutenant, Baron in 1809. Inactive in 1815, reinstated in 1831 until 1853.

CLAPAREDE'S BRIGADE

Claparède had been responsible for intelligence under Moreau. General in 1802, Count and Major General in 1808. Wounded three times in 1809, wounded at the Beresina, GdCxLH in 1815, Pair de France in 1819 and GdCxSL. Died in 1842.

17th Light (two battalions and elite companies of the 3rd)

Commanded by colonel *Cabanes de Puymisson*, Baron, OLH, General in 1810, retired in 1815.

- *Devilliers*, Major, received a Sabre of Honour. General in 1811, went to Russia, fought at Ligny, Viscount and CrSL in 1823, GdOLH in 1836.

- *Roger*, Battalion commander, OLH in 1807, killed at Oporto.

- *Cardeilhac*, Captain, mentioned at Rivoli, LH. Wounded at Jena. Battalion commander, OLH, Chevalier in 1808, wounded at Lützen. Half-pay, died in 1834.

- *Deschamps*, Captain, Sabre of Honour, OLH, Retired 23th November 1806, covered in wounds.

- *Goudaux*, captain, Italian campaign, LH. Wounded at Jena and Battalion commander. Retired in 1807.

- *Dedoual*, Captain, mentioned at Rivoli, LH. Battalion commander in 1808, OLH in 1811, retired in 1813.

- *Fourtet*, captain, hero of Italy, LH. Mentioned at Saalfeld with his voltigeurs, congratulated by Lannes. Twice wounded at Jena, Battalion commander in 1811, mentioned in Portugal, then in Russia, then at Dantzig. Half-pay, retired in 1818.

- *Lejosne*, Lieutenant, Rivoli, Musket of Honour, LH. Battalion commander of the Young Guard in 1813. OLH in 1815, retired in 1827 wit the rank of Lieutenant colonel.

- *Wallerand*, Second lieutenant, Rivoli, Musket of Honour. Captain in 1809 and retired.

- *Lacomblée*, Musket of Honour, promoted Second lieutenant 21th December 1806. Lieutenant, First Eagle-bearer in 1809, retired in 1811.

- *Huc*, Italy, LH. Seriously wounded at Jena and retired in 1808.

- *Hanetin*, Italy, LH. Second lieutenant in December 1806, Captain in 1813, retired in 1814.

This regiment, always at the front at Saalfeld and Jena, used up all its ammunition each time. At the beginning of October, it had 57 officers and 1, 990 men for the two battalions. Five officers commanded 180 elite soldiers from the 3rd battalion. Only the casualties for the officers are known: 3 dead and 15 wounded.

Claparède, a brigade commander in the 5th Corps.

Reille, a brigade commander in the 5th Corps.

REILLE'S BRIGADE

Reille, Masséna's aide de camp in Italy, was promoted General in 1803, then Major General after Jena. Count in 1808, GdCxLH, served at Waterloo, then retired. Pair de Frace in 1819. He married Masséna's daughter in 1814. Maréchal de France in 1847.

34th Line (three battalions)

Commanded by colonel *Dumoustier*, present on 18th Brumaire and at Marengo. Wounded at Jena, promoted General in December 1806 and replaced Reille. Baron. Transferred to the Guard. Count and Crown of Iron in 1813, exiled and watched in 1815, reinstated in 1830, GdOLH in 1831, died in an accident.

- *Remond* 'Remonda', Major. Baron, CtLH, General in 1811.

- *Tridoulat*, Battalion commander, Sabre of Honour, CtLH. Captured three cannon at Austerlitz. Mentioned at Jena. Baron, then Colonel in 1811.

- *Gritte*, Captain, LH, wounded at Jena. OLH in 1810, Spain.

- *Bouillet*, Captain, mentioned at Novi, wounded at Jena, killed at Arcis in 1814.

- *Hersant*, Captain, LH, Battalion commander in Spain. OLH in 1813. Wounded five times and took part in 53 fights.

At the beginning of October, the regiment had 3,032 officers and men. Losses at Saalfeld were two officers killed and two wounded, with 60 wounded soldiers. At Jena there were 4 officers killed and 19 wounded.

40th Line (two battalions)

Under the command of colonel *Chassereaux*, wounded at Jena and replaced by Dupeyroux, baron in 1809, Spain, General in 1811. Wounded at Lützen and inactive in 1815.

- *Dupeyroux*, Battalion commander, former captain in the Maltese Legion in Egypt. Colonel in 1808, OLH in 1810 in Spain. Inactive in 1817.

- *Lepage*, Captain, Adjudant major, at Arcole, LH. Wounded at Jena, retired in 1809.

- *Millet*, Captain, mentioned at Saalfeld. Colonel in 1810, OLH in 1811, General and Baron in 1813. Half-pay in 1815.

- *Bardeuux*, Captain, LH, wounded at Jena. Retired in 1809, with rank of Battalion commander.

- *Draye*, Sergeant-major, Italian campaign, LH. Lieutenant in 1811 and First Eagle bearer of the regiment. Captain in 1813.

- *Piquenot*, Musket of Honour, LH. Retired with rank of Second lieutenant in 1806.

- *Simon*, Drum-major, decorated in 1807.

Bugeaud, a second lieutenant in the 64th Line. *Cambronne, a battalion commander in the 88th Line.* *Gazan, a division commander in the 5th Corps.*

At Jena, there were six officers wounded, 28 men killed and 80 wounded among the two battalions.

VEDEL'S BRIGADE
Vedel was wounded at Rivoli and three times in 1807. CtLH and Count in 1808. Emprisoned after Baylen and disgraced. Reinstated from 1813 to 1815. Died in 1848.

64th Line
Commanded by Colonel *Chauvel*, Baron in 1808. General and CtLH in 1809, half-pay in 1811 and retired in 1815.

- *Joubert*, Battalion commander. Joubert's aide de camp in Egypt, with the camels in Egypt, wounded at Austerlitz. Baron and Colonel in 1808, wounded at Wagram. General in 1811, Russia, CtLH, Viscount in 1822 and retired in 1835.

- *Voirol*, Captain, LH in 1807, became Major General then Governor General of Algeria in 1833.

- *Lorrain*, Lieutenant, Musket of Honour, hero of Italy, OLH in 1807, killed in Spain.

- *Bugeaud*, Second lieutenant, future Maréchal de France.

88th Line (two battalions)
Under the orders of Colonel *Veilande*, Baron, OLH, Crown of Iron, General in 1810, CtLH in 1814, retired in 1815. Deputy in 1825, reinstated from 1830-1832.

- *Cambronne*, Battalion commander, mentioned at Jena, OLH 1807, transferred to the Guard. Baron, General and CtLH in 1813, followed Napoleon to Elba. Count, Pair de France and GdOLH in 1815. Arrested, aquitted and struck-off without pay. Reinstated in 1818, Viscount in 1822, retired in 1823. Died in 1840.

- *Blaizat*, Captain, Egypt, LH. Badly wounded at Jena, died in 1834.

- *Gilles*, Captain, Egypt, Sabre of Honour, OLH. Battalion commander in 1811 in Spain. Sacked in 1815.

- *Bachelier*, Captain, Egypt, LH. Retired in 1807.

- *Hurel*, Lieutenant adjudant-major, Egypt, LH. Served in the 6th Voltigeurs of the Guard in Russia. OLH and Colonel in 1814. 3rd Voltigeurs at Waterloo. Maréchal de Camp in 1823. CrLH, Lieutenant General in 1835.

- *Joubert*, Lieutenant, Egypt, LH. Captain in 1808, OLH in 1810 and retired due to wounds in 1811. Died in 1813.

- *Gelly*, Lieutenant, Egypt, LH. Retired in 1807.

- *Guimard*, Second lieutenant, Egypt, LH. Captain in 1809, killed at Ocana.

- *Lecomte*, Second lieutenant, LH. Captain in the Guard in 1814. Two horses killed under him at Waterloo, cashiered.

- *Gilbain*, Sergeant, Egypt, LH. Lieutenant in 1813, retired in 1816.

- *Laroche*, Sergeant, Egypt, LH. Lieutenant in 1813, retired in 1814.

✥ GAZAN'S DIVISION
Gazan, promoted general on the battlefield at Zürich, Count in 1808, Spain. GdCxLH in 1815, inactive 1816. Pair de France in 1831, died in 1845.

His Chief of Staff: *Fornier d'Albe*, Egypt, in command of the Surveyors. Wounded at Jena. Baron then General in 1809, CrLH in 1814, sacked in 1815.

General *Graindorge*, wounded at Jena, CtLH in 1809 and killed at Bussaco, was with the 21st Light.

21st Light
Commanded by Colonel *Duhamel*, Italy and Egypt, Battalion commander OLH. CtLH in 1806, died 1st March 1807 from wounds received at Ostrolenka.

- *Leblanc*, Battalion commander, LH. Captured at Baylen, escaped from the prison-ship *La Vieille Castille* on 15th May 1810, taken back in 1812, retired in 1814.

- *Laroche*, Captain, Egypt, LH, died in Spain in 1811.

- *Boissard*, Captain, Egypt, LH. Battalion commander after Jena, killed at Saragossa.

- *Rougirelle*, Lieutenant, Egypt, Sabre of Honour, OLH, retired in 1807.

Opposite.
French light infantry 1806. The camp-follower is giving a drink to two carabiniers wearing bearskins and one chasseur wearing a shako. (Original water-colour by Lucien Rousselot, Author's collection)

CAMPANA'S BRIGADE

General *Campana*, born in Turin, was with Masséna in Italy, CtLH, served at Jena, killed at Ostrolenka.

100th Line (three battalions with eight companies)

Commanded by colonel *Quiot du Passage*. Wounded at Rivoli, served at Marengo. Former aide de camp of Lannes, wounded at Jena. Baron, Spain, General in 1811. Captured wounded at Kulm. Served at Waterloo, GdOLH in 1822, Lieutenant General in 1823, died in 1849.

- *Henriod*, major, OLH, colonel of the 14th Line on 30th December 1806. CtLH, Baron, General in 1810, retired in 1815.
- *Barraud la Pècherie*, Lieutenant, Sabre of Honour. Captain 22th December 1806. Spain, retired in 1811.
- *Guillot*, Second lieutenant, LH. Lieutenant, Eagle bearer in 1808, retired in 1811 due to wounds.
- *Barbier*, Sergeant, LH. Wounded at Jena, retired in 1808.

103rd Line (two battalions)

Commanded by colonel *Taupin*, wounded at Marengo. Sabre of Honour, OLH then CtLH in 1805. General in 1807, Spain and Portugal, wounded eight times at Toulouse where he died.

- *Berger*, Battalion commander, LH at Jena. OLH and retired in 1809.
- *Gauderon*, Captain, LH. Battalion commander in 1808, died in Spain.
- *Dudoyer*, Lieutenant, LH. Captain in 1807, retired in 1812.

- *Gastebois*, Second lieutenant, LH. Lieutenant after Jena, Battalion commander in 1815.
- *Evrard*, Corporal, LH retired in 1810.
- *Lerouge*, Corporal, LH, killed at Saragossa.

❖ 5th CORPS' CAVALRY

Commanded by General *Treillard*, CtLH, Major General in December 1806. Baron, retired 1815.

- *Delaage*, Chief of Staff, Spain, Russia, wounded at Borodino, General in Moscow, CrLH in February 1815, then inactive.

9th Hussars

Commanded by colonel *Barbanègre*, killed at Jena.

- *Lambert*, Major, OLH, General in 1811, died 1814 in the Jura.
- *Donop*, Captain, came from Murat's staff on 25th August. General and OLH in 1813, killed at Waterloo.
- *Point*, Captain, died from wounds received at Saalfeld.
- *Ordonnet*, Lieutenant, captured two cannon at Saalfeld.
- *d'Escrivieux*, Second lieutenant in 1809, Captain in 1815, CrLH in 1831, Colonel of the 13th Chasseurs in 1840.

The regiment numbered 29 officers and 561 horsemen. At Saalfeld, one officer was killed and four wounded. At Jena, the colonel was killed and three officers were wounded. Nine officers had horses killed under them.

10th Hussars

Commanded by colonel *Briche*, Marengo. General in Spain,

The charge of the 9th Hussars at the battle of Saalfeld, by Edouard Detaille. (© Musée de l'Armée Photograph, Paris).

Corporal, 9th Hussars   Trumpeter, 9th Hussars   Trooper, 10th Hussars   Trumpeter, 10th Hussars

André Jouineau © Histoire & Collections 1998

Baron, Major General in 1813, Viscount in 1815, CrSL in 1816, GdOLH in 1821, died 1825.

- *Corbineau*, Major. Colonel in 1807, Baron, General in 1811. Russia, at the Beresina, found the Studianka passage. Aide de camp to Napoleon, Major General and Count. Inactive in 1815, reinstated in 1830, Pair de France and GdOLH.

- *Guindey*, Sergeant, born at Laruns, signed up at Cahors in the 10th Hussars whose colonel was Lasalle, wounded several times in 1805. At Saalfeld, he fought Prince Louis. Ordering him to surrender and receiving two sabre strokes in reply, he wounded the Prince six times; two of the wounds were fatal. Promoted Sergeant-major, then in 1807 Second lieutenant with the LH, he transferred to the Horse Grenadiers of the Guard. In Russia he was Captain adjudant-major of the regiment. OLH in 1813, he was killed at Hanau, surrounded by the bodies of the many enemy soldiers he had killed before falling.

21st Chasseurs

Commanded by Colonel *Berruyer*, OLH, congratulated by Napoleon at Jena. Baron, retired in 1808.

- *Gaydon*, Major. He commanded the squadrons in 1807. OLH in 1810 in Spain, retired in 1812.

- *du Coëtlosquet*, Lieutenant adjudant-major, Lasalle's aide de camp before and after Jena. Colonel in 1812, wounded at Boro-

Gourgaud, aide de camp, 5th Corps' artillery.

dino, General in 1813, wounded at Leipzig, mentioned at Montereau, Lieutenant General in 1821, CrSL, Minister of War, retired in 1831.

At Saalfeld, this brigade captured four flags and 33 cannon; followed by 8 flags and 15 cannon at Jena.

✠ 5th CORPS' ARTILLERY

Commanded by General *Foucher du Careil*. Baron 1808, followed Lannes to Spain. Russia, GdOLH in 1813, retired in 1818.

- *Gourgaud*, aide de camp, Polytechnicien, aide de camp to Napoleon in 1811. Elba, Saint Helena. Lieutenant General in 1835, Deputy in 1849.

- *Fruchard*, commanding officer for the 1st division. Italy, LH, with the 6th Horse Artillery, then the 5th Foot Artillery, OLH. Colonel in 1809, retired in 1814.

- *Saint-Loup*, 2nd division, chief of staff. Baron, General in 1809, Crown of Iron, Waterloo. GdOLH 1821, died in 1839.

- *Humbert de Fercourt*, commanding the pool. Baron, General 1813, retired in 1814.

- *Sibille*, Captain, commanded three guns at Saalfeld and had one horse killed under him at Jena.

- *Simmonet*, Lieutenant, had two guns, mentioned at Saalfeld. Two horses killed under him.

One officer and three men were killed, 23 wounded. More than 60 horses were killed.

Michel Ney, Duke of Elchingen, Prince of the Moskowa (Borodino), Maréchal de France, 1769-1815. (Oil on canvas by Charles Meynier, Château de Versailles, © Réunion des Musées nationaux photograph).

NEY'S 6th CORPS

Maréchal Ney was only able to bring up a small part of his corps to the battle, i.e. the cavalry, the 25th Light and an elite unit. He committed them in rather a hazardous way, wanting to show off without really having the means to do so.

- *Dutaillis*, Chief of Staff, Count, mentioned at Castaglione, Pistols of Honour. Hero of Italy, Egypt, Marengo. Major General in 1807, Crown of Iron. Retired in 1815, Pair de France in 1832, GdCxLH in 1845, died in 1851.

- *Destabenrath*, Deputy Chief of Staff, served at Marengo. Adjudant commandant. General in 1807, Baron, six wounds in 1809, CtLH. Inactive in 1816, died in 1853.

The aides de camp were:

- *Jomini*, the Maréchal's guru. A former broker and commandant in the Swiss national guard, he published a '*Traité des grandes opérations*'. This theoretical strategist impressed Ney whose culture was rather limited. He became his Chief of Staff in Spain and his advice was rather ill-omened. He impressed the General Staff, was made a General, then Baron and began his '*Histoire des guerres de la Révolution*', finished in 1824. Put

in the Historical Department by Berthier, arrested in 1813, he went over to the enemy and captivated the Tsar, Nicholas I, who made him his General in chief. He retired in 1848. He wrote among other things a '*Mémoire sur la Défense de la Russie par un bon système de forteresses*'. As a precursor of Maginot, he had forgotten the basic adage of the real strategists: '*the history of fortifications is all mixed up with the history of capitulations*'.

- *Béchet de Léocour*, Squadron commander, adjudant commandant in 1807, OLH. Baron, Chief of Ney's staff in Spain. General in 1814. At Mézières in 1815, then inactive, honorary Lieutenant General in 1825.

- *Chodron*, Captain, wounded three times. LH. Sent to the 25th Light, aide de camp to Ney at Jena, a cannonball shattered one of his legs. Battalion commander, retired in 1815.

- *Daicker*, Captain, in the 3rd Hussars' suite, LH. Squadron commander and OLH, Major in the Hanoverian Legion in Russia, committed suicide in Moscow.

- *Laboissière*, Lieutenant. Colonel in Russia, General in 1813. OLH, Baron, wounded at Dresden, died of his wounds.

✣ MARCOGNET'S DIVISION (elements)

The division in the front was the third, Marcognet's. It arrived at the end of the battle, but the 25th, which was part of it, accompanied Ney with a battalion of grenadiers and a battalion of voltigeurs.

Marcognet was only a Brigadier General, but he was in command temporarily due to Vandamme's absence. Baron, Major General in 1811. OLH, at Waterloo, retired in 1815.

25th Light

Commanded by colonel *Morel*, CtLH, Baron. He retired in 1807 because of wounds.

- *Gleizes*, Battalion commander, OLH after Austerlitz. Captured at Baylen, he escaped from the prison-ship *La Vieille Castille*. Major, retired in 1826. Honorary Colonel.

- *Amy*, Battalion commander, LH. Colonel, Baron and OLH, killed at Bussaco.

- *Croutelle*, Lieutenant, LH. Battalion commander and OLH in 1813. At Waterloo, then inactive in 1816.

Grenadiers and Voltigeurs (two battalions)

- *Lovizé*, Major, from the 3rd Hussars.

- *Arnauld*, Battalion commander. Came from the Staff, Adjudant commandant in 1807, General in 1808, Baron, Crown of Iron. GdOLH in 1821.

- *Lamour*, Battalion commander, hero of Switzerland and Germany. Commanding the Voltigeurs, he was likewise detached from Ney's staff. Colonel, he was killed at Lützen while awaiting his promotion to General.

✣ 6th CORPS' CAVALRY (COLBERT)

General *Colbert de Chabanais, Auguste*. One of three Colberts. He fought in Italy and Egypt, and was Murat's aide de camp at Marengo. Baron, he was killed by a bullet in the head whilst charging in Spain in 1809.

Trooper,
3rd Hussars

Trumpeter,
3rd Hussars

Trooper,
10th Chasseurs
in full dress

Lieutenant, 10th Chasseurs
in full dress

Trumpeter,
elite company,
10th Chasseurs
in full dress

Trooper,
elite company,
10th Chasseurs
in full dress

Corporal,
centre company,
10th Chasseurs
in full dress

Trooper,
centre company,
10th Chasseurs
in full dress

Corporal,
centre company,
10th Chasseurs
in marching dress

André Jouineau © Histoire & Collections 1998

10th Chasseurs

Commanded by colonel *Subervie*, Lannes' aide de camp in Italy. With Lasalle in Spain. Baron, General in 1811. Russia, wounded at Borodino. Lieutenant General in 1814 on half-pay. At Waterloo then inactive. Took part in the Revolution of 1830. Deputy of Lectoure, Minister for War in 1848. Grand Chancellor of the LH and GdCxLH, died in 1856.

- *Levesque*, Major, Count *de la Ferrière*, mentioned 7th October 1806, wounded at Jena. Colonel of the regiment in 1807, baron. General in 1811. Réunion and Crown of Iron. Major with the Horse Grenadiers of the Guard in 1813. Major General, chamberlain to Napoleon in 1814, inactive in 1818. GdCxLH in 1821. GdCxSL in 1823. Pair de France in 1832. Wounded about 13 times including the loss of his left leg at Craonne.

- *Lapointe*, Squadron commander, wounded at Jena, one horse killed, mentioned in despatches. Colonel and retired in 1809.

- *Lahuberdière*, Captain. Italy and Marengo, LH. Colonel of the regiment in 1811. Russia, Baron. Inactive in 1815. CrLH in 1830, retired in 1833.

- *Saint-Léger*, Captain, mentioned at Jena. Squadron commander in Spain, mentioned at Ocana where he was in command of the Brigade.

- *Clerget*, Captain, Italy, LH. Wounded at Jena, at Hof, at Friedland and in Spain, retired in 1809.

- *Boulle*, Captain, Italy, LH. OLH in 1807, retired and died in 1808.

- *Falguière*, Captain, Italy, LH. Wounded at Eylau, OLH. Squadron commander, killed in Spain in 1813.

- *Latour-Maubourg*, Lieutenant, aide de camp to the general, LH in 1807, Maréchal de camp in 1821. Lieutenant General in 1835, GdOLH in 1845.

- *d'Astorg*, Second lieutenant. Mentioned in despatches, LH. Colonel of the 6th Hussars in 1821.

- *Baer*, Second lieutenant, Italy, Sabre of Honour, retired in 1808.

- *Subervie*, Sergeant. LH in 1807.

- *Bailly*, LH, Second lieutenant. Captain in 1814, half-pay.

One officer and 13 chasseurs were killed at Jena with one officer and 23 chasseurs wounded.

3rd Hussars

Commanded by colonel *Lebrun*, son of the Duke of Plaisance, mentioned at Jena, aide de camp to Napoleon and general in 1807, wounded at Friedland. Major General in Russia, Waterloo. Inactive, then Pair de France in 1824 on the death of his father. GdCxLH in 1833, Grand Chancellor of LH in 1853. Military Medal, died in 1859

- *Domon*, Squadron commander. Colonel in 1809, Baron, General in 1812, entered the service of Naples, resigned in 1814.

Auguste de Colbert, commanding officer of the 6th Corps' cavalry.

Lieutenant General. Waterloo, exiled to Péronne, reinstated in 1820. Cavalcadour Equerry, CrSL, Saint-Ferdinand in 1823, GdOLH.

- *Nicolas*, Captain, LH. OLH in 1807. Colonel of the 11th Chasseurs in Russia, Baron CtLH in 1814. Cashiered in 1815, Maréchal de camp in 1823, GdOLH in 1834.

- *d'Hollosy*, Captain wounded at Jena. Squadron commander after Eylau, OLH, retired in 1813.

The regiment casualties were eight officers wounded, five hussars killed, and many wounded.

✥ 6th CORPS' ARTILLERY

Ney's artillery was commanded by Major General *Séroux*, GdOLH in 1807. Baron, retired in 1815. GdCxSL in 1819. He was not present at Jena, but marching with the divisions. His chief of staff was with the vanguard, and made the reports.

- *Bicquilley*, Chief of Staff. CtLH in 1807. Baron and General in 1808. Killed in Spain in 1809. Séroux's son in law.

- *Brasseur*, Captain, commanded the vanguard's two 8-pounders, two 4-pounders and two howitzers. Served by the 5th company and a squad from the 2nd Horse artillery regiment.

- *Masson*, Lieutenant. He dismantled one enemy gun and blew up two limbers. They had a 4-pounder and a howitzer dismantled. A limber exploded, killing 13 men and 23 horses. Lieutenant Masson was able nevertheless to equip two guns with which he followed the vanguard during the rest of the battle.

The two divisions which Ney had at his disposal and which tried to get there but only arrived at the end were the following:

✥ MARCOGNET'S DIVISION (3rd)

This has already been mentioned. It detached the **25th Light** and arrived with the:

- **50th Line**, under Colonel Lamartinière.
- **27th Line**, under Colonel Bardet.
- **59th Line**, under Colonel Dalton.

These troops arrived completely exhausted from their forced march.

✥ MARCHAND'S DIVISION

It included the **6th Light** and the **39th**, **69th** and **76th Line**.

SOULT'S 4th CORPS

Only a part of this Corps was used, on Napoleon's right wing and in a brilliant manner: this was mainly Saint-Hilaire's division, the cavalry and a part of the artillery. The other divisions arrived gradually.

- *Compans*, Chief of Staff, wounded at Austerlitz. Major General 23rd November 1806, Count. In Russia, he and his division captured the redoubt at Schwardino on the 5th September 1812.

Wounded in 1813, fought in 1814. GdCxLH. Retired by Napoleon, Pair de France on the 17th August 1815, he voted for the death of Ney. Died in 1845.

- *Binot*, Deputy Chief of Staff, former aide de camp to Friant in Italy and Egypt. CtLH, General on the 22nd November 1806 and transfered to the 7th Corps, he was killed at Eylau.

- *Asselin de Williencourt*, Captain. Battalion commander in November 1806. In Russia with Prince Eugène. General in 1814, LH. OLH in 1832.

In September 1806, lacking a Deputy Chief of Staff, Soult had borrowed the Adjudant-commandant *Cosson*, Legrand's own Chief of Staff. Baron and General in 1808, Cosson was badly wounded at Wagram, and inactive in 1815.

Soult's aides de camp were:
- *Ricard*, Adjudant commandant, first aide de camp, mentioned at Jena. General on the 13th November 1806. Returned in 1810 for '*intriguing*', reinstated as Major General in 1812. In Russia and 1813 and 1814 campaigns. Followed the King to Gand, Pair de France, then Count, retired in 1830.

Jean de Dieu Soult, Maréchal de France, Duke of Dalmatia.
(Painting by Louis Henri de Rudder after Jean Broc,
Château de Versailles, © Réunion des Musées nationaux photograph).

- *Lameth*, Captain, son of the Constituant, LH. Wounded at Heilsberg, Squadron commander, killed in an ambush in Spain in 1809.

- *Hulot*, Battalion commander. In command of the Tirailleurs of the Pô who belonged to Legrand's division, whilst still keeping his function of aide de camp. Wounded at Eylau, Colonel in 1808. General in 1812, Baron, wounded at Leipzig, served at Ligny. Inactive in 1815, retired as honorary Lieutenant General in 1825. Reinstated in 1831, GdOLH in 1834, retired in 1848.

- *Brun de Villeret*, Captain. With Soult in Spain, General in 1813. Torgau, retired in March 1815. Deputy, Lieutenant General in 1831. Pair de France and GdOLH.

- *Dalachau*, Squadron commander, OLH, Chevalier, retired in 1811.

Compans, Chief of Staff of the 4th Corps.

- *Saint-Chamans*, author of memoirs.

✤ SAINT-HILAIRE'S DIVISION

General *Saint-Hilaire*, Toulon and Italy. Wounded at Austerlitz, Grand-aigle of LH, Commander of the Crown of Iron, Count. He had his left foot shot off at Essling, died as a result.

- *Baillod*, Deputy Battalion commander. Wounded at Eylau, Adjudant-commandant, CtLH. General in 1811, seriously wounded at Leipzig, Crown of Iron. Inactive in 1815. Retired honorary Lieutenant General in 1825.

- *Lacroix*, Chief of Staff from 1st October, Colonel, OLH. Captured in Russia, retired as honorary Maréchal de camp in 1818.

His aide de camp was:
- *Boudin de Roville*, Captain, wounded at Eylau and Wagram. Colonel wounded at Lützen and Montmirail. CrSL in 1821, GdOLH in 1825, retired in 1835.

CANDRAS' BRIGADE

Commanded by General *Savetier de Candras*, CtLH, Baron. Served at Polotsk and was killed at Beresina.

10th Light

Commanded by Colonel *Pouzet*, OLH, wounded at Austerlitz, then at Jena and at Eylau. Baron, killed by a bullet in the head at Essling.

- *Lafitte*, Battalion commander, wounded at Eylau, then Eckmühl, promoted Colonel in the field. Wounded in Russia, General in 1813. Inactive in 1815. Came back 1830 to 1836.

- *Pichon*, Second lieutenant, Sabre of Honour. Lieutenant in 1807, retired in 1815.

- *Geisse*, LH. Wounded at Austerlitz, Second lieutenant after Jena.

- *Malizieux*, LH. Wounded at Austerlitz, lieutenant in 1813, retired in 1815.

36th Line

Commanded by Colonel *de Lamothe*, Egypt, LH, mentioned at Austerlitz, killed at Jena.

French Army

ARTILLERY 8-POUNDER,
GRIBEAUVAL SYSTEM,
DRAWN BY A DOUBLE TEAM.

- *Lecaret*, Battalion commander, replaced the Colonel at Jena.
- *Abadie*, Captain adjudant-major, killed at Jena. Hero of Austerlitz.
- *Ducros*, Captain, LH. Retired in 1808.
- *Bergon*, Captain, LH. Mentioned at Austerlitz then at Eylau. Killed in Spain.
- *Morin*, Lieutenant. Became Major of the 55th.
- *Pegon*, Musket of Honour, died in 1834.
- *Piquet*, Musket of Honour, retired in 1808.
- *Aubail*, LH, grenadier, wounded at Eylau and retired.

VARÉ'S BRIGADE
General *Varé*, CtLH, died from his wounds in 1807.

43rd Line
Commanded by Colonel *Lemarois*, OLH, killed at Eylau.
- *Lefebvre*, Battalion commander, LH. Retired in 1807.
- *Jacquot*, Captain. Italy, mentioned at Marengo, Sabre of Honour, mentioned at Austerlitz, OLH. Wounded at Jena, transfered to the Guard, Chevalier. Russian campaign, Battalion commander of the 9th Tirailleurs. Lieutenant-Colonel at Waterloo. Cashiered without pay.

55th Line
Commanded by Colonel *Silbermann*, killed at Eylau.
- *Buquet*, Major. Colonel and OLH in 1807, captured in Spain, escaped from the prison-ship *La Vieille Castille*. Baron and

General in 1812, badly wounded at Borodino, then at Bautzen, CtLH. Served during the 100-Days, then inactive. Retired in 1831.
- *Chartener*, Battalion commander, LH, wounded at Austerlitz. Wounded twice in 1809 and three horses killed under him. OLH, Spain, retired in 1811.
- *Coeffé*, Captain, Sabre of Honour, hero of Italy. Killed at Eylau.
- *Lacroix*, Second lieutenant, Sabre of Honour, mentioned at Jena. Captain in 1807, taken in Spain, died at Cabrera.
- *Plomion*, Second lieutenant, hero of La Trebia, saved the flag, Sabre of Honour. Lieutenant in 1807. Battalion commander and OLH in 1813 at Dresden. Retired in 1814.
- *Hugo*, Captain, uncle of Victor. He inspired the verses about Eylau and his campaigns.
The regiment lost four killed and 150 wounded of which two officers.

✣ 4th CORPS' CAVALRY
General *Guyot*, OLH, killed in June 1807. At Jena, he only had the 8th Hussars under his command.

8th Hussars
Under the command of Colonel *de Laborde* who continued to fight in spite of being wounded. Killed at Wagram.
- *Perceval*, Major, LH. Killed in June 1807.
- *Rebillot*, Squadron commander, wounded at Eylau.
- *Becker*, Squadron commander, hero of Switzerland, LH. Retired in January 1807, OLH.

The harnessing
of the rear horses

The driver rode on the
carrier horse and lead the
horse with a switch.
The harnessing of the front
pair of horses was identical
except for the bit and the
leading-rein which were
replaced by a back-strap.

Ammunition limber

André Jouineau © Histoire & Collections 1998

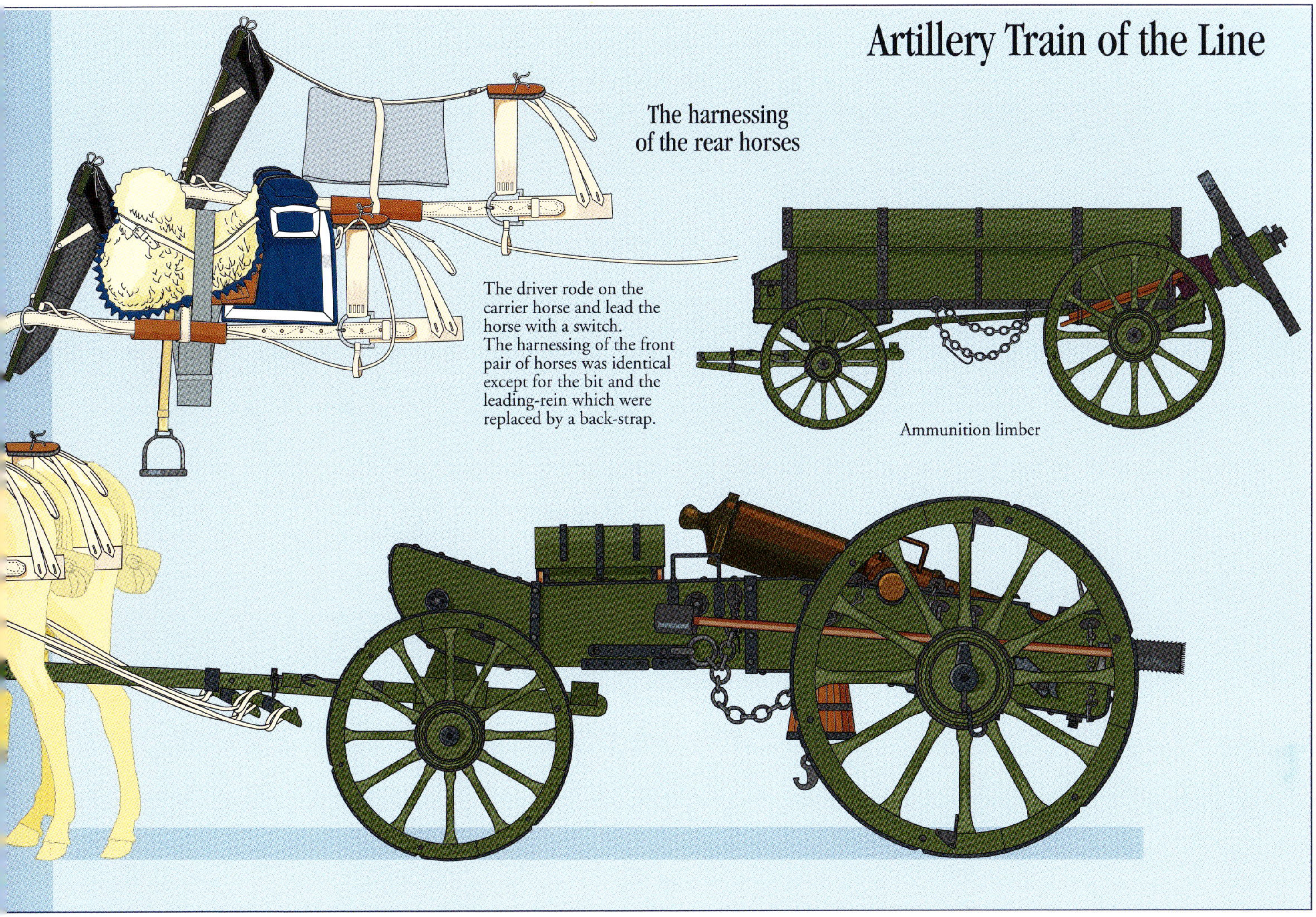

- *Thurot*, Captain. Squadron commander in 1808, OLH, Colonel in 1813. Commanded the 12th Cuirassiers at Waterloo, mayor of Haguenau in 1820.

- *Maréchal*, Captain, killed at Wagram.

- *Petit*, Captain, LH in 1807, killed at Wagram.

- *Juet*, Lieutenant, wounded at Jena. Decorated in 1807, wounded at Eylau and killed at Wagram.

- *Decalonne*, Second lieutenant, LH. Captain in 1813, killed at Wachau.

- *Bergeret*, Second lieutenant, wounded at Jena, LH in 1807. Captain, killed at Essling.

- *Blin*, Adjudant. Captain in 1808, Squadron commander, OLH 1815, Lieutenant-Colonel in 1821, CrLH in 1831, retired in 1841.

- *Soury*, Carbine of Honour, killed at Jena.

The regiment lost one officer and 12 hussars killed at Jena, with 13 officers and 63 men wounded; the total for the three squadrons at the beginning was 31 officers and 464 men. The officers of the 4th squadron had been sent back to the depot.

The **22nd Chasseurs** completed the brigade on the 16th October, after the battle.

MARGARON'S BRIGADE

General *Margaron*, CtLH, wounded twice at Austerlitz. Baron, Major General in 1813, inactive in 1815.

*Margaron, a cavalry brigade commander
in Soult's 4th Corps.*

11th Chasseurs

Commanded by Colonel *Jacquinot*, wounded four times at Jena. Baron, General in 1809, Major General in 1813. At Waterloo, CrSl in 1826, GdCxLH in 1844, died in 1848.

- *Pinteville*, Squadron commander, LH. Colonel in 1810, Baron. Wounded at Borodino, OLH. In the Guard in 1813. Honorary Maréchal de camp in 1815.

- *Beuvière*, Squadron commander, LH. OLH at the end of 1806, retired in 1811.

- *Meuziau*, Captain. He was entrusted with the vanguard before Jena and his reports were excellent. Colonel of the 5th Hussars in Russia, wounded at Borodino, then at Winkowo. Transfered to the light cavalry of the Guard, General. Retired in 1825, taken back in 1831, honorary Lieutenant-Colonel and GdOLH in 1833.

- *Jacquinot*, Captain, brother of the Colonel, Squadron commander 22th November 1806.

- *Picard*, Captain. He captured an enemy convoy on the 4th November 1806.

- *Lejeune*, Second lieutenant. With his trumpeter and 80 horsemen, he made his way round a wood, took the Prussians by surprise and captured six cannon and a standard. (continued on page 78)

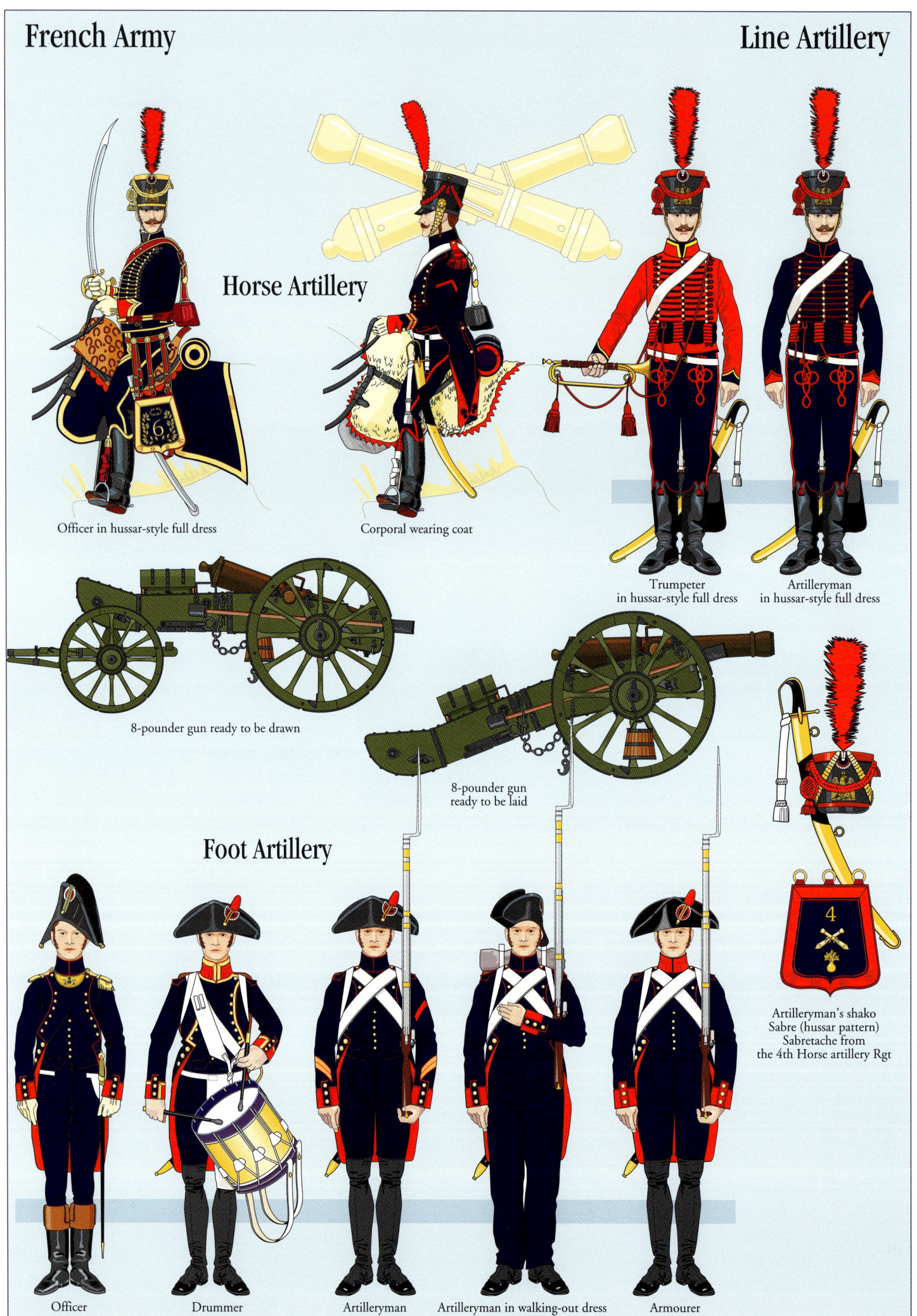

Horse Artillery

Officer in hussar-style full dress

Corporal wearing coat

Trumpeter
in hussar-style full dress

Artilleryman
in hussar-style full dress

8-pounder gun ready to be drawn

8-pounder gun
ready to be laid

Artilleryman's shako
Sabre (hussar pattern)
Sabretache from
the 4th Horse artillery Rgt

Foot Artillery

Officer

Drummer

Artilleryman

Artilleryman in walking-out dress

Armourer

André Jouineau © Histoire & Collections 1998

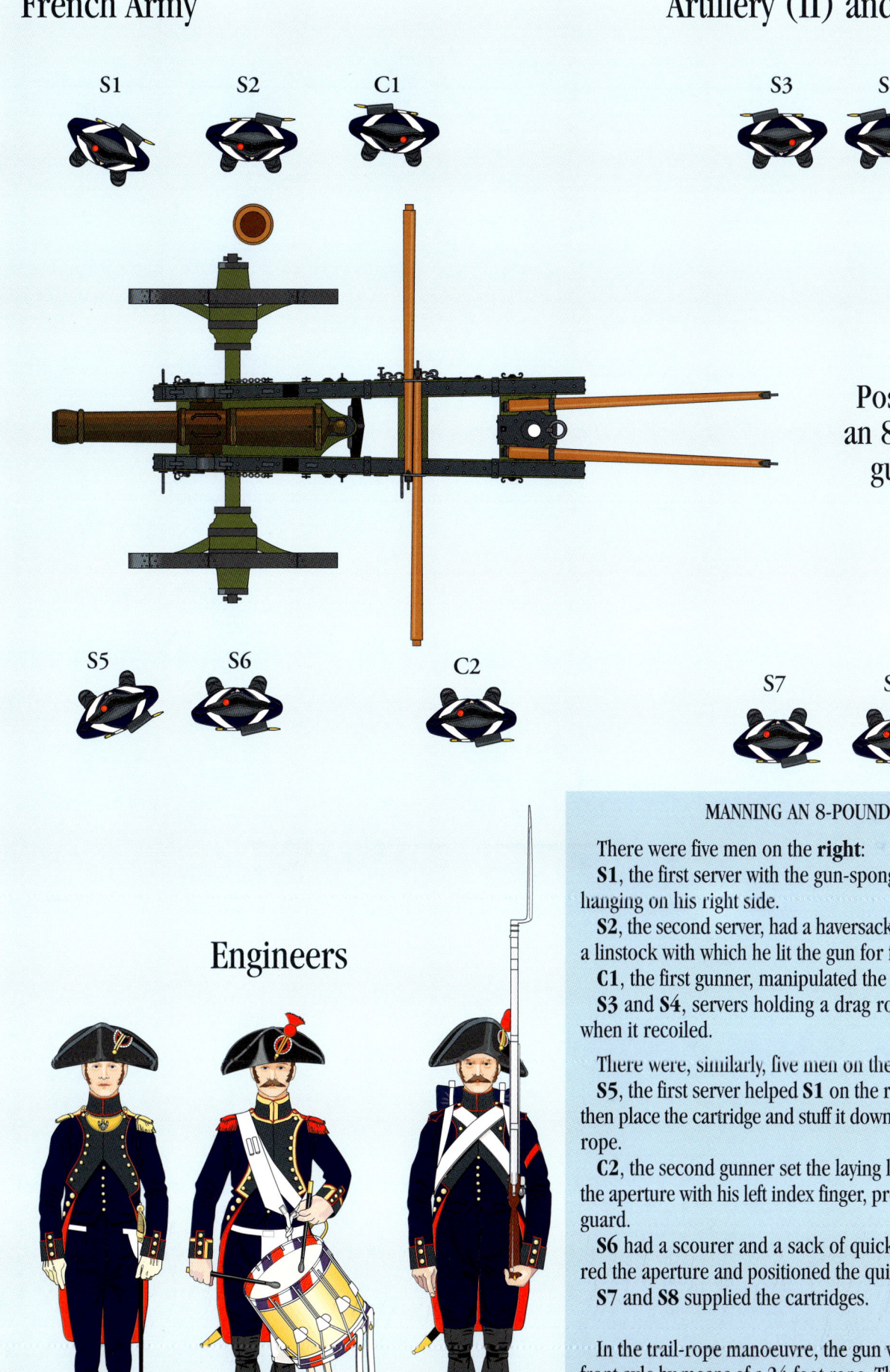

S1　S2　C1　S3　S4

S5　S6　C2

S7　S8

Positions of
an 8-pounder
gun crew

Engineers

Officer　Drummer　Soldier

MANNING AN 8-POUNDER

There were five men on the **right**:

S1, the first server with the gun-sponge and a drag rope hanging on his right side.

S2, the second server, had a haversack full of lighters and a linstock with which he lit the gun for firing.

C1, the first gunner, manipulated the laying levers.

S3 and **S4**, servers holding a drag rope to pull the gun when it recoiled.

There were, similarly, five men on the **left**:

S5, the first server helped **S1** on the right to sponge out, then place the cartridge and stuff it down; he too had a drag rope.

C2, the second gunner set the laying lever whilst closing the aperture with his left index finger, protected by a finger-guard.

S6 had a scourer and a sack of quickmatches. He cleared the aperture and positioned the quickmatch.

S7 and **S8** supplied the cartridges.

In the trail-rope manoeuvre, the gun was attached to the front axle by means of a 24-foot rope. This enabled the gun to be pulled back in an emergency. In this case the laying levers were pulled out and the gunners ensured that the butt didn't get caught on any obstacles.

André Jouineau © Histoïre & Collections 1998

French Army

Guyot's Cavalry (Soult's 4th Corps) at Jena

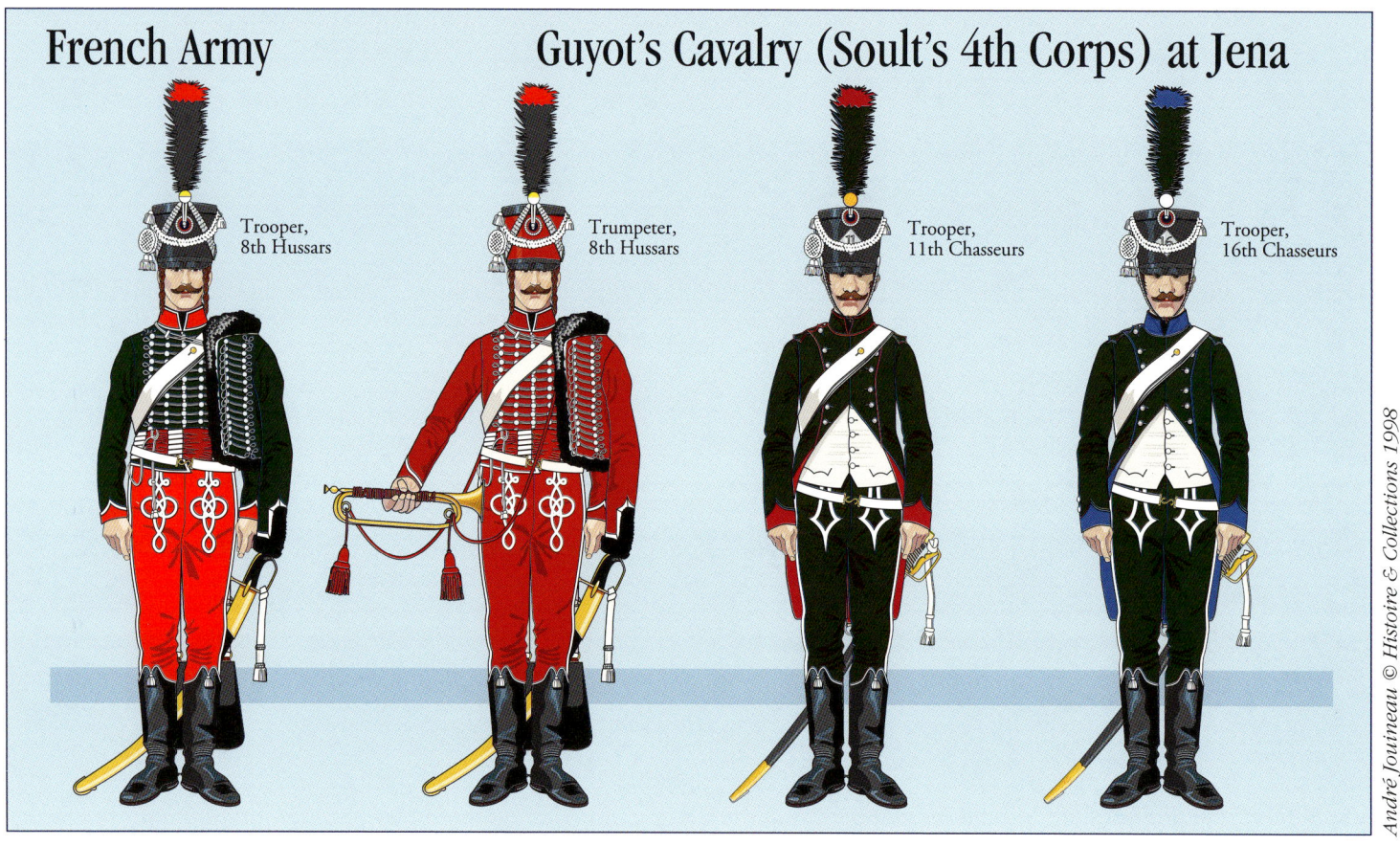

Trooper,
8th Hussars

Trumpeter,
8th Hussars

Trooper,
11th Chasseurs

Trooper,
16th Chasseurs

André Jouineau © Histoire & Collections 1998

(continued from page 75)

The regiment had 25 officers and 423 men. It lost one officer and 15 horsemen killed, 5 officers and 60 men wounded.

Having noticed that the Saxon dragoons had little steel chains sewn into the sleeves of their jackets, the colonel ordered his troops to '*aim for the face or the hands*'.

16th Chasseurs

On the 22nd October, there was only one Squadron commander to command this regiment.

- *Maupoint*, Colonel, Baron in 1808, General in 1811 in Spain. CrLH in 1814, retired in 1816.

- *Bertèche*, captain, LH. Squadron commander in November 1806, OLH, sacked in 1815.

Lariboisière, commanding the 4th Corps' artillery.

✤ 4th CORPS' ARTILLERY

Commanded by General *Lariboisière*, Major General, wounded at Danzig, Count and GdOLH. GdCX of the Crown of Iron. Commander in chief of the artillery in 1812, he died as a result of the retreat from Russia, at Königsberg. In his report, he said that only the six guns from the light artillery were engaged, but that they created havoc in the enemy ranks, which was their objective. 17 men were wounded. The rest of the artillery only arrived after mid-day.

Of the 48 guns of the 4th Corps, 42 had been seized on the Austrian army after Austerlitz.

The other divisions of the 4th Corps only arrived for the end of the battle. They were the following units:

✤ LEVAL'S DIVISION consisted of:
24th Light with General Schiner.
FEREY'S BRIGADE
4th Line, under Colonel Boyeldieu.
28th Line, under Colonel Edighoffen.
VIVIES' BRIGADE
46th Line, under Colonel Latrille.
57th Line, under Colonel Rey.

✤ LEGRAND'S DIVISION included:
LEDRU'S BRIGADE
26th Light, under Colonel Pouget.
18th Line, under Colonel Ravier.
75th Line, under Colonel Lhuillier.

Also included in Legrand's Division:
Tirailleurs corses, under d'Ornano.
Tirailleurs du Pô, under Hulot.

These tirailleurs were used a lot on the march to Jena and they fought with distinction afterwards at Lübeck. They marched at the head of the Corps which explains why some were wounded.

In his report after the battle, Soult announced the following losses in his 4th Corps:

- for the Saint-Hilaire division, seven officers and 36 men killed, 21 officers and 544 men wounded.

- for the cavalry, 27 dead, 209 wounded and 39 lost. This was obviously less than the real figure because a lot of the wounded died as a result of their wounds.

Cavalry charges at Jena have greatly inspired military painters, sometimes beyond reality. This is the case, for instance, with L. Malespina who exhibited in the 'Salon des Artistes français' in 1910 a powerful charge by the 16th Dragoons (top).
In fact, this regiment from Beaumont's Division did not get to Apold a before the evening of the 14th October. The 16th Dragoons only participated in the pursuit of the beaten Prussians.
Similarly, in 1891, Edouard Detaille painted the charge of the 1st Hussars at Jena (right). But at the time of the battle, this regiment was serving as a horse guard by the Emperor and did not see action. The Guard cavalrymen themselves were absent. They were still marching and joined Napoleon only four days after Jena.
(Copyright Musée Saint-Rémi, Rheims).

MURAT'S CAVALRY RESERVE

- *Belliard*, Chief of Staff, promoted General on the battlefield at Arcole, hero of Egypt. Made Major General by Kléber, Governor of Madrid in 1808, Chief of Staff to Murat in Russia, wounded. Colonel General of the Cuirassiers in 1812. Pair de France and GdCxLH in 1814. Struck off and arrested in 1815. Pair de France again in 1819. Ambassador to Brussels, died in 1832.

- *Girard*, Deputy Chief of Staff. Italy, Marengo. General in November 1806. Baron, Major General in 1809 in Spain. GdOLH in 1811. Russia, wounded at the Beresina. GdCx of the Réunion, wounded at Lützen, trapped in Magdeburg. Mortally wounded on the 16th June 1815.

- *Rogniat*, Battalion commander, in command of the Engineers. Wounded at Saragossa, General in 1809, Baron. Major General in Spain in 1811. He commanded the Engineers of the Grande Armée in 1813. Waterloo. GdCxSL in 1820. Viscount, CrSL. Pair de France in 1831, died in 1840.

Murat's aides de camp were:

- *Beaumont*, Egypt, General in 1805, Baron, Spain, Russia, CtLH and Crown of Iron, died in 1813.

- *Déry*, Squadron commander, colonel of the 5th Hussars in December 1806. OLH, General in 1811, killed in Russia.

- *Levasseur*, OLH, retired in 1809 as Adjudant-commandant.

- *Geither*, Egypt, Colonel, commanding Berg's Infantry. General in 1811. OLH, he lost right arm at Beresina. Retired in 1820, then again in 1832.

- *Flahaut de la Billarderie*, probably the son of Talleyrand, Marengo, Colonel. Baron in 1809, Grand Equerry to Queen Hortense who bore him a son: the Duke of Morny. General in Russia then Count, Major General and aide de camp to Napoleon in

1813, served at Waterloo. Outlawed. Pair de France in 1831, GdCxLH, Senator, Grand Chancellor of the LH in 1864, Military Medal in 1866.

THE LIGHT CAVALRY

It did not fight at Jena, but was instrumental in the pursuit afterwards.

THE DRAGOONS

✢ KLEIN'S DIVISION

General *Klein*, Senator, Count and Governor of the Palace in 1808. Retired, he was made Pair de France in 1814, then GdCxLH in 1834.

- *Bertrand*, Chief of Staff, wounded at Eylau and Friedland, General in 1808, CtLH. Russia, retired in 1815.

- *Bachelet-Damville*, Captain. Received seven sabre strokes at Jena then eleven wounds at Heilsberg. OLH in 1811, Baron, Brigadier General in 1813, killed at Leipzig. Received in all 22 wounds.

FORNIER'S BRIGADE

General *Fornier* called '*Fénérols*', CtLh, killed at Gloymin.

1st Dragoons (three squadrons)
Commanded by colonel *Oullenbourg*. General in 1807, Baron, Russia, CtLH in 1814, retired in 1815, honorary Lieutenant General.

- *Haugeranville*, Squadron commander, Berthier's nephew. Colonel in 1807, Baron. Wounded at Essling and Wagram. Transfered to the Chasseurs of the Guard in 1811. Russia, General, wounded and captured at Leipzig. Followed the King to Gand, died in 1817.

- *Vaudeville*, Second lieutenant, LH. Lieutenant in 1809, Russia, Squadron commander in 1813, wounded, OLH. Retired in 1816. Entered Holy Orders, canon at Nancy.

- *Gontard*, Second lieutenant, LH. Wounded at Jena, Captain retired in 1815.

On the 27th September, the regiment numbered 26 officers and 400 men.

2nd Dragoons (four squadrons)
Commanded by Colonel *Pryvé*, CtLH. At Jena, he charged three times with his regiment and captured a battalion, a flag and 12 cannon. Baron, General, captured at Baylen. Returned from England and retired in 1818.

On the 27th September there were 31 officers and 600 troopers.

FAUCONNET'S BRIGADE

- *Fauconnet*, Major General, city commanding officer in 1808. Baron, retired in 1815.

Belliard, Chief of Staff of Murat's Cavalry Reserve.

Klein, in command of the 4ᵗʰ Dragoon Division.

14th Dragoons (three squadrons)
Commanded by colonel *Bouvier des Eclaz*, given the command on the 20th September 1806. Wounded at Eylau, then at Heilsberg. Baron and General in 1810. CtLH in 1811, Crown of Iron. Russia, capitulated in Holland, arrested and inactive 1814, retired 1815.

- *Dumesnil*, Lieutenant, LH. Captain after Jena, OLH. Retired in 1814.

On the 27th September, the regiment had 30 officers and 500 men.

PICARD'S BRIGADE

General *Picard*, invalided out in 1809, retired in 1815.

26th Dragoons (three squadrons)
Commanded by colonel *Delorme*, Rivoli, CtLH after Austerlitz. Baron, retired.

- *Vial,* Squadron commander, Egypt. Colonel in 1807. Baron, General in 1813, Waterloo. Cashiered, retired in 1825, honorary Lieutenant General. Reinstated, GdOLH in 1850.

- *Vimont*, Second lieutenant. Wounded, he got through a square and captured the commanding officer.

The regiment had on the 27th September:

1st squadron: 17 officers, 148 dragoons, 184 horses;

2nd squadron: eight officers, 157 dragoons, 157 horses;

3rd squadron: eight officers, 141 dragoons, 155 horses;
making a total of 33 officers and 433 men.

Four officers were wounded, one dragoon was killed and two wounded.

20th Dragoons (three squadrons)
Commanded by colonel *Reynaud*, Egypt, CtLH. General in December 1806, Baron, Russia, inactive in 1814, retired.

- *Coulon*, Squadron commander, LH. Chevalier, Adjudant-commandant in 1812, retired in 1818.

- *Baudin*, Lieutenant, Egypt, LH. Captain in 1807, killed at Madrid.

- *Dereume*, Second lieutenant in November 1806. Spain, captain in 1813. Present at Danzig, sacked in 1815.

- *Labalette*, Egypt, wounded six times, LH. Second lieutenant in 1809. Lieutenant in 1813, wounded. Waterloo, retired in 1816.

On the 27th September, the regiment had 29 officers and 400 horsemen.

The total strength for the division at that date was 149 officers and 2,252 dragoons together with a hundred artillerymen with

Dragoons

Corporal, 1st Dragoons

Trooper, 2nd Dragoons

Sergeant,
26th Dragoons

Cuirassiers

Trumpeter,
10th Cuirassiers

Corporal
wearing coat

Corporal,
10th Cuirassiers

NB : this dress
has been
reconstructed.

Chasseurs

1st Rgt

2nd Rgt

7th Rgt

11th Rgt

20th Rgt

21st Rgt

André Jouineau © Histoire & Collections 1998

8-pounders and a howitzer followed by four 8-pounder limbers, three for the howitzer and one for the infantry, and one forge.

THE CUIRASSIERS

✤ D'HAUTPOUL'S DIVISION

This was the only division to arrive in time, and even then only two regiments, the 1st and 10th. The others were delayed in the defiles.

General *d'Hautpoul* died as a result of his wounds at Eylau. He was Grand-Aigle of the LH and Senator.

D'Hautpoul, commanding a Cuirassier Division.

1st Cuirassiers
Commanded by colonel *Guiton*, CtLH. General in 1807, Baron, served at Waterloo, retired in 1815.
- *Roize*, Squadron commander, former aide de camp to Davout, wounded, LH. Wounded again in 1807, Major.
- *Daudiès*, Squadron commander, LH. Chevalier, Colonel in 1813, wounded twice at Leipzig.

The regiment had 24 officers and 510 horsemen. Two cuirassiers were killed, one officer and 20 men wounded.

10th Cuirassiers
Commanded by colonel *Lhéritier*, who took command on the 5th October. OLH in 1807, Baron, General in 1809, Russia, Major General in 1813. CtLH in 1814, wounded at Waterloo, then placed on the inactive list.
- *Boyer*, Captain, mentioned at Jena.

The regiment had 25 officers and 487 men. It charged in support of the 1st cuirassiers.

The rest of the cavalry reserve included:

✤ 2nd DRAGOON DIVISION (Grouchy)
3rd , **6th**, **10th**, **11th**, **13th** et **22nd Dragoons**.
Total strength on the 27th September: 192 officers and 2,745 dragoons.

✤ 3rd DRAGOON DIVISION (Beaumont)
5th, **8th**, **9th**, **12th**, **16th** et **21st Dragoons**.
Total strength: 183 officers and 2,872 men.

✤ 4th DRAGOON DIVISION (Sahuc)
15th, **17th**, **18th**, **19th**, **25th** et **27th Dragoons**.
Total strength: 179 officers and 3,009 dragoons.
The artillery was the same as for the other divisions.

✤ 2nd BRIGADE OF D'HAUTPOUL'S DIVISION
5th (understrength) and **11th Cuirassiers**.
Strength 49 officers and 835 cuirassiers.

✤ NANSOUTY'S CUIRASSIER DIVISION
2nd, **3rd**, **9th** et **12th cuirassiers**
(also including **1st** and **2nd Carabiniers**)
Total strength: 145 officers and 2,842 cuirassiers.
The horse artillery included 13 guns for the whole of the heavy cavalry.

Murat leading the charge of the 1st Cuirassiers at Jena, part of the Panorama of Jena, by Poilpot.

The victorious commander: Maréchal Davout,
in command of the 3rd Corps.

One of the defeated generals:
the Duke of Brunswick.

The battle of Auerstaedt, on the 14th October 1806 at 10 a.m. with Morand's infantry squares, water-colour by Gobaut. (SHAT, Vincennes)

PRELUDE TO AUERSTAEDT

The name appears with various spellings on the maps, such as Auerstadt or even Auerstedt, but the name used by Davout for his title of Duke, was Auerstaedt.

D URING THE NIGHT of 13th to 14th October 1806, the Duke of Brunswick wrote to Hohenlohe about his intentions in the following terms:

'H.M. the King's army has advanced to Auerstaedt and is camped there. The enemy has taken the bridges at Kösen and is now in and around Naumburg. According to a Jäger, Maréchal Davout is in command of these troops; reports differ greatly on the strength of these troops. The King's army will cross the Unstrutt tomorrow at Freyburg and Laucha, and will try to reach Weissenfels with its vanguard…'

Davout actually was at Naumburg, awaiting the latest orders which arrived at 3 a.m. He was to reach Apolda and fall upon the rearguard of the Prussian army. This, Napoleon believed, was directly in front of him, all of it. Bernadotte could have marched with Davout, but it was better for him to come out of Dornbourg, so he decided to head for this passage.

The generals regrouped around Davout received their orders, except for Vialannes who decided not to stay; he rejoined his brigade which was with Morand's Division at Freyburg; they would have some ground to cover to join up again. A detachment of the

Prince Frederick-William Charles of Prussia, the youngest son of King Prince-Frederick III.

Field Marshall Blücher, commanding the Prussian vanguard.

Lieutenant General von Möllendorf, badly wounded at Jena.

13th Light was ordered to watch the bridge at Freyburg and to destroy it if necessary.

The Maréchal didn't know what to expect in front of him. He knew he had to march on Apolda to fall upon the Prussian rearguard. So he thought he was to block its passage by trying to throw the enemy forces back on to Napoleon who was coming up from Jena. In fact, Davout came across the main army whose only objective was to reach Magdeburg, crushing on the way if necessary, Davout's weak forces who were the tip of the French right wing.

At 4 a.m., the 3rd Corps got moving with Gudin's Division at the front. One of his battalions from the 25th had already occupied the bridge at Kösen. This division included Gauthier's Bri-

THE PRUSSIAN GUARD (I)

THE FOOT GUARD

This included:
— the **Guards Regiment (n° 15)**
It was made up of several different elements:
— the *Leibgarde* (Ist battalion) consisting of six grenadier companies of which two were carabiniers (for flanking).
— Battalions II and III.
— the units of back-up troops, dressed without braids.
— the **Guard Grenadier Battalion (n° 6)**
Il consisted of six companies including one of carabiniers.

THE UNIFORMS OF THE GUARD ON FOOT

The **Guards Regiment (n° 15)** had a bright red distinctive. The **grenadiers** of the *Leibgarde* battalion wore a silver grenade on their bonnet, above the frontal plaque with the spread eagle. The bonnet top was bright red edged with two silver stripes, the plume was white.

Their blue coat had a bright red distinctive, and the collar was edged with the silver stripe and eight buttonholes on each side, ending in a point. The silver edged facings also had vertical silver buttonholes, but this was peculiar to the Guard. Two silver button-holes on the pockets and below the lapels. Silver buttons and a black cravate. The trousers and gaiters were white, but in the field the soldiers wore overtrousers of a washed-out greyish-yellow colour.

Other companies apart from the flanking grenadiers of the regiment, wore a hat with silver stripe with a black cockade and silver braid, and pompoms with white horns and a black centre like the NCOs. The rest of the uniform was similar to that of the flanking grenadiers.

The **officers** had a very high hat, edged with a scalloped silver stripe, silver tassels and a cockade of silver braid. On their coat there was embroidery on the collar and on the lapels only of the button-holes which had silver floches. On the right shoulder a silver shoulder strap and lanyard. Black cravate. In the field, the uniform was stricter: no sabre-knot, no lanyard, no floches; the hat was often protected by waxed cloth.

The **Guard Grenadier Battalion (n° 6)** wore a uniform based on the same principle but the distinctive was scarlet (instead of bright red), with golden buttons, stripes and ornaments.

THE FLAGS

They had a white background, without a cross, with a blue central motif for Battalion n° 6, and the regimental flags had golden embroidery and a yellow shaft. The colonel flag had a central motif with a white background.

For Regiment n° 15, the cloth was white, but with silver stripes, the central escutcheon was blue for the regimental flags and silver for the colonel flag. All the embroidery was silver and the shaft white.

Grenadier
of the Guard
Grenadier
Battalion, n° 6
in full dress

Officer
of the Guards
Regiment,
IR n° 15
2nd battalion
in full dress

Grenadier NCO
of the Guards
Regiment,
IR n° 15
2nd battalion
in full dress

Grenadier
of the Guards
Regiment
IR n° 15,
2nd battalion
in full dress

Musketeer
of the Guards
Regiment
IR n° 15,
2nd battalion
in full dress

Grenadier
of the Guards
Regiment
IR n° 15,
1st battalion
in full dress

Musketeer
of the Guards
Regiment
IR n° 15,
1st battalion
in field dress

Garde Gren. Bat n° 6

Garde IR n° 15

André Jouineau © Histoire & Collections 1998

*Marshall Count
von Kalckreuth.*

*General Gerhard Johann David
von Scharnhorst.*

*General Count Tauentzien.
He fought at Jena, not at Auerstaedt.*

*Marshall Prince Blücher (insert), a horse killed under him in the fighting
at Hassenhausen, during the battle of Auerstaedt.*

gade (25th and 85th) and Petit's Brigade (12th and 21st) with 10 cannon. The Maréchal marched along with Gudin and sent forward a reconnaissance party under the command of his aide de camp, Colonel Bourke, together with a squadron from Captain Hulot's 1st Chasseurs, the only cavalry present.

Passing through Hassenhausen, Bourke met the first Prussians at Poppel, and he returned to report this.

The Maréchal got the 25th followed by the 12th to march to the right of the road going to Hassenhausen. On the left, the 85th preceded the 21st and the artillery used the road itself.

Blücher who was in command of the Prussian vanguard, only had the Queen's Dragoons with him. The Graumann battery had got lost somewhere in the thick fog but managed somehow to

THE PRUSSIAN GUARD (II)

THE HORSE GUARD

This included two regiments:

— the **Garde du Corps Regiment (n° 13)** with red and silver distinctives was the most distinguished. Its colonel flag, unique in the Prussian cavalry, consisted of a vexillum with a great silver eagle; a horizontal bar was suspended from this eagle from which the standard hung: in silver cloth with silver embroideries studded with little dabs of red on the ribbons and the bottom of the crown. Another distinction peculiar to the Gardes du Corps was the cartridge box bearing the silver star of the same type as that of the order of the Black Eagle.

— the **Gendarmes Regiment (n° 10)** with red and gold distinctives, had a ordinary type of standard.

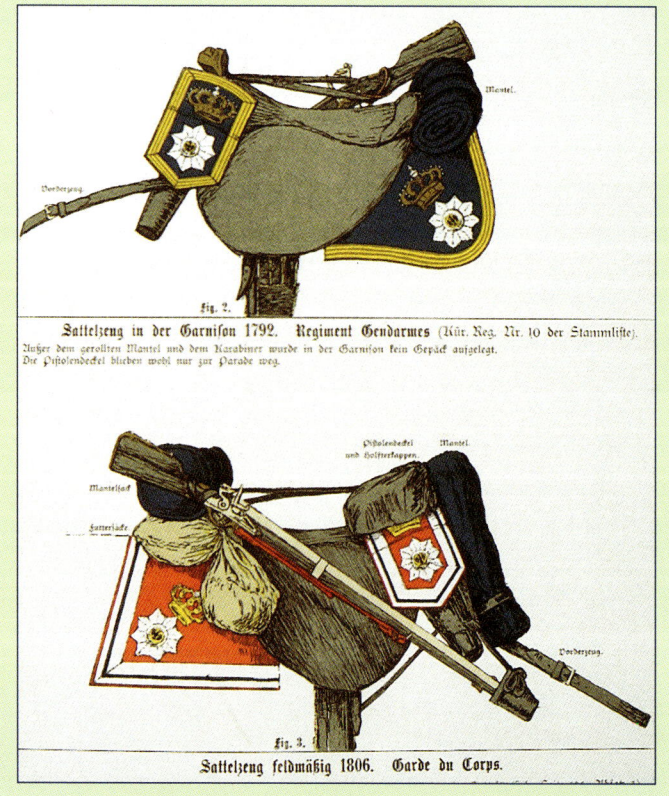

*Prussian Guard harness and saddlecover: top, the
Gendarmes Regiment. Below, the Gardes du Corps Regiment.*

Officer
Gardes du Corps
Regiment,
in full dress

NCO
Gardes du Corps
Regiment,
in full dress

Gardes du Corps
in full dress

Sword-knots of the Gardes du Corps Regiment

NCOs

Companies

Gardes du Corps
Regiment n° 13

Gendarmes
Regiment n° 10

André Jouineau © Histoire & Collections 1998

catch up with him. He passed through Hassenhausen and came across the 25th who immediately formed up into squares; its artillery took up position on the road and sent off a volley of grape-shot. Blücher got his dragoons deployed and the Graumann battery set up to the north of the road where it was quickly taken to task by the skirmishers of the 25th Line.

Captain Lagoublaye, Gauthier's aide de camp, attacked the battery with two companies of grenadiers and one of voltigeurs from the 25th, helped by Hulot's Chasseurs. The Prussians were only able to fall back with three out of their eight cannon and even lost another one, which broke a wheel whilst going through the village.

In the fog, Davout had no idea that he was about to face the 50,000 elite troops of the main Prussian army. It consisted of the following units:

THE KING OF PRUSSIA'S PRINCIPAL ARMY

The vanguard division of the Duke of Saxony-Weimar was detached off to the west and did not take part in the battle. The remaining units were on the battlefield.

✜ VON SCHMETTAU'S DIVISION
VON ALVENSLEBEN'S BRIGADE
Malchitz and Schimonski Regiments, Krafft Grenadier battalion and Stankar 12-pounder battery.
VON SCHIMONSKI'S BRIGADE
Prince Henry and von Alvensleben Regiments, Schack Grenadier battalion and Röhl 12-pounder battery.

Malschitzki IR n° 28

Alvenseiben IR n° 33

Schimonsky IR n° 40

Prince Henri IR n° 35

André Jouineau © Histoire & Collections 1998

Kleist IR n° 5

Renouard IR n° 3

Prince Louis Ferdinand
IR n° 20

Duke of Brunswick
IR n° 21

Rollendorf IR n° 25

Wartensleben IR n° 59

André Jouineau © Histoire & Collections 1998

VON BUNTING'S CAVALRY BRIGADE

Heising and Bunting Cuirassiers, Schorlemmer horse artillery battery.

LIGHT TROOPS

2nd battalion of Würtemberg Hussars (five squadrons), Greiffenberg Fusilier battalion and the Weimar Sharpshooters battalion.

A total of 12 battalions, 15 squadrons and three batteries (to which must be added the battalion guns as well).

✤ VON WARTENSLEBEN'S DIVISION

VON RENOUARD'S BRIGADE

Duke of Brunswick and Louis-Ferdinand Regiments, Alt-Braun Grenadier battalion, Lange and von Hauser batteries of 12 pounders.

VON WEDEL'S BRIGADE

Renouard and Kleist Regiments, Hanstein Grenadier battalion and Wilkens 12-pounder battery.

VON QUITZOW'S CAVALRY BRIGADE

Quitzow and Reitzenstein Cuirassiers, Merkatz hose artillery battery.

LIGHT TROOPS

Irwing Dragoons and Koch Fusilier battalion.

A total of 11 battalions, 15 squadrons and four batteries.

✣ THE PRINCE OF ORANGE'S DIVISION

VON LUTZOW'S BRIGADE

Möllendorf and Wartensleben Regiments, Knebel Grenadier battalion and Lehmann 12-pounder battery.

PRINCE HENRY OF PRUSSIA'S BRIGADE

Puttkamer and Prince Ferdinand Regiments, Rheinbaben Grenadier battalion and Reiner 12-pounder battery.

PRINCE WILHEM'S BRIGADE

Life Cuirassiers, Life Carabiniers and Willmann horse artillery battery.

Puttmaker IR n° 36

Prince Ferdinand IR n° 34

Arnim IR n° 13

Pirch IR n° 22

André Jouineau © Histoire & Collections 1998

LIGHT TROOPS

1st battalion of Würtemberg Hussars and Oswald Fusilier battalion.

A total of 11 battalions, 15 squadrons and three batteries.

GRAF VON KALCKREUTH'S RESERVE

✣ FIRST DIVISION, VON KUNHEIM

VON HIRCHFELD'S BRIGADE

Guard Grenadier Battalion, Guards Regiment and Faber 12-pounder battery.

VON ZASTROW'S BRIGADE

The King's Regiment, Prince Augustus and Rabiel Grenadier battalions, Alkier 7-pounder howitzer battery.

VON BEEREN'S CAVALRY BRIGADE

Gardes du Corps Regiment.

✣ SECOND DIVISION, VON ARNIM

VON ZENGE'S BRIGADE

Arnim and Pirch Regiments, Gaudy and Osten Grenadier battalions and Heiden battery of 12-pounders.

VON MALSCHITSKY'S BRIGADE

Zenge Regiment, Hulsen and Schliffen Grenadier battalions and Bychelberg battery of 12-pounders.

VON IRWING'S CAVALRY BRIGADE

Ten squadrons of the Queen's Dragoons and Graumann horse artillery battery.

Add to this the Gendarmes of the Guard and the Beeren Cuirassiers, together with the Scholten horse artillery battery.

A total for von Kalckreuth's reserve of two divisions of 18 battalions, 25 squadrons and three batteries, all elite units.

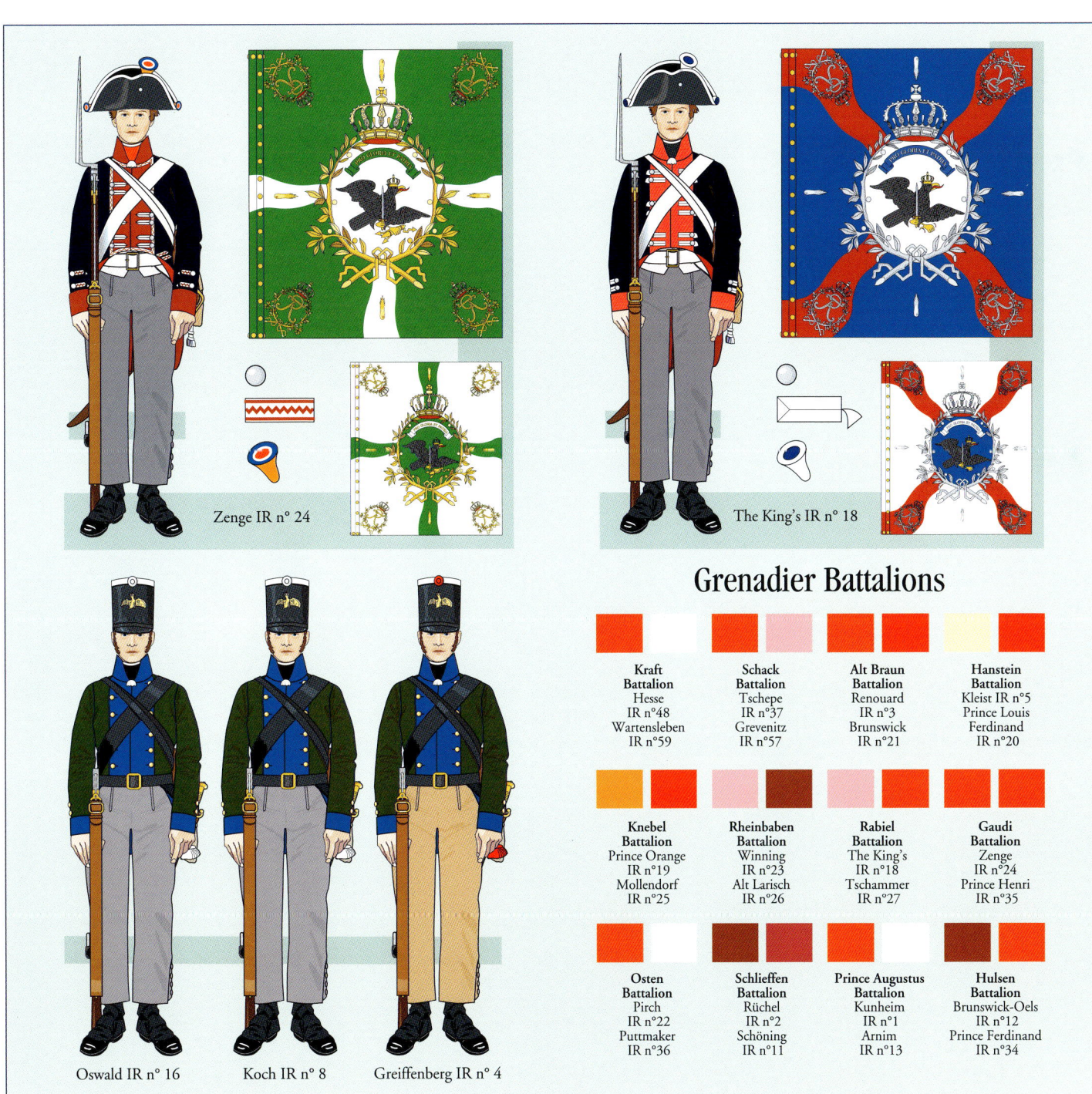

Zenge IR n° 24

The King's IR n° 18

Oswald IR n° 16

Koch IR n° 8

Greiffenberg IR n° 4

Grenadier Battalions

Kraft Battalion
Hesse
IR n°48
Wartensleben
IR n°59

Schack Battalion
Tschepe
IR n°37
Grevenitz
IR n°57

Alt Braun Battalion
Renouard
IR n°3
Brunswick
IR n°21

Hanstein Battalion
Kleist IR n°5
Prince Louis
Ferdinand
IR n°20

Knebel Battalion
Prince Orange
IR n°19
Mollendorf
IR n°25

Rheinbaben Battalion
Winning
IR n°23
Alt Larisch
IR n°26

Rabiel Battalion
The King's
IR n°18
Tschammer
IR n°27

Gaudi Battalion
Zenge
IR n°24
Prince Henri
IR n°35

Osten Battalion
Pirch
IR n°22
Puttmaker
IR n°36

Schlieffen Battalion
Rüchel
IR n°2
Schöning
IR n°11

Prince Augustus Battalion
Kunheim
IR n°1
Arnim
IR n°13

Hulsen Battalion
Brunswick-Oels
IR n°12
Prince Ferdinand
IR n°34

André Jouineau © Histoire & Collections 1998

Hussars

Würtemberg n° 4

Blücher n° 8
in full dress

Blücher n° 8
in field dress

Trumpeter,
Blücher n° 8

Blücher n° 8
NCO in field dress

Dragoon's saddle,
Queen Louise's
Regiment n° 5

Dragoons

Trooper,
Queen Louise's
Dragoons n° 5

Trooper,
Von Irwing
Dragoons n° 3

NCO and trumpeter,
Von Irwing Dragoons n° 3

André Jouineau © Histoire & Collections 1998

Cuirassiers

von Beeren n° 2

Standard

Coat's stripe

NCO's stripe

Life Cuirassiers n° 3

Quitzow n° 6

Rietzenstein n° 7

Heising n° 8

Officer, Bünting Regiment n° 12 in full dress

Life Carabiniers n° 11

Bünting n° 12

Officer, Bünting Regiment n° 12, wearing frock-coat

André Jouineau © Histoire & Collections 1998

THE BATTLE OF AUERSTAEDT

DAVOUT ONLY HAD his three divisions (Morand, Friant and Gudin) and the 1st, 2nd and 12th Chasseurs of Vialannes with which to oppose the enormous Prussian army. He had 25,000 men of which 1,200 were cavalry; a further 1,000 men from the 17th who were guarding the bridge at Kösen could not be used in the battle.

FIRST PHASE: GUDIN FIGHTING ALONE

After losing Graumann battery, Blücher took his cavalry off towards the left of the road. With him were the Queen's Dragoons and the Heising Cuirassiers, with a little troop of infantry made up of Alvenleben 2nd battalion and a unit of skirmishers. Meanwhile, Gudin occupied Hassenhausen with the three elite companies of the 25th which had taken the Prussian cannon; he then positioned two battalions of the regiment to the north of the village. Scharnhorst came to see Blücher, saw the French line and returned to headquarters; Schmettau's Division was sent up on the double. It arrived at Taugwitz towards 8.15.

Cavalry reinforcements were sent to Blücher with the Reitzenstein Cuirassiers and the Merkatz horse artillery battery, which set up to the south of Spielberg and began the day brilliantly by firing on Blücher's cavalry! The fog began to lift; now that he could see a good deal better, Blücher began to prepare an attack on Gudin's infantry.

Davout got the right hand battalion of the 25th to form a square; the 21st did the same. A little further back, the 12th formed a third square at full strength. The cannon were placed at the corners of the squares. Friant's Division was approaching, with Lochet's 11th and 108th in the front, followed by Kister's 33rd and 48th.

Blücher ordered the cavalry to attack, Merkatz continued firing but he again fired on his own side, in this case cuirassiers from the Heising Regiment. The few chasseurs present fell back very quickly, but whilst pursuing them, General Reitztenstein was wounded. At any rate, Gudin's squares held fast. Davout and Gudin went from square to square in between the successive waves of attacks, which Blücher kept up unceasingly until he had a horse killed under him; he took the horse off a trumpeter. His cavalry losses were very high and the horses were exhausted; the remaining horsemen gave up the fight, falling back on Eckartsberg, to the west of the Spielberg, where they tried to regroup.

Meanwhile, near Taugwitz, the King and the Duke of Brunswick were in the process of deploying Schmettau's Division, preceded by the skirmishers, the Alvensleben 2nd battalion and the Krafft Grenadier battalion, who forced the French skirmishers gradually back towards the village.

It was 9 a.m. when Schmettau's Division moved forward ready for the attack. But Brunswick held it back, waiting for Wartensleben's Division, which had to get hold of the plateau to the south of Hassenhausen, to reach the Lissbach between Taugwitz and Rehausen. This occurred at about 9.30. The movements of this division remained concealed for a long time, and it caught Davout by surprise when it suddenly emerged on his left.

Before they got there, the 85th supported by two 8-pounders, drove off an attack by the Krafft Grenadiers, in front of Hassenhausen.

THE ARRIVAL OF FRIANT'S DIVISION

To support Gudin, Davout sent Friant towards the right, having the 108th occupy Spielberg and attempt to get round the Prussian left. Vialannes' chasseurs, having now arrived, supported this action. The 111th extended the line of the 25th between Hassenhausen and Spielberg; three batteries, one between the two regiments and two on the wings completed this deployment. The 12th and the 21st were kept in reserve; the 33rd and the 48th moved up towards the right. To the rear of Hassenhausen, the 12-pounders lined up on the right of the road.

The Maréchal had chosen to spread out towards the right for two reasons: he could thus cover the road leading to the Unstrutt crossings and in particular, Freyburg; on this side he also could extend his line as much as he wanted, whereas towards the south he would have been blocked by the valley of the Ilm. To the right, he could also very easily to try to turn the Prussian left wing.

Meanwhile, Morand, on a forced march, was getting closer to the battlefield. So for the moment, they had to hold on.

First the Merkatz battery had to be taken: it was firing nonstop. Although it was also protected by two squadrons reformed from the Reitzenstein Cuirassiers, a combined attack by the 108th, the 25th and the chasseurs succeeded. The Prussians only managed to get one gun away in time and elsewhere the Prussians now got themselves organised in preparation for a general attack, set for 9.30 a.m.

THE PRUSSIAN LEFT WING

The Stankar battery took up its position at the end of the line, but as it was rather isolated, the French chasseurs immediately attacked it. Schmettau had to send the Malschitzky 1st battalion to free it. Three squadrons of the Quitzow Cuirassiers had been requested by Blücher in the morning; they had been kept by Schmettau because he had run out of cavalry. This cavalry now went in to attack the French, but when they came under heavy fire from the French cannon, they turned away and went off towards Lisdorf where they rallied with Blücher's cavalry, lea-

Davout at the beginning of the battle, on the road down Hassenhausen to Auerstaedt. Behind him can be seen a cannon with a broken wheel, which had been abandoned by the retreating Prussian Graumann battery. Around the Maréchal commanding the 3rd Corps, Gudin's soldiers are taking their new positions, north of Hassenhausen.
(Original plate by J. Girbal, the Authors' Collection).

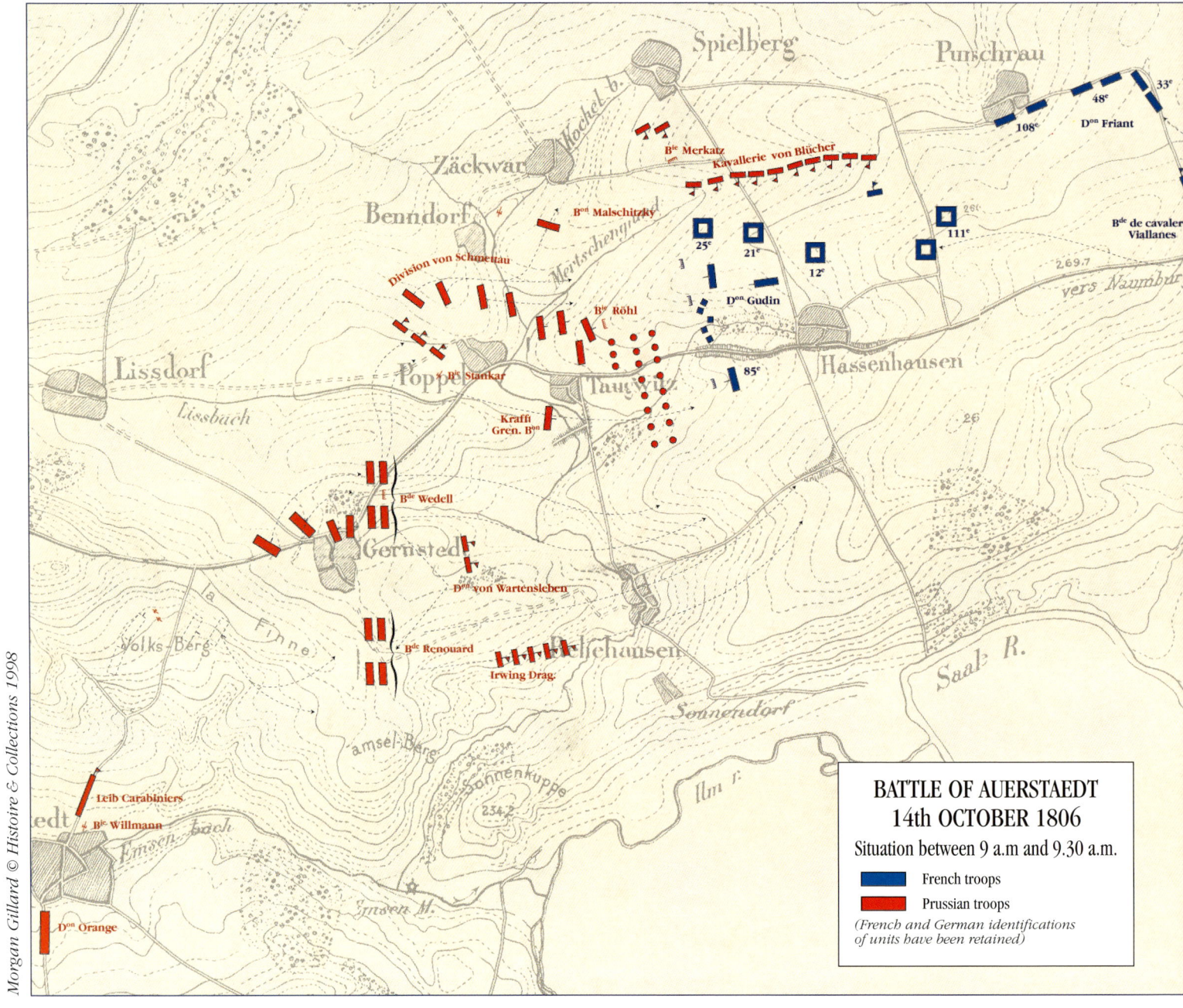

BATTLE OF AUERSTAEDT
14th OCTOBER 1806

Situation between 9 a.m and 9.30 a.m.

■ French troops

■ Prussian troops

*(French and German identifications
of units have been retained)*

ving the Prussian left without cavalry cover once again.

Brunswick had just sent Scharnhorst to deal with this sector; he soon had to take over the left because Schmettau had been wounded twice and taken from the battlefield.

The new commander raised merry hell to get cavalry support for his action; but he didn't get any because all available squadrons were being concentrated by Brunswick on the right wing with Prince William, behind Wartensleben's Division. All these manoeuvres removing cavalry units from their divisions only added to the congestion. Crossing Auerstaedt was complicated and the Prince of Orange's Division coming to reinforce the centre was delayed. Cannon got bogged down or slithered into ditches, reinforcements were moving up only very slowly and the two reserve divisions didn't budge an inch. Confused orders and congestion caused the huge numerical advantage that the Prussians had over the French to be lost.

THE ATTACK BY THE PRUSSIAN RIGHT WING

On the Prussian right wing however, they still had the advantage. The attack got off at 10 a.m. The 85th which was fighting

the Krafft battalion, suddenly saw the mass of the Wartensleben Division moving on to the plateau, accompanied by an imposing force of cavalry. The Irwing Dragoons charged the exposed French regiment positioned in front of Hassenhausen. Encouraged by this, the Krafft battalion pushed home the attack.

The 85th was routed. It rushed through the village, and managed to form up behind it into a square, incomplete on the north side. During their attack however, the Irwing Dragoons lost 8 officers, 182 men and 200 horses. By the time the Bunting and Beeren Cuirassiers also tried to charge the 85th's square, it had formed up completely. This action failed because Gudin's troops were hard, well commanded and had got over the effect of the surprise. But the village was abandoned; fortunately for the French, the Krafft battalion didn't occupy it.

The Wartensleben Division was now deployed on the plateau and squadrons were moving all around Prince William. The Life Carabiniers and the Willmann battery arrived, with the Life Cuirassiers, the Garde du Corps, elements from the Queen's Dragoons, two squadrons of the Quitzow Cuirassiers, Blücher's hussars, and the Würtemberg Hussars; not forgetting the Irwing Dra-

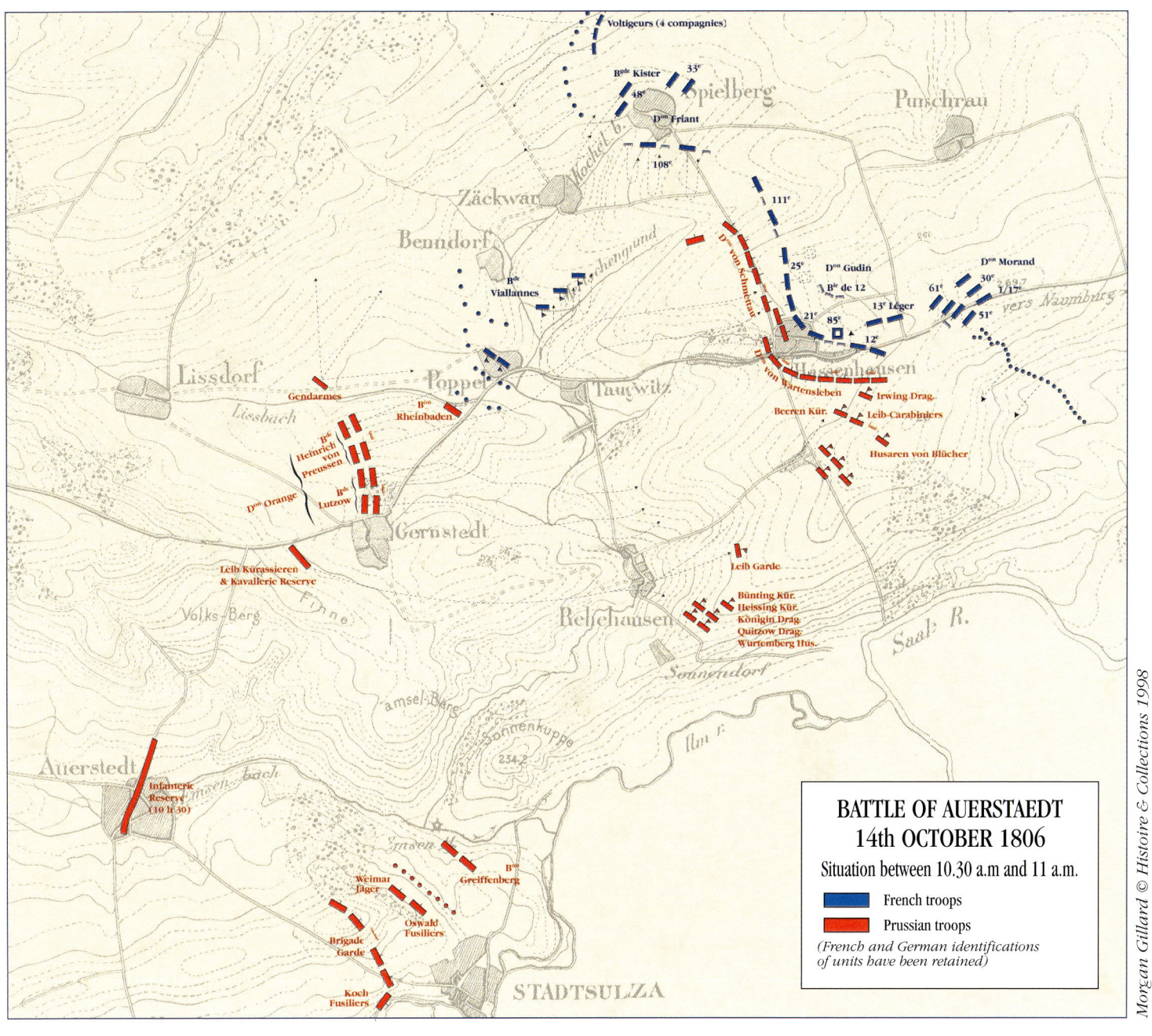

goons, and the Bunting and Beeren Cuirassiers. All these squadrons formed up, but this took time.

Davout reacted immediately and sent the 12th in support of the hard-pressed 85th. The 21st moved into Hassenhausen and pushed back the Prussians. The 12-pounders helped as much as they could.

Brunswick went over to the Haustein Grenadiers and ordered them to attack the village. At this precise moment he was hit in the face by a bullet which mortally wounded him. He was taken to the rear. With the Commander-in-chief gone and the Quartermaster out on the left wing, there was nobody with the King except old Marshall Möllendorf; operations were disorganised enough already as it was: now there was no longer a firm hand to control the situation. However, there remained that mass of squadrons and Wartensleben's Division; the Prince of Orange's Division now emerged behind the Prussian centre. The Heuser 12-pounder battery, which had just arrived, started firing on the 12th. Fearing an attack from the squadrons it could see in the distance, the 12th formed up into a square.

Casualties in the 12th were heavy and the men sheltered as best they could. Well-protected, these defenders of Hassenhausen managed to push back several assaults. They were covered by the village whereas the Prussians had to approach across totally open ground.

Wartensleben's horse was killed and Wedell was wounded. Hassenhausen was increasingly under threat because units from Scharnhorst's right were getting closer and closer. This was the critical moment for Davout who no longer had any reserves left.

It was 10.30 and the Prince of Orange's Division now appeared. On the left, the Rheinbaben battalion and the Puttmaker Regiment tried to repel the 108th's skirmishers, but their artillery was still in the rear and didn't appear. Four other battalions reinforced Schmettau's line. Lutzow's Brigade moved up behind Wartensleben's Division.

The attack on Hassenhausen had gathered momentum to the north and to the south. The 21st clung on desperately, hiding among the last houses left standing in the village. There was a risk of the 12th and the 85th being turned. It was at this moment that things began to go the other way: Morand had appeared on the scene. It was 11 a.m.

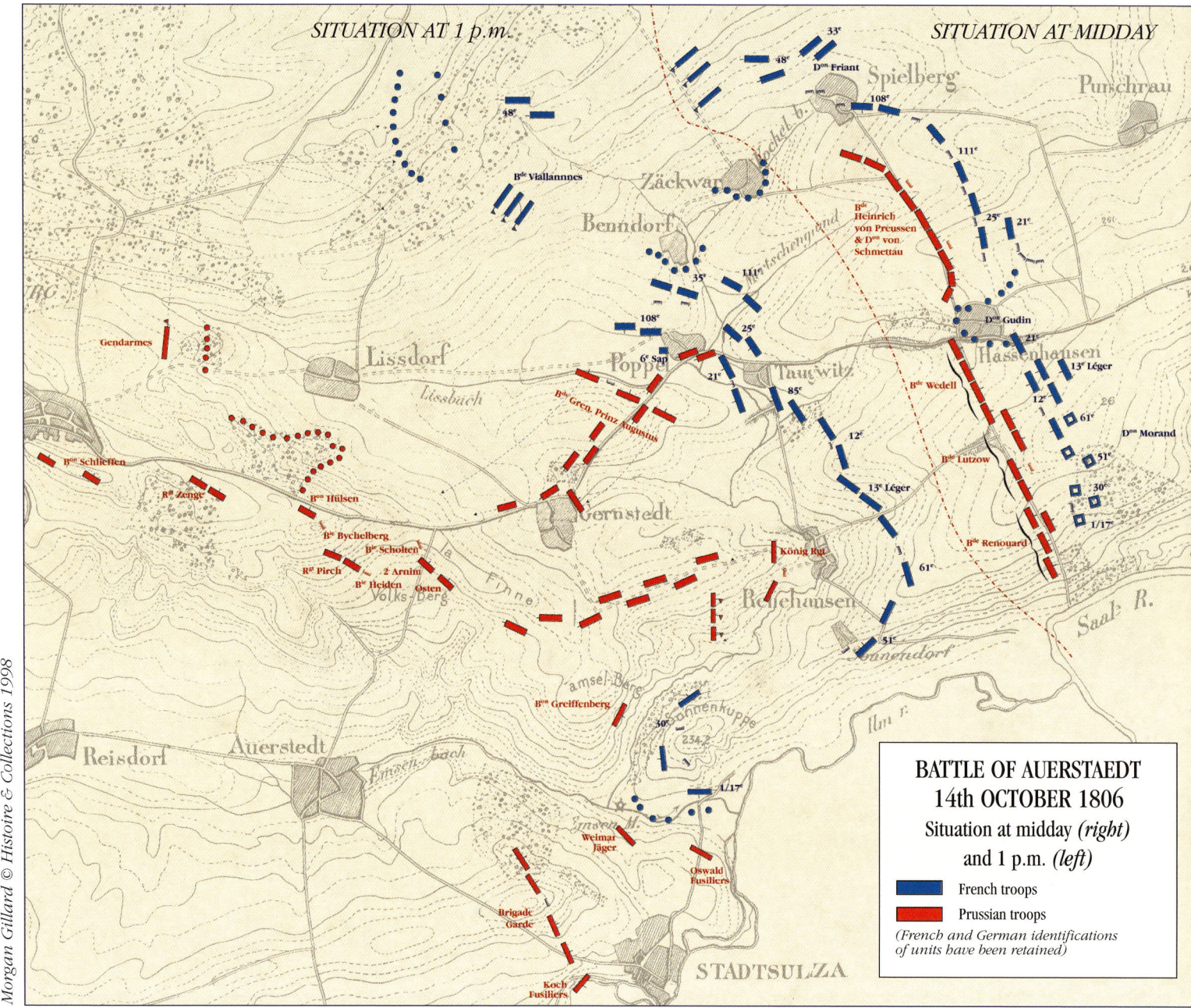

SITUATION AT 1 p.m.   SITUATION AT MIDDAY

BATTLE OF AUERSTAEDT
14th OCTOBER 1806
Situation at midday *(right)*
and 1 p.m. *(left)*

█ French troops
█ Prussian troops
(French and German identifications of units have been retained)

THE ARRIVAL OF MORAND'S DIVISION

The 13th Light was immediately sent into the village with its two 4-pounders; it relieved it but could not get back out due to enemy artillery fire; leaving the 21st to hold the position, it placed itself just to the rear of the village.

Scharnhorst gathered together 150 Queen's Dragoons who charged the French lines. They managed to reach one of the batteries, but only 50 got back and this sacrifice only gave a moment's improvement; Davout's line had barely receded. There was no Prussian reserve on the way on this side.

The Maréchal went to meet Morand and marched with him to the left of Hassenhausen, straight towards Wartensleben's Division.

General Debilly opened up the way with the 51st and the 61st. Brouard followed with the 30th and the 17th reduced to one battalion; it went along the slopes of the valley with swarms of skirmishers; the artillery was placed in the centre of the division. This deployment was carried out on the left of the 12th of the line, now well covered.

The Prussian cavalry now went into action. Blücher's hussars attacked first with Prince William at their head.

Morand's squares formed up with their cannon on the corners. They let the red horsemen get as near as possible and then opened up at the last moment. The Prince's horse was killed, he himself wounded and the charge driven back. A further charge failed and half of the hussars were out of action. The Prince was evacuated. The Life Carabiniers were no more successful and only the Willmann battery succeeded in getting a square to move back a little.

All the other Prussian squadrons charged unsuccessfully in turn until they were exhausted. This beautiful cavalry, which claimed to be the best in the world, came thus to fall in front of the walls of Davout's troops, reminding the veterans of Egypt of the brilliant Mameluks they had so often fought off.

The Prussian cavalry broken up, exhausted and all mixed up, fell back on Auerstaedt where it rallied as well as it could. Now completely without any effective cavalry cover, Wartensleben's Division had to fall back too, drawing Lutzow's Brigade with it. Victory had changed sides.

Morand moved on and detached hosts of skirmishers on his

98

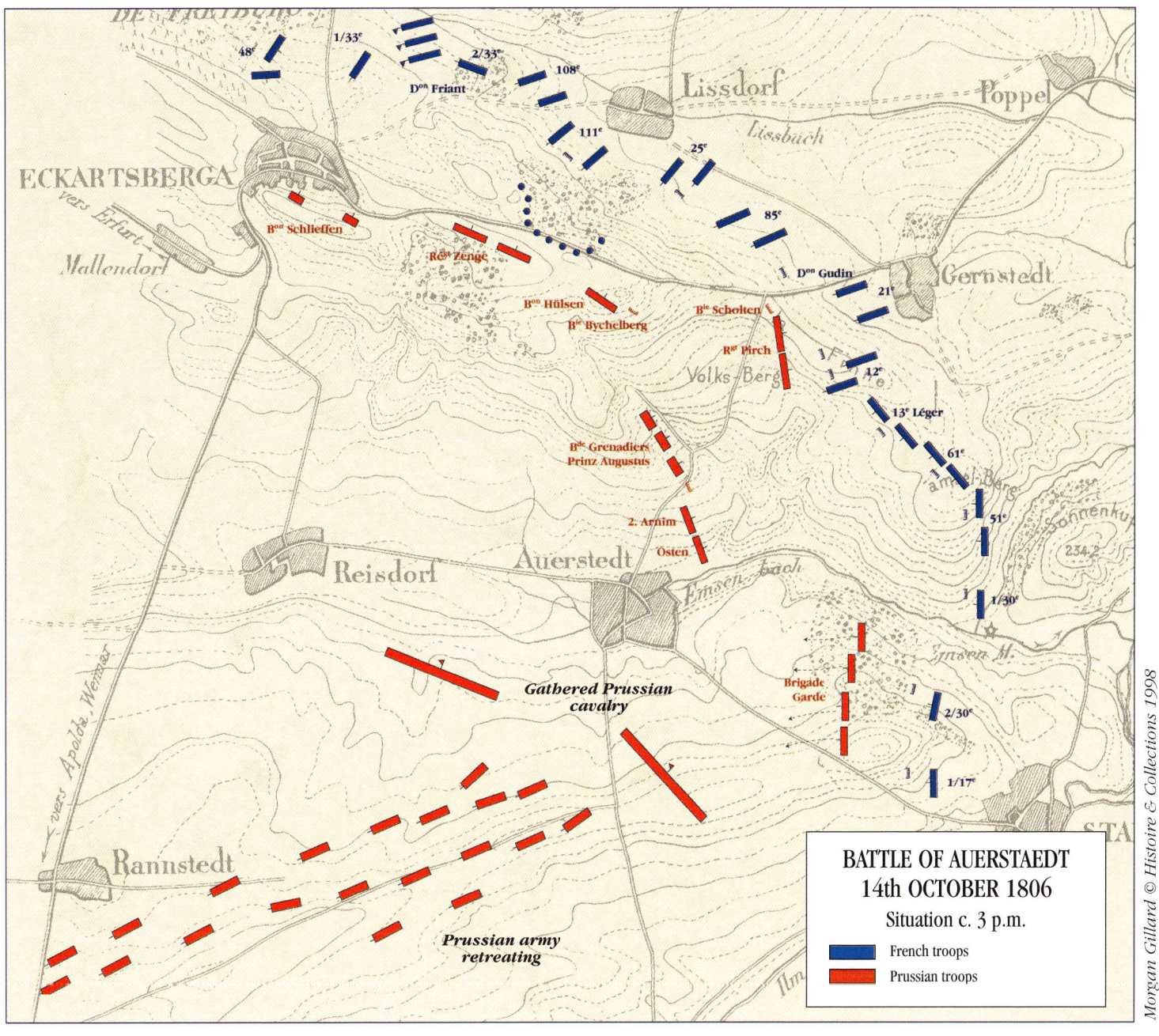

BATTLE OF AUERSTAEDT
14th OCTOBER 1806
Situation c. 3 p.m.

█	French troops
█	Prussian troops

Morgan Gillard © Histoire & Collections 1998

left to turn the Prussian line. Gudin got going as well. The 21st left Hassenhausen with the 12th on its left, the batteries joined in. It was midday.

THE RETREAT OF THE PRUSSIAN RIGHT WING

Very hard fighting took place on a level with the Rehausen ravine, but Debilly's Brigade finished by pushing back Lutzow's regiments. They fell back towards the Lissbach leaving a lot of artillery on the field. The Hanstein battalion did its best to hold on, but then went and joined the troops on the left wing. The King's Regiment coming up in reinforcement found everybody retreating. It positioned itself on the right bank of the stream in order to cover the exit from Rehausen with its guns.

At that moment, Davout and Morand saw the four Guards battalions with the Faber battery and three squadrons of the Würtemberg Hussars up on the heights. The Oswald battalion, the Weimar Jägers and the Koch battalion had also taken up position. The top of the Sonnenberg was now occupied by the Greiffenberg battalion.

The Maréchal ordered the 30th and the battalion of the 17th

to move against the Sonnenberg. The bigger part of the division came up in support of Gudin near Rehausen and Taugwitz. The Sonnenberg was taken and 300 men in the battalion holding it were killed, wounded or captured. Morand immediately set up a battery on these heights in order to attack the Prussians on their the flank and fire on the guard. The King's Regiment managed to hold off the French for a moment, enabling a retreat to be made.

THE RETREAT OF THE PRUSSIAN LEFT WING

Friant's Division had also been ordered to attack. Four voltigeur companies cleaned out the wood and pushed back the survivors from Blücher's cavalry. The 48th moved into the wood but couldn't find any of the enemy; an aide de camp was sent off to bring it back to the battlefield where it arrived at about 3 p.m.

The 108th took Poppel and this cut the retreat for Prince Henry's four battalions which had attacked from the east at the same moment as the Knebel and Prince Augustus Grenadiers, led by the Prince in person, arrived in reinforcement. The 108th was obliged to give way and the Prussians were therefore able to fall

Brunswick, mortally wounded, was evacuated from the battlefield of Auerstaedt by a group of grenadiers. Struck by a bullet which took his left eye out and shattered his eye-socket, the Duke was sent to Ottensee, where he died on the 10th November 1806, after the wounds inside his brain worsened. (Drawing by R. Knötel, from 'Die Deutschen Befreiungskriege 1806-15').

back on Auerstaedt. The 11th and the 33rd advanced around Poppel which fell again, once and for all. The 108th, aided by Captain Pradeau's 6th company of engineers, took a flag, several cannon and a thousand prisoners. It was 2 p.m.

The King hesitated a lot; he did notice however that his remaining intact reserves did not number more than 10,000 men and that his only cavalry consisted of the Gendarmes Regiment. The rest were all spread out in a huge muddled-up retreat. He gave the order to retreat giving the command to general Kalckreuth. For the moment the reserve was covering the position on the Eckartsberg. It was 3 p.m.

Davout now had his troops in front of Gerstedt and decided to follow up the attack. Morand's target was Auerstaedt; Gudin's was the Eckartsberg and Friant's, the Prussian left, through Lissdorf.

Morand's soldiers followed the retreat of the Prussian right wing reserve; the guns and the skirmishers were firing all the time. The division won through to Auerstaedt, which was burning, and settled itself on the neighbouring heights. The soldiers were completely exhausted.

In the centre, the Pirch Regiment began its retreat and the Scholten battery fired off a last salvo before leaving.

In front of Gudin, General Malschitzky, who had not received the order to retreat, continued defending his position; but General Petit, with the 12th and the 21st forced the Hülsen battalion back into the Zenge Regiment. Seeing that he had been thus left alone, the Prussian General fell back. He then came across Friant and the 48th at last coming out of the wood. There was now a

general retreat and the French entered Eckartsburg taking 20 cannon and a lot of prisoners.

Only the skirmishers and Vialannes' cavalry started to chase them, followed by the battalion of the 17th which had been guarding the bridge at Kösten and which had now been called up.

Davout's soldiers, totally exhausted, collapsed in a heap. They had won the day by sheer courage and efficiency, so they chose to leave the chase to others. They bivouacked on the battlefield with their Maréchal and his generals. Only Debilly had been killed. The wounded streamed into Naumburg and Davout had to threaten this reluctant community with reprisals if it didn't help Chambon, the ordnance officer who was completely snowed under.

The 3rd Corps' losses were enormous; Davout's report gave 258 officers and 6,790 men out of action, being about a third of the troops engaged. The losses however varied from unit to unit.

Gudin's Division suffered the most: 134 officers and 3,500 men out of action. Morand's with 98 officers and 2,189 killed or wounded; and Friant's with only 20 officers and 900 men out of action, mainly in the 108th and 11th who had thrown themselves so utterly into the fight.

Prussian losses were also very heavy. They left behind them 3,000 prisoners, with 150 cannon taken. The number of men put out of action was estimated between 10,000 and 15,000. This last figure, put forward by the Maréchal, was contested by the Prussians, but not by others.

At any rate, the elite Prussian troops were in full flight: they soon joined and mixed with Hohenlohe's, fleeing from Jena.

THE FRENCH COMBATANTS AT AUERSTAEDT

THESE WERE THE UNDISPUTED HEROES of this awful day. They fought alone two against one and despite totally unfavorable conditions, they defeated the elite of this arrogant Prussian army.

DAVOUT'S 3rd CORPS

Davout's Chief of Staff was *d'Aultane, Fournier de Loisonville,* Marquis, officer under the Ancien Régime. Major General on the 31th December 1806, Baron. Spain. GdOLH, GdCxSL, GdCx of Baden. Retired in 1815, loyal to the King.

- *Hervo*, Deputy Chief of Staff, General and CtLH in 1807. Baron, killed at Eckmühl in 1809.

- *Allain*, CtLH, Marengo, Adjudant commandant. Given responsibilities by Davout on the 17th October. Retired in 1810 (also mentioned with the 5th Corps ?).

- *Chambon*, Commissary, responsible for the many wounded. OLH in 1807, Saint-Henri of Saxony, Baron and CtLH in 1809. Retired in 1816.

- *Lalance*, Inspector of Parades, Toulon, Italy, ex-General, LH. Served with Rapp, transfered to the auxiliary officers in 1817.

- *Tousard*, in command of the Engineers, Egypt, OLH. General in 1807, city commanding officer in Hamburg with Davout. Died there in 1813.

- *Saunier*, Squadron commander, in command of the Gendarmerie. Wounded at Eylau, Saint-Henry of Saxony, Polish Order, Baron, General in 1811, with Davout in Russia. CtLH in 1813. Retired in 1819 with rank of honorary Lieutenant General.

The aides de camp were:

- *Bourke*, Adjudant commandant, wounded at Auerstaedt. Baron then General in 1809. Spain, then caught in Wesel in 1813. Spain in 1823, GdCx de Saint-Ferdinand, CrSL, Pair de France, GdCxLH, died in 1847.

- *Davout*, Colonel, brother of the Maréchal. CtLH in 1807, General in 1811, retired for reasons of health.

- *Falcon*, Squadron commander. OLH in 1807, Baron, Colonel, killed in Silesia in 1813.

- *Musquinet de Beaupré*, Davout's father in law, Friant's uncle, aide de camp to Leclerc at Saint-Domingue. General in 1807 following Davout's staff. Baron, wounded at Wagram, Russia, died from wounds from the retreat in Berlin, January 1813.

Morand, a division commander in the 3rd Corps.

Debilly, killed at Auerstaedt at the head of his Brigade. On this portrait, he wears his Cross of Commandeur of the Légion d'Honneur.

✣ MORAND'S DIVISION

Morand, General in Egypt, wounded at Austerlitz, Major General in 1805. Wounded at Auerstaedt, at Eylau, at Wagram and at Borodino. Count in 1808, GdCx of the Réunion, Cr of Saint-Henry of Saxony, trapped in Mainz. Aide de camp to Napoleon in 1815, Colonel of the Chasseurs à pied of the Guard, Pair de France, Waterloo. Exiled to Poland, condemned to death, reinstated in 1819. GdCxLH in 1830, Pair de France in 1832, died in 1835.

- *Coehorn*, Adjudant commandant, Chief of Staff. Already wounded 12 times, wounded at Auerstaedt then in 1807. General then Baron, CtLH. Wounded at Wagram. Commander of the Military Merit of Bavaria. Wounded at Leipzig, died from amputation.

- *Lagarde*, Battalion commander, aide de camp to Morand. Italy and Egypt, Colonel in 1807. Baron, General in 1813. Wounded in 1815, inactive, died in 1822.

BONNET D'HONNIERES' VANGUARD

This General, OLH, was later killed at Eylau. He marched with the vanguard with two 4-pounders and the 13th Light.

13th Light

Commanded by Colonel *Guyardet*, wounded at Auerstaedt, OLH in 1807. Baron and General in 1811. Russia, died from

wounds during the retreat from Thorn on the 5th January 1813.

- *Thévenet*, Battalion commander. Wounded at Marengo, LH. Wounded at Auerstaedt, then at Eylau. Colonel, Chevalier and OLH in 1809. Wounded twice in Spain, General in 1813, wounded in 1814. Served in 1815, on half pay then retired in 1825, reinstated in 1831.

- *Hanetin*, Rivoli, LH. Second lieutenant in December 1806. Captain in 1813, retired in 1814.

DEBILLY'S BRIGADE

General *Debilly*, CtLH, was killed during the battle of Auerstaedt.

- *Christophe*, Squadron commander, aide de camp, wounded at Auerstaedt, Davout's aide de camp in 1809, Baron and Colonel in 1811, General in 1815, inactive in 1816.

51st Line (two battalions and the elite of the 3rd)

Under Colonel *Baille*, Italy, Egypt. Wounded at St John of Acre, mentioned at Aboukir, LH. Wounded at Golymin, OLH in 1807, Baron. General in 1811 in Spain. CrLH in 1815 and retired.

- *Gallo*, Battalion commander, LH. Wounded at Auerstaedt, promoted Colonel and retired.

- *Devez*, Battalion commander, in Spain in 1810.

- *Bony*, Captain, mentioned at Castiglione, at Arcole, then at Hohenlinden. Wounded at Auerstaedt, Battalion commander on the 28th October 1806. Brilliant in Spain. Wounded at Lützen, General in 1813, Chevalier, Réunion, OLH. Wounded at Leipzig, served at Waterloo. Inactive, CrLH in 1820, retired in 1825 then 1835.

- *Aulard*, Captain, Italy. Battalion commander in January 1807. Colonel, wounded at Wagram, OLH, Baron, General in 1814, killed at Waterloo.

- *Robin*, Captain, Battalion commander in 1810, hero of Spain, major and OLH in 1813.

- *Bosse*, Lieutenant, hero of Arcole, LH. Battalion commander and OLH in 1813, retired in 1816.

- *Ladrières*, Musket of Honour at Hohenlinden, killed in Spain in 1811.

At Auerstaedt the regiment had two battalions and the 180 voltigeurs and grenadiers of the 3rd battalion, making a total of 62 officers and 1,200 men.

Six officers and 70 men were killed. Six officers and 300 men were wounded.

61st Line (two battalions plus 186 men of the 3rd's elite)

Comanded by Colonel *Nicolas*, CtLH. General on the 23th Octo-

Drum-major

Drum-major, 88th Line

Drum-major in field dress

Drum corporal 88th Line

Young fusilier drummer

Grenadier drummer

Fusilier drummer

Drummer, 88th Line

Voltigeur cornet

Drum-major, 16th Light

Light infantry carabinier drummer

Cornet, 17th Light

André Jouineau © Histoire & Collections 1998

ber 1806. Because he had received three serious wounds at Auerstaedt, Garrison commander. Inactive in 1814.

- *Chemineau*, Major, Baron, Brigadier in 1811. Major General in 1813, CtLH in 1813, retired 1815.

- *Peynet*, Battalion commander, Sabre of Honour, OLH. Wounded and one horse killed at Auerstaedt. Baron, seriously wounded in 1809, Colonel, city commanding officer, sacked in 1816.

- *Bodelin*, Battalion commander, Italy, Egypt. Transfered to the Guard on the 28th October 1806. OLH, Russia, General, retired in 1813.

- *Balavoine*, Captain adjudant major, Egypt, LH. Killed at Eylau.

- *Hervieu*, Captain, Egypt, LH. Baron, Battalion commander, Russia, Hamburg, died at Ligny.

- *Clément*, Captain, mentioned at Auerstaedt, Battalion commander on the 28th October 1806, killed at Valoutina.

- *Joubert*, Captain, Egypt, LH. Wounded at Auerstaedt, retired in 1807.

- *Bejet*, Lieutenant, Egypt, LH. Captain 28th October 1806, missing in action in Russia 6th December 1812.

- *Jaboulet*, lieutenant, LH, Captain 28th October 1806, died in 1808.

- *Bourgeois*, Egypt, LH. Captain in 1811, retired in 1814.

Friant, a division commander in the 3rd Corps.

Barbanègre, commanding the 48h Line from Friant's Division.

voltigeurs companies. Retired in 1810, Major and OLH.

- *Kerveiller*, Second lieutenant, Musket of Honour at Marengo, LH, wounded and mentioned at Austerlitz. Died from the many wounds received at Auerstaedt.

On the 1st October 1806, Morand's Division had 9,370 soldiers and 317 officers. It was the most numerous with five regiments, but one battalion of the 17th was left at Kösen and a company of the 13th Light at Freyburg, which represented 1,100 men who did not participate directly in the battle.

✧ FRIANT'S DIVISION

General *Friant* was one of the former French Royal Guards. Major General with Desaix in Upper Egypt. Hero of Austerlitz, Grand Aigle of the LH. Wounded at Eylau, Count. Wounded at Wagram, wounded in Russia three times, Colonel of the Grenadiers of the Guard. Chamberlain to Napoleon, commander of the Old Guard. Pair during the Hundred-Days, wounded at Waterloo, retired in 1815, died in 1829.

- *Leclerc des Essarts*, Adjudant commandant, Chief of Staff, brother of Pauline Bonaparte's husband. Wounded at Wagram, CtLH, Count. Wounded in Russia, in Hamburg with Davout. Lieutenant General and inactive in 1815. Married d'Hautpoul's widow in 1809.

- *Bonnaire*, Deputy Battalion commander, wounded at Austerlitz. Colonel, Baron then General in 1813. Commanding Condé in 1815, he was accused of firing on a group of enemy parliamentaries, disgraced and imprisoned. His aide de camp Mietton was shot. He died of grief in prison in 1816.

KISTER'S BRIGADE

General *Kister*, CtLH, Captain under the Ancien Régime, mentioned at Austerlitz. Retired in 1812.

33rd Line (two battalions and 210 men from the 3rd's elite)

Commanded by Battalion commander *Cartier*, mentioned at Novi, LH, who was killed at Auerstaedt.

- *Thoulouse*, Battalion commander, Italy, Egypt, mentioned at Aboukir. LH. Was also in command of the regiment at Eylau where he was wounded. Wounded at Wagram, promoted Colonel of the 12th on the battlefield. Baron, OLH, killed at Valoutina.

- *Thierry*, Captain adjudant-major, Italy, Sabre of Honour, OLH, Battalion commander killed at Ratisbonne.

- *Lieutaud*, Captain, captured two flags in Italy, Sabre of Honour. Captain after Austerlitz, OLH in 1807. Retired in 1810.

- *Léonard*, Lieutenant, mentioned at Mondovi, LH. Wounded

BROUARD'S BRIGADE

General *Brouard*, Italy, Egypt, OLH. He lost an eye at Czarnowo on the 23th December 1806. Baron, Department commander, Lieutenant General during the Hundred-Days, sacked, reinstated in 1831, retired in 1832.

17th Line (two battalions only)

Commanded by colonel *Lanusse*, aide de camp to his brother in Italy and in Egypt. Wounded at Heilsberg, Crown of Iron, General in 1808. Grand Marshall of the Palace and Major General at Naples, Baron. Married the daughter of Pérignon. Russia, CtLH, Major General in 1813, inactive in 1815. Retired in 1833.

- *Lanier*, Captain, LH. Battalion commander after Auerstaedt. OLH and Major in 1807, Chevalier. Colonel in Russia, wounded twice. CtLH. On inactive list in 1815, retired in 1817.

One of the regiment's battalions was at the bridge at Kösen; it was called back only for the chase at the end of the battle. The total strength was 2,080 men.

30th Line (two battalions plus 179 men from the 3rd's elite)

Commanded by colonel *Valterre*, CtLH, wounded at Eylau, General in 1808, inactive in 1814.

- *Gibassier*, Battalion commander, LH, in the front with two

French Army   Line Infantry Band

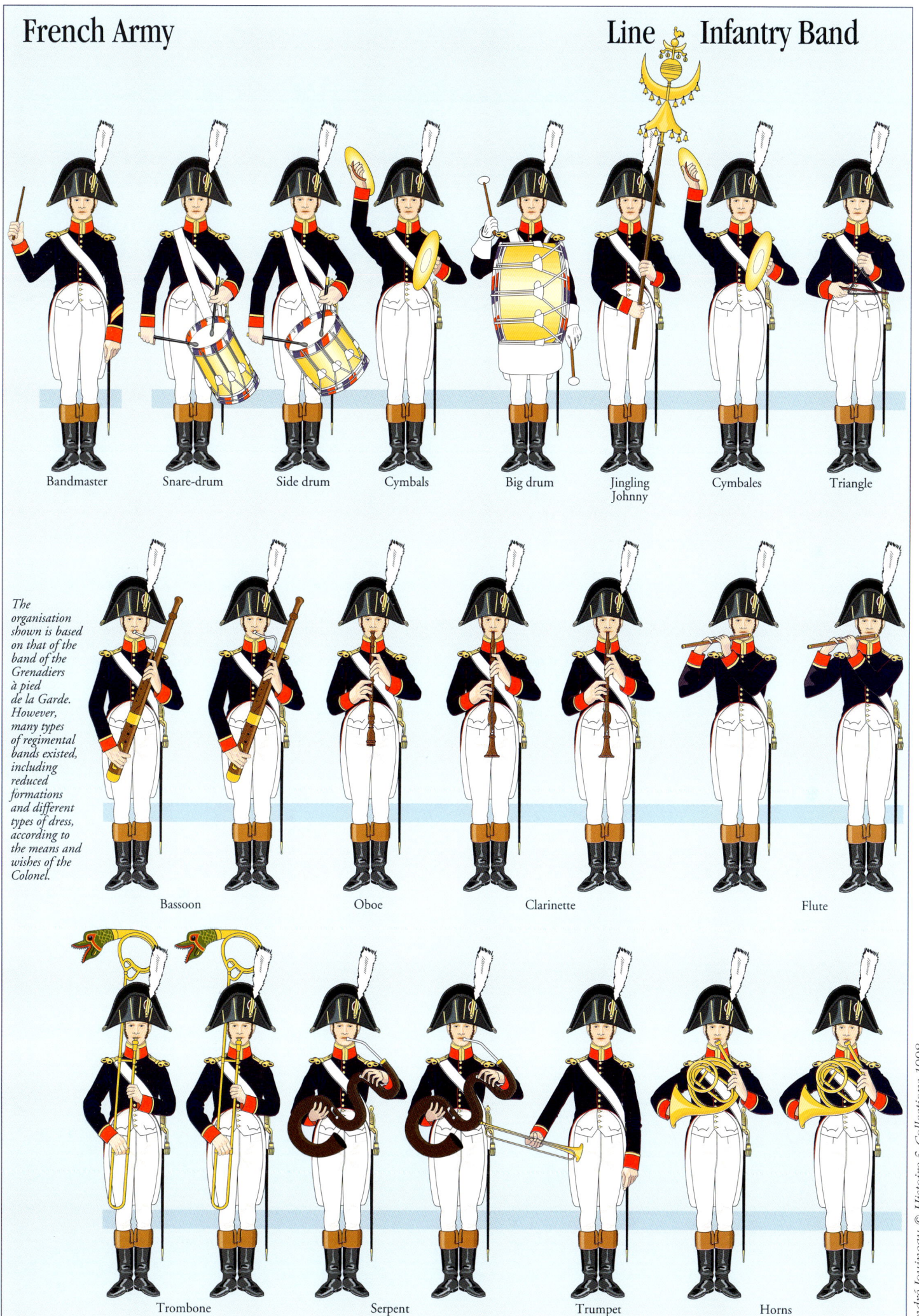

The
organisation
shown is based
on that of the
band of the
Grenadiers
à pied
de la Garde.
However,
many types
of regimental
bands existed,
including
reduced
formations
and different
types of dress,
according to
the means and
wishes of the
Colonel.

Bandmaster | Snare-drum | Side drum | Cymbals | Big drum | Jingling Johnny | Cymbales | Triangle

Bassoon | Oboe | Clarinette | Flute

Trombone | Serpent | Trumpet | Horns

André Jouineau © Histoire & Collections 1998

at Eylau, Captain. Taken in Russia, returned home, retired in 1818.

Casualties were 11 killed and 192 wounded in this battle.

48th Line (two battalions only)

Under colonel *Barbanègre*, came from the Guard, CtLH. Baron, then General in 1809. Russia, wounded twice at Krasnoë, where he was mentioned. Trapped in Stettin. In command of Hunningen in 1815 with 135 men. His defence of this town became famous and he surrendered with full military honours (recorded on the famous painting by Detaille). Inactive in 1815. CrSL in 1820. Went mad and locked away after 1829.

- *Glachant*, Battalion commander, LH. Retired in 1807.

The regiment had four officers wounded, eight soldiers killed and 72 wounded.

LOCHET'S BRIGADE

This general, CtLH, was killed by a bullet in the head at Eylau. He was in command of one regiment only.

108th Line (two battalions only)

Commanded by Colonel *Higonet*, killed at Auerstaedt.

- *Chevalier*, Battalion commander, Italy, LH. Died from his wounds at Auerstaedt.

- *Schmitz*, Captain, mentioned and wounded in Switzerland, OLH. Mentioned at Austerlitz. At Auerstaedt, where the Colonel and the two Battalion commanders were out of action, he assumed command on the orders of Friant, who reported on the capabilities of this brilliant captain. Colonel of the Illyrian Regiment in 1811, Russia, General in 1813. Served at Waterloo, retired in 1815. His son was Trochu's Chief of Staff in 1870.

- *Baudoz*, Lieutenant, Sabre of Honour, OLH, killed at Eylau.

- *Quenet*, Sergeant-major, Second lieutenant in Russia. Died in February 1813.

- *Turpin*, Sergeant, wounded at Auerstaedt, LH in 1809, Lieutenant in 1813. Wounded in Russia, his legs froze making walking almost impossible.

- *Lapersenne*, Grenadier corporal, LH, retired in 1811.

- *Simon*, Sergeant, Lieutenant in Russia, Hamburg, sacked in 1815.

The regiment lost two officers killed, and five wounded as well as 29 men killed and 213 wounded.

GRANDEAU'S BRIGADE

General *Grandeau* was made a Baron in 1808 in Russia with Friant. Major General on the 24th August 1812, Governor of Smolensk. Trapped in Stettin, GdOLH in 1814. Cashiered in 1815, retired in 1825. At Auerstaedt, he too was in command of only one regiment.

111th Line (two battalions and 178 men from the 3rd's elite)

Commanded by colonel *Gay*, OLH. Mentioned at Austerlitz, hero of the fighting in Sokolnitz. Mentioned at Auerstaedt. Appointed Inspector of Parades on the 29th October 1806, replaced by Husson, transferred from the 85th of Gudin's Division. Baron in 1808, retired in 1811.

- *Guigue*, Battalion commander, LH. Adjudant commandant after Auerstaedt, died of fever in 1807.

- *Guinand*, Battalion commander, LH. Colonel of the 69th in Spain, killed in an assault in 1813.

- *Massaroil*, Captain, mentioned at Austerlitz, wounded at Auerstaedt. LH in 1807.

- *Ardoyn*, Captain, wounded at Auerstaedt. LH in 1807.

- *Giusiana*, Captain, took a battery at the head of his grenadiers. LH in 1807, Battalion commander in Russia, wounded at Krasnoë, Major in 1814.

- *Richeri*, Captain, LH in 1807, Battalion commander in Russia, wounded at Schwardino on the 5th September 1812 attacking the redoubt, retired in 1814.

- *Denis*, Captain, wounded at Auerstaedt, LH in 1807.

- *Mensa*, Captain, wounded twice at Auerstaedt. LH in 1807.

- *Vacca*, Lieutenant, LH in 1807. Captain at Borodino, he was wounded six times there and sent home. Battalion commander in 1814, sacked in 1815.

- *Pinto*, Lieutenant, mentioned. LH in Russia, disappeared during the retreat.

- *Ferrero*, Lieutenant, mentioned and wounded at Auerstaedt. LH in 1809, mentioned at Eckmühl, mentioned in 1813, Battalion commander in 1814, mentioned at Hamburg. Naturalised in 1816.

- *Pécoul*, also known as 'Printemps', Second lieutenant, Sabre of Honour, mentioned at Auerstaedt. Captain after Essling, died 6th September 1812.

- *Moser*, Drum major, marched into the attack at the head of his drummers. A load of shot flattened them all. He got up, picked up the nearest drum and beat the charge at the head of the 1st battalion. LH in 1807. Wounded in Russia, Eagle bearer, retired in 1814.

- *Longuet*, Drummer with Moser, wounded in the legs, he lost consciousness, came to, picked up his drum and, covered in blood, he continued to beat the charge. LH in 1807.

- *Annes*, LH, wounded at Auerstaedt, wounded at Eckmühl, Second lieutenant in 1813, inactive in 1814, retired in 1819.

- *Robin*, Sergeant, remained at his post in spite of being wounded three times. Lieutenant, killed at Borodino.

- *Campana*, Quartermaster, took three prisonners. Lieutenant, killed at Borodino.

- *Novana*, Grenadier, captured a colonel. LH in 1807.

The village of Hassenhausen, keypoint of the battle of Auerstaedt, photographed in the second half of the XXth Century.

Prussian artist Geissler produced several 'life' drawing depicting the entrance of Davout's soldiers in Leipzig. Here, light infantrymen are shown, loaded with loaves and various provisions. (© Musée de l'Armée Photograph, Paris).

- *Canavesio*, continued fighting although wounded twice. LH in 1807.

- *Berletti*, Eagle bearer at Auerstaedt where he lost three fingers off his right hand and where the shaft of his Eagle was broken. Saved by Corporal Vercella and his grenadiers.

The regiment had three officers killed and twenty wounded as well as 61 soldiers killed and 339 wounded. It numbered 2,346 men of which a third were conscripts.

On the 1st October 1806, Friant's Division numbered 7,034 men and 259 officers.

✣ GUDIN'S DIVISION

General *Gudin*, one of the most brilliant generals of them all, was killed at Valoutina in Russia whilst attacking the Russian rear-guard which other corps commanders hadn't dared to do. *Charles Gudin de la Sablonnière*, born at Montargis, had been an officer of the King. Grand Aigle of the LH, Commander of the Order of Saxony, he was Count of the Empire. A hero of several battles, he played a major role at Auerstaedt.

His aides de camps were:

- *Gudin des Bardelières*, brother of the General, Battalion commander, Colonel then Baron. Wounded at Wagram, then in

Gudin, a division commander in the 3rd Corps.

Spain at Sagonta. General in 1812, with Rapp in 1815. CrLH then Major General in 1821, Viscount in 1822, CrSL. Died in 1855.

- *Creutzer*, Lieutenant, Captain in 1807. Russia, General in 1813, OLH in 1813, inactive in 1815. He married Lefebvre's niece.

PETIT'S BRIGADE

This general, CtLH, was wounded at Auerstaedt. Baron, killed in 1809.

12th Line (two battalions plus 178 men of the 3rd's elite)

Under the command of Colonel *Vergez*, mentioned in Italy, wounded three times at Auerstaedt, General on the 23th October 1806. Baron, Spain, wounded, CtLH. Retired in 1815, honorary Lieutenant Colonel in 1825.

- *Teulet*, Major, hero of Castiglione, Sabre of Honour, OLH. Wounded four times in Spain, Colonel in 1813, Maréchal de camp in 1815 by Napoleon, fired, retired in 1821 as a Colonel.

- *Aubry*, Battalion commander, Egypt, LH. Colonel in 1809, killed at Polotsk.

- *Sensenbrener*, Lieutenant, Sabre of Honour, killed at Auerstaedt.

- *Leblanc*, Second lieutenant, Sabre of Honour, OLH, killed at Auerstaedt.

- *Fougery*, Sergeant-major. Second lieutenant on the 12th November 1806. Wounded at Borodino. OLH in 1812, sacked in 1815.

- *Michelet*, Sergeant-major. Second lieutenant in January 1807. Wounded in 1809, Captain adjutant major in 1811, wounded at Borodino, at Kulm and at Dresden, sacked in 1815.

21st Line (two battalions and 178 men of the 3rd's elite)
Commanded by colonel *Decouz*, Toulon, Italy, Egypt, mentioned at Auerstaedt. Baron, then General, CtLH in 1809. Major General in 1813. In the Guard, killed at Brienne.

- *de Vaugineuse*, Battalion commander, mentioned. Colonel of the 1st regiment of the Paris Guard.

- *Grognet*, Battalion commander, wounded at Arcole, mentioned at Hohenlinden, Sabre of Honour, OLH. One leg shot off at Auerstaedt. Retired as Colonel in 1807.

- *Ducrest*, Battalion commander, mentioned at Arcole, LH. Wounded at Wagram, Colonel of the regiment, commanding Barcelona, retired 1815, then again in 1821.

- *Rome*, Captain, wounded at the head of his grenadiers at Auerstaedt. Wounded twice in 1807. Colonel in 1811, mentioned at Valoutina, wounded at Borodino. CtLH and General in 1813, served at Ligny, inactive in 1815.

- *Duthoya*, Captain, LH in March 1806. Battalion commander, killed at Borodino.

- *Camusat*, Captain. LH in 1807, killed at Valoutina.

- *Métraud*, Captain. LH in 1807, Major in 1812, wounded at Valoutina, wounded seven times at La Fère-Champenoise.

- *Farette*, Lieutenant, LH. Captain in 1807, taken at Baylen, died in prison.

- *Caillebotte*, Lieutenant, LH and Battalion commander in 1812, sacked in 1816.

- *Corne*, Second lieutenant, Italy, LH, Spain, retired as Captain in 1813.

- *Vuillemot*, Second lieutenant. LH, wounded 1807, taken at Baylen, died in captivity.

- *Guilmard*, Sergeant major. Second lieutenant on the 28th October 1806, Captain in 1809, wounded at Borodino. LH at Moscow. Battalion commander, wounded at Bautzen, half-pay in 1814, retired in 1823. Mayor of Isigny in 1831.

- *Guilmard*, Sergeant-major, brother of the above, died of illness in 1807.

- *Guilmard*, Quartermaster, the third of the brothers. Sergeant-major, died of fever in Mainz in 1809.

- *Rossy*, Sergeant-major, wounded at Auerstaedt, wounded at Valoutina, Captain. LH. Sacked in 1815.

- *Jobert*, Sergeant-major, wounded at Auerstaedt, Battalion commander and LH in 1812. Major on half-pay.

- *Chaboisseau*, Sergeant, wounded at Auerstaedt. Second lieutenant and LH in 1812, killed in 1813.

- *Arnefaut*, Sergeant, LH in An XII. Wounded twice at Valoutina as Second lieutenant, captured, returned in March 1815, sacked in 1815.

- *Moreau*, Sergeant, wounded. LH in 1807, Captain in 1812, sacked in 1815.

- *Hérel*, Sergeant, wounded. Lieutenant in 1812, disappeared at Viasma.

- *Froissard*, Sergeant, wounded. LH. Lieutenant in 1812, woun-

ded at Valoutina, sacked in 1815.

- *Demédy*, Sergeant. Captain at Moscow, died burnt in an isba at Orcha.

- *Féton*, Sergeant, wounded, Second lieutenant in 1812, wounded at Borodino, veteran of 1813.

- *Magnin*, Sergeant, wounded, Lieutenant in 1812, wounded at Borodino, Captain in 1813.

- *Sénéchal*, Sergeant, wounded, mentioned in 1807, LH. Wounded at Valoutina, retired as Captain in 1813.

- *Boutloup*, Corporal, wounded. LH in 1812, Captain in 1813 half-pay.

- *Doignon*, wounded. Second lieutenant and LH in 1813. Taken at Dresden, later a Major in the Belgian army.

GAUTIER'S BRIGADE
General *Gautier* was Masséna's aide de camp in Zurich. OLH, wounded at Auerstaedt, killed at Wagram.

25th Line (two battalions only)
Commanded by Colonel *Cassagne*, hero of Italy, wounded at Auerstaedt. General then Baron. Taken at Baylen opposing Dupont. CtLH in 1811, Major General in 1813. Crown of Iron, Cross of the Réunion, taken at Dresden. Inactive in 1815.

- *Ranchon*, Captain, Egypt, Sabre of Honour, mentioned at the head of the grenadiers at Auerstaedt. Transfered to the Imperial Guard. Russia, Major in 1813, Crown of Iron. Served at Waterloo, retired in 1816.

- *Lavallée*, Lieutenant adjutant-major, Egypt, LH. Killed at Eylau.

- *Croutelle*, Battalion commander and OLH in 1813, retired in 1816.

- *Lajoye*, Lieutenant, wounded. Captain in 1807, retired in 1811.

- *Deshameaux*, Second lieutenant. LH in 1809, Battalion commander in 1812, OLH in 1814.

- *Garand*, Sergeant. As a child, reared by the army in the regiment, in the Guard in 1809, LH. Lieutenant in Russia with the 15th Light, captured, returned from Russian jail in 1814.

- *Adin*, Sergeant, LH, seriously wounded at Auerstaedt, retired in 1808.

The regiment had a strength of 61 officers and 1,774 men at the beginning of 1806.

85th Line (two battalions plus 179 men from the 3rd's elite)
Under the command of Colonel *Viala*, mentioned at Toulon, at Rivoli and in Egypt where he was wounded, OLH. Badly wounded at Auerstaedt, left for dead. General on the 23th October 1806. Chevalier, retired in 1811. Mayor of Rodez.

- *Fournier*, Battalion commander, was the first to enter Regensburg, wounded several times at Wagram. Chevalier then Colonel. CtLH and General in 1813. On half pay, honorary Lieutenant Colonel in 1826.

- *Husson*, Battalion commander, Egypt, LH. Colonel of the 111th on the 28th October 1806. OLH in 1807, General in 1811. Captured at Danzig. Served at Waterloo, honorary Lieutenant General in 1826.

- *Filanchier*, Captain, Egypt, LH, wounded at Auerstaedt. Bat-

Top.
On this second drawing by Prussian artist Geissler depicting the entrance of Davout's soldiers in Leipzig, French infantrymen are selling their war booty — any sorts of dress and equipment taken from the defeated Prussians — to the local Jewish merchants. (© Musée de l'Armée Photograph, Paris).

Opposite.
The same action has been reproduced, in a much more naïve way on this third document which has not been published before. (Christian Blondieau Collection).

talion commander in Russia, OLH in 1813. Taken at Dresden. Waterloo, inactive 1815, retired in 1821.

- *Denou*, Captain, Italy, wounded in Egypt, wounded at Auerstaedt, at Wagram and at Smolensk. Battalion commander, OLH retired in 1813.

- *Gaubert*, Lieutenant, Egypt, LH. Captain in December 1806, OLH in 1811, killed at Borodino.

- *Salmon*, Second lieutenant, Egypt. Russia, Battalion commander and LH in 1813, wounded five times.

- *Barlier* and *Duplaine*, two Second lieutenants, Arms of Honour, both killed at Auerstaedt.

- *Gély*, Corporal, Egypt, Musket of Honour, taken at Auerstaedt. Retired in 1808 because of his wounds.

- *Fraissignes*, Toulon, wounded at Auerstaedt. Captain in Russia, disappeared in the retreat.

- *Charlot*, Sergeant, wounded at Auerstaedt. Lieutenant wounded in Russia, returned.

According to the roll of 1st October, Gudin's Division numbe-

red 272 officers and 8,201 men. It was they who suffered the heaviest casualties and who were responsible for the victory at Auerstaedt.

✥ 3rd CORPS' CAVALRY (VIALANNES)

General *Vialannes*, mentioned at Marengo, CtLH, Baron. Put on sick leave and retired in 1815.

In a letter of 10th November 1806, Davout complained about Vialannes because he hadn't waited for the Emperor's orders during the night of the 13th and 14th October. Whereas all the other generals were already on the march with their orders, he could not be found; as a result, the cavalry instead of being first to arrive (except for the Maréchal's service squadron) only got there between 9 and 10 a.m. Davout also accused Vialannes of encouraging looting and horsetrading. During the course of the battle, his performance was only average although his horsemen gave a good account of themselves.

For these reasons, Vialannes was transfered to the dragoons and followed them to Spain.

1st Chasseurs

Under the command of Colonel *Exelmans*, born at Bar-le-Duc in 1775. Murat's aide de camp, Colonel of the regiment after Austerlitz. General in 1827, aide de camp to Murat, Baron, Grand Dignitary of the Order of the Two Sicilies. Took Valence in 1808, escaped from England in 1811. Major of the Horse Grenadiers in 1812, Major General, replaced Pajol, wounded at Vilna. Count in 1813. A letter written by him to Murat was confiscated and he was taken off the active list in December 1814; tried and acquitted. Served at Ligny, beat the Prussians at Rocquencourt. Exiled until 1819, he took part in the Revolution of 1830. Pair de France, Grand Chancellor of the LH, Maréchal de France in 1831.

- *Ayet*, Squadron commander. Wounded at Eylau, died in Spain in 1809.

- *Hulot*, Captain, always mentioned in the vanguard.

- *Tavernier*, Captain. Squadron commander of the 12th Chasseurs in 1809.

- *Cabot* or *Cabat*, Captain, decorated in 1807.

- *Simoneau*, Lieutenant. Captured the first Prussian cannon, wounded at Auerstaedt. LH in 1807, aide de camp to Exelmans in 1812, Colonel of the regiment in 1815, wounded at Waterloo. Maréchal de camp, sacked, taken back as General in 1830, CrLH, Saint-Ferdinand, CrSL, Cross of Leopold. Retired in 1848.

- *Coquerelle*, Captain. Killed at Wagram with his brother, a Second lieutenant.

- *Riquet*, Lieutenant, wounded at Auerstaedt. LH in 1807, wounded at Borodino as a Captain.

- *Gaillac*, Lieutenant. LH in 1807, Captain, killed in 1809.

- *Caunay* or *Chaunez*. Wounded at Borodino, Squadron commander in 1813, wounded twice at Leipzig, OLH, retired in 1816.

- *Hubert*, Lieutenant. Colonel in 1812, General in 1814, then inactive, taken back in 1823 in Spain as Lieutenant General. Retired in 1832.

- *Ratelle*, Lieutenant. OLH in 1813, Colonel of the 9th, half-pay in 1815.

- *Bertaux*, Second lieutenant and LH in 1807, Captain with the Lancers of the Guard in 1813, OLH in 1822, Colonel of the 2nd Carabiniers in 1832, CrLH in 1837.

The three squadrons numbered 420 horsemen on the 5th October 1806. One officer and 17 horsemen were killed, and four officers and 53 men were wounded.

2nd Chasseurs

Under the command of Colonel *Bousson*, CtLH, badly wounded in the left thigh at Auerstaedt, retired in April 1807.

- *Thuilier*, Squadron commander, charged and had his coat peppered with bullets.

- *Jacquet*, LH, Squadron commander, had two horses killed

Exelmans, commanding the 12th Chasseurs at Auerstaedt. (A much later portrait by Charles-Philippe Larivière, Château de Versailles, © Réunion des Musées nationaux photograph).

under him at Auerstaedt. Retirement due to seniority.

- *de Lacroix*, Captain adjutant-major, mentioned at Novi, LH. He commanded the 1st squadron of the regiment and captured 40 dragoons. The senior officers being out of action, he took command of the regiment. Squadron commander in 1809, Major in Russia, CtLH in 1813 and Colonel of the 3rd Cuirassiers. Died as a result of wounds after charging with the 2nd Cuirassiers at Waterloo.

- *Locharda*, Captain, took command of the 2nd squadron during the battle. Mentioned at Borodino. Captured in Russia, disappeared ?

- *Decoutz*, Captain, LH. Two horses were killed under him and he rode off on a third.

- *Demaille*, Lieutenant. Marengo, Sabre of Honour, OLH. Retired in September 1807.

- *Vénière*, Lieutenant. LH in 1809, Captain in Russia, OLH in 1814, Squadron commander in Hamburg, wounded and sacked in 1815.

- *Sautard* and *Dubourg*, Lieutenants wounded and LH in 1807.

- *Merle*, Lieutenant. Captured 60 carriages on the 26th November 1806. LH in 1807, Captain in Russia, retired in 1815.

- *Forjonel*, Second lieutenant, commanding the ordnance of Maréchal Davout, supported the front line of the skirmishers. LH in 1807, Squadron commander in 1813.

- *Langlais*, Second lieutenant, LH, escaped from *La Vieille Castille*. Captain in Russia. Sacked in 1815.

- *Pion*, Second lieutenant. LH in 1809, Captain in Russia in 1812, wounded and retired.

- *Imbert*, Sergeant, continued to fight on foot. Lieutenant in Russia and LH at Moscow. OLH in 1827, Colonel in 1833, CrLH in 1840, Maréchal de camp in 1846, retired in 1850, died in 1864.

- *Monchamp*, Lieutenant in Russia, wounded at Borodino, Captain in 1813, Squadron commander and OLH in 1830.

The regiment had 507 horsemen present at the battle. It lost 27 killed and 76 wounded.

12th Chasseurs

Commanded by Colonel *Guyon*, absent at Auerstaedt. Italy, Egypt, Sabre of Honour. Baron in 1809, General in 1811, GdOLH in 1825, on leave in 1829.

- *Deschamps*, Squadron commander (came from the 1st Chasseurs), temporarily in command while Guyon was absent. Wounded in 1806 and 1807, LH. Major at the depot in 1808.

- *Dejean*, Captain, LH in 1807, killed at Borodino.

- *de Tascher*, Captain, wounded at Auerstaedt, LH in 1807. Died in January 1813 as a result of the retreat from Russia, in the hospital in Berlin.

- *Duperron*, also known as *Pourlant* after his village, Lieutenant adjudant major, LH. Appointed captain in November 1806, retired in 1809. Served during the French campaign.

- *Delpy*, Lieutenant, LH in 1807, became outfitting Captain in 1811.

- *Fauvelet*, Lieutenant. LH and retirement in 1807.

- *Receveur*, Second lieutenant, LH in 1807, OLH in 1809, Squadron commander in the regiment in Russia. Retired in 1814.

- *Gaulier*, Second lieutenant. LH in 1809, Captain in Russia, wounded at Borodino, Squadron commander in 1813, OLH in 1814, retired in 1816.

- *Duregard*, Second lieutenant, LH in 1807, wounded at Borodino as a Captain.

- *d'Hénin*, Second lieutenant. LH in 1807, Russia, Captain in 1813, retired in 1815.

- *Minville*, Second lieutenant, LH in 1807, Captain in 1809.

- *Aubry*, Adjudant. Was at Marengo and Austerlitz. Wounded at Auerstaedt, LH and Second lieutenant in 1807, Captain in 1810, wounded at Borodino, taken by the Russians. Returned, wounded at Ligny. Retired in 1816. Author of memoirs.

- *Ferard*, Adjudant, LH in 1806, Russia, wounded, Captain in 1813, retired in 1815.

- *Grobert*, Sergeant, brilliant at Auerstaedt. LH in 1807, killed at Wagram.

- *Rumeau*, camp follower, gave her first blow with a sabre 1st March 1807.

The regiment had about 420 horsemen present at the battle. Three officers and 11 chasseurs were killed, five officers and many chasseurs wounded.

✢ 3rd CORPS' ARTILLERY

Chief of Staff: Colonel *Charbonnel*, Italy and Egypt. Baron and General in 1809, Peninsular war, Russia, Major General in 1813, Count in 1814. GdCxLH in 1824, Pair in 1841, died in 1846.

- *Jouffroy*, Colonel in command of the pool. CtLH in 1807, Baron in 1809, General in 1811. With Davout in Russia and in Hamburg, retired in 1815.

When Gudin advanced, he was accompanied by a half-company of the 5th Horse artillery commanded by Lieutenant Roy with two 8-pounders and a howitzer, supported by Lieutenant Manguin with two 8-pounders and one 4-pounder. They dismantled three enemy cannon from a recently abandonned battery.

A 12-pounder battery, commanded by Lieutenants Micquel and Osella got into position behind Hassenhausen (15th company of the 7th). Micquel was killed.

With Morand, a horse artillery battery reinforced the corners of the squares and then positioned itself forward in the centre. It was under the command of Captain Séruzier, whose hand was wounded. Lieutenant Laporte was wounded and his horse killed. Adjudant major Alphand, with the 1st company of the 7th, positioned four guns forward and two others between the 30th and the 17th, thus supporting the offensive.

On Friant's side, three batteries formed up. Captain Chemin with two 8-pounders, Lieutenant Jouault with two 4-pounders and the third with Captain Jarry, who had three 8-pounders and a 6-pounder howitzer.

The 3rd Corps only had 44 guns of different calibres, inclu-

Davout's soldiers in Leipzig, selling their war booty to the Jewish merchants. The inspiration of this naïve engraving is the same as that noticeable in Geissler's work reproduced in the previous pages. (Christian Blondieau Collection).

ding the reserve. Here is the breakdown of this artillery on the 1st October, according to Foucart.

Morand: 11th company of the 7th Foot and companies 1 and 6 of the 1st transport battalion. With five 8-pounders, two 4-pounders and a 6-pounder howitzer, together with 15 artillery limbers and 18 infantry limbers, and 53 carriages.

Friant: 2nd company of the 7th Foot and the 2nd of the 5th Horse. Companies 4 and 5 of the 1st transport battalion. With five 8-pounders, two 4-pounders and a 6-pounder howitzer together with 15 artillery limbers and 15 infantry limbers, and 41 carriages.

Gudin: companies 3, 4, 5 of the 7th Foot and the 2nd of the 5th Horse. Companies 4 and 5 of the 1st transport battalion. With five 8-pounders, two 4-pounders and a 6-pounder howitzer, together with 15 artillery limbers and 15 infantry limbers, and 48 carriages.

THE RESERVE POOL

Two companies of the 7th Foot and one from the 5th Foot, companies 1, 2, 3 and 6 of the 3rd *bis* tranport battalion and a further one from the 1st. With six Austrian 12-pounders, three 8-pounders and three 6-pounder howitzers, 65 artillery limbers and 47 infantry limbers, 152 carriages. One officer and 21 artillery workers, 20 commandered drivers.

This represented 35 officers and 1,531 men with 1,500 horses.

✢ ENGINEERS

The 6th company of enginners from the 2nd battalion, i.e. two officers and 71 men. After the battle, only 36 engineers remained standing.

The Prussian prisoners of Hohenlohe's army under French escort, by Geissler. (Brunon Collection).

THE PURSUIT

AT THREE IN THE MORNING, Napoleon wrote to Joséphine. He thought he had defeated an army of 150,000 men and that he had nearly captured the King and Queen of Prussia…

Squadron commander Falcon, Davout's aide de camp, arrived with the Maréchal's report. The Emperor then said to his entourage: '*Davout has had a terrible time…*' adding '*Bernadotte behaved badly*'.

THE BERNADOTTE PROBLEM

This problem has already been brought up. Historians have always insisted up on the conflict between Bernadotte and Davout, and the Trobriand report sent by Davout to Bernadotte, requesting his support. Some have defended the future King of Sweden, using Napoleon's order to move to the village of Dornburg as an excuse. But nobody has ever bothered to ask, if he wouldn't help Davout, why didn't he go and help out at Jena…?

He claimed that the paths and the roads were difficult to use. Holtzendorff's detachment nevertheless managed to pass through on the evening of the 13th. Bernadotte helped neither Davout nor Napoleon; he kept well away from the cannon and did not even send out scouts from among his numerous cavalry. Napoleon wasn't taken in and began to have his Maréchal watched. Reille was given this task for a while. Later at Baylen, the behaviour of Dupont, a Major General in Bernadotte's Corps, only made things worse, and the Saxon case at Wagram didn't exactly help things either.

MAKING USE OF THE VICTORY

Now that the full extent of the victory was known, it had to be exploited to the full by pursuing the Prussians who were fleeing to Magdeburg.

The King of Prussia sought refuge with the Russians, leaving the command in Hohenlohe's hands; he had two divisions with

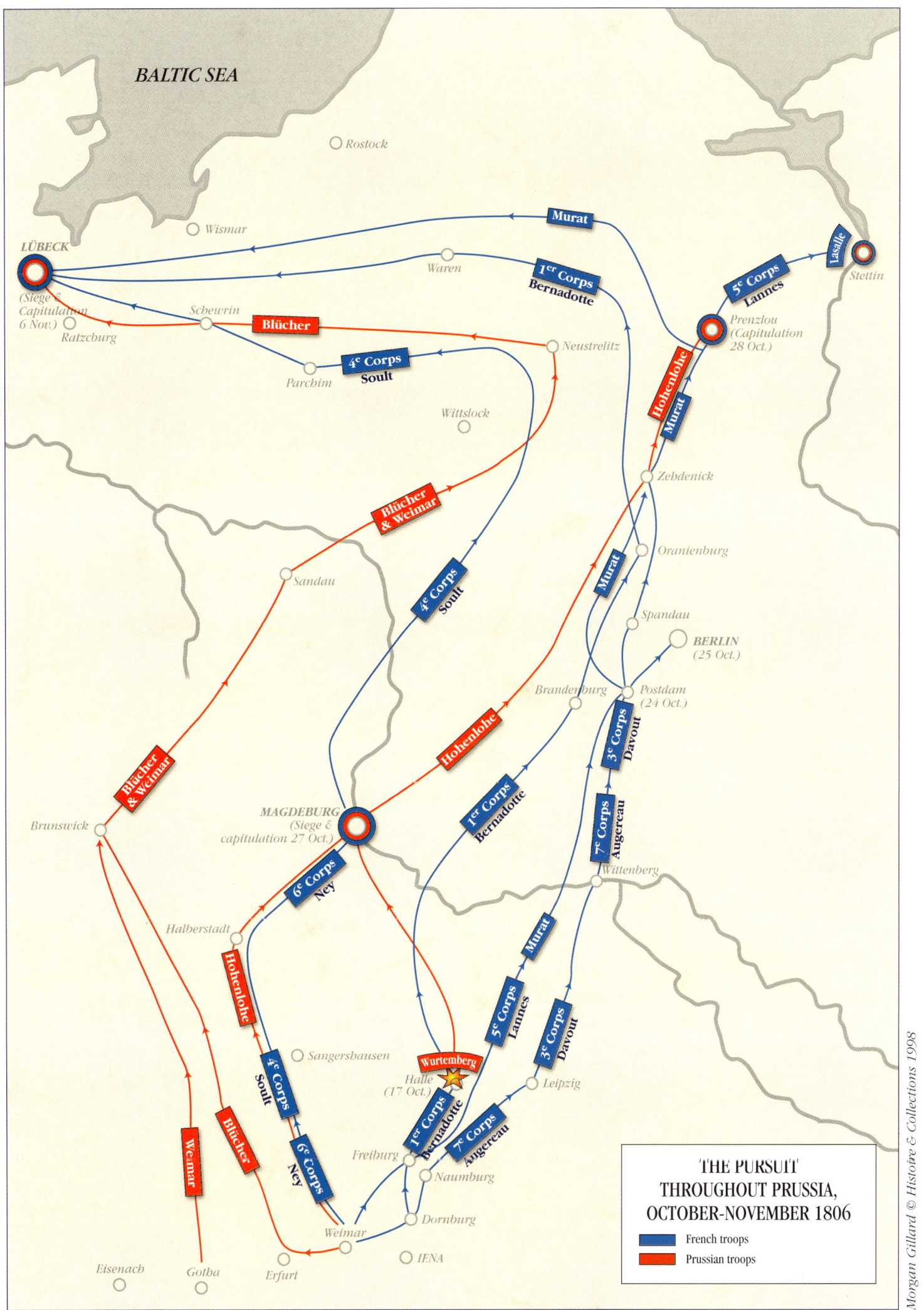

BALTIC SEA

LÜBECK
(Siège &
Capitulation
6 Nov.)

Rostock

Wismar

Waren

Murat

1er Corps
Bernadotte

5e Corps
Lannes

Lasalle

Stettin

Ratzeburg

Schewrin

Blücher

Parchim

4e Corps
Soult

Neustrelitz

Wittslock

Prenzlou
(Capitulation
28 Oct.)

Hohenlohe

Murat

Blücher
& Weimar

Zebdenick

Murat

Oranienburg

Sandau

4e Corps
Soult

Spandau

BERLIN
(25 Oct.)

Hohenlohe

Brandenburg

Postdam
(24 Oct.)

Blücher
& Weimar

MAGDEBURG
(Siège &
capitulation 27 Oct.)

1er Corps
Bernadotte

3e Corps
Davout

Brunswick

6e Corps
Ney

7e Corps
Augereau

Wittenberg

Halberstadt

Hohenlohe

Sangershausen

4e Corps
Soult

Murat

5e Corps
Lannes

3e Corps
Davout

Leipzig

Weimar

Blücher

6e Corps
Ney

Wurtemberg

Halle
(17 Oct.)

1er Corps
Bernadotte

7e Corps
Augereau

Freiburg

Naumburg

THE PURSUIT
THROUGHOUT PRUSSIA,
OCTOBER-NOVEMBER 1806

French troops

Prussian troops

Eisenach

Gotha

Erfurt

Weimar

Dornburg

IENA

Morgan Gillard © Histoire & Collections 1998

113

The retreating Prussians.
(Illustration by Richard Knötel).

Opposite.
The capture of the
Queen's Dragoons standard at
Zehdenick par Lasalle's troopers.
(Plate by Jack Girbal from the
Author's book 'Lasalle').

Kalckreuth, Blücher with his cavalry and Duke of Weimar's troops who were still intact. The Prince of Würtemberg's reserve moved towards Halle.

Napoleon sought to arrange things with the Saxons so that they would come over to his side. He sent the 6,000 that had been captured at Jena back home, but kept their horses to equip his foot dragoons. Their Elector became king and an ally of the Emperor.

As far as the chase was concerned, there were plenty of units left over from the regiments that had not been employed in the battle. Murat's cavalry reserve had Lasalle's and Milhaud's four light regiments; Klein's, Sahuc's, Grouchy's and Beaumont's dragoons, and Nansouty's and d'Hautpoul's cuirassiers and their associated light artillery.

Even Bernadotte's Corps which until now had not been of any use, made itself useful. Soult and Ney, who also had fresh regiments, set off. Lannes who had been fighting non-stop, wanted to march as well. Only Davout's exhausted Corps advanced directly to Berlin because the Emperor, in recognition of their exceptional merit, had reserved the supreme honour for them: the men of the 3rd Corps would be the first to enter Berlin, one day before the Emperor and the Grande Armée. Augereau followed to Berlin

Goethe witnessed the French entering Weimar, which was then sacked by Ney's troops as a form of contribution towards *'arrears in payment'*. Napoleon was furious when he heard of this. General Schmettau was buried. When they entered Erfurt, the French found huge resources and 7,000 wounded and stragglers who were made prisoner. Old Möllendorf was there with the Prince of Orange. Rüchel was found seriously wounded in a nearby village. He survived.

On the 17th, Blücher gave his word to Klein and Lasalle that an armistice had been signed, which deceived them completely. This trick enabled him to get away for the time being. Bernadotte marched on Halle with Dupont's Division in the lead where they earned fame by upsetting the Prince of Würtemberg.

On the 19th October, Hohenlohe reached Magdeburg and

managed to get the army into a semblance of order. Blücher and the Duke of Weimar were more to the west. Hohenlohe left Kleist in Magdeburg and moved on towards Stettin with the main part of the army.

On the 24th, Napoleon reached Potsdam with the Guard, Murat and Lannes. Davout's soldiers cleaned their kit because the following morning they were marching alone, into Berlin as the vanguard. They deserved this honour and more than 500 medals were given out to them.

Enormous ressources were found in Berlin: 500 cannon, thousands of rifles and equipment of all sorts. Horses were recovered, as were harnesses and sabres, to make up the losses of the French cavalry. Skin riding breeches were found and these were given to the dragoons and cuirassiers. Coats were made, as were greatcoats and shoes. Everything was taken; Prussian cavalrymen were obliged to exchange their high boots for shoes.

Augereau arrived and covered Berlin from the east with Davout. Encircling Magdeburg, Ney waited for Kleist to surrender. Bernadotte moved up towards Brandenburg. Soult left Ney alone and went for Rathenau; the Bavarian division with Jérôme was in Saxony. Lasalle and Grouchy moved from Potsdam to Zehdenick and the Stettin road, with Murat following. Spandau capitulated to Lannes. Hohenlohe, who had found Blücher and the Duke of Weimar again, was also marching in that direction, leaving Blücher on his left.

Napoleon entered Berlin on the 26th.

On the 27th October, Kleist surrendered and abandoned Magdeburg and its riches. At that moment, at Zehdenick, Lasalle's hussars fell upon the Queen's Dragoons whose standard was captured by Hussar Studer of the 7th, aided by Adjudant Wilmuth and by Second lieutenant Dam. Grouchy's dragoons had charged as well.

Napoleon said to Murat: '*Let your troops eat the bread that the enemy has made; that bread is far tastier for our brave soldiers than pieces of our own brioche*'... War fed war.

Lannes caught up with the cavalry, marching at full speed, with his legendary 17th Light and all the voltigeurs of his corps.

Hohenlohe fled towards Prenzlow, whereas at Boitzenburg, the 10th Dragoons surrounded and forced a detachment of the Gendarmes Regiment to surrender, the very same horsemen who had sharpened their swords of the steps of the French embassy in Berlin.

Lasalle saw the Prussians entering Prenzlow but, alone, he couldn't do anything. He had Murat warned. Murat arrived at 9 on the 28th with Grouchy's and Beaumont's dragoons.

Called on to surrender, Hohenlohe hesitated, then finally capitulated. Lasalle then threw himself on to the Stettin road with his hussars; a wagon loaded with cartridges followed him.

In front of this stronghold, Lasalle did his best to bluff, dragging his wagon around on all sides, creating clouds of dust to make believe there was a large force. At night he called on the Governor to surrender, but was turned down; Lasalle repeated his summons, threatening to lay the town to waste. This made the inhabitants think. The Governor finished by capitulating before 500 hussars.

There remained only Blücher and the Duke of Weimar, now close to home; he left his men with Blücher. They headed off towards Lübeck. Against them, the cavalry of Murat, Soult's men and Bernadotte's. They quickened the pace and on the 6th November, Lübeck was finally taken. The Corsican and Pô Tirailleurs made a name for themselves by taking the Mühlen Gate. Blücher who had tried to reach the Danish frontier, was surrounded and captured. He had saved his honour and capitulated.

Having no more enemies to fight, Murat, Lasalle and Bernadotte rallied the main army. They went off to fight the Russians on the other side of the Vistula; other fights, other victories. But the price was to be dear for '*it wasn't enough to kill a Russian, you had to push him to make him fall over*'.

In his final report, the Emperor announced that 140,000 Prussians had been captured, as well as 4,000 cannon and 250 flags or standards.

The King of Prussia, who had taken refuge in Königsberg, only had ten thousand soldiers which he handed over to Lestocq, to join the Russians.

ABOUT THE UNIFORM OF NAPOLEON'S SOLDIERS AFTER JENA

Precious information can be found on this subject in the letters of the Emperor or his corps commanders.

In a letter of orders to Berthier, Napoleon asked Kellermann to form eight temporary battalions with companies of 140 men and added in the letter:

'*It won't be necessary to train the conscripts; they will only need eight or ten days' instruction. Make sure that they are armed, that they have a jacket, trousers, gaiters, the uniform hat and a greatcoat. Don't wait for the coat.*'

These battalions were sent to Cassel or to Magdeburg where their instruction was completed and their equipment was found at Prussian expense.

In the equipment found in Berlin, there were 6,000 hats which were distributed.

As early as 27th October, Davout requested 6,000 greatcoats and shirts, 12,000 pairs of shoes, cooking pots, axes, etc.

From Stettin, Lannes requested shoes and greatcoats, especially for the 21st Light, '*which goes around all naked*'.

From Lübeck, the 96th's Colonel requested 1,700 pairs of shoes, greatcoats and 600 hats.

The Emperor gave orders for shoes and greatcoats to be made everywhere, because winter was approaching in this country, where shoes didn't last very long. He ordered Prussian cloth to be used to make up clothing, etc. All that could be found was used.

Here we can realise that the picture we have of the French soldier going off to fight the Russians in a regulation uniform is a long way from reality.

As with these examples, discussion concerning hats is unnecessary. The men had the same hats as at Austerlitz; shakos were only worn by the Light infantry regiments, and even then they were the old pattern. Likewise, even if a lot of the grenadiers wore bearskins, many of them still wore a hat. During this campaign, Napoleon's principal concerns were the soldier's footwear, which wore out very quickly, and the greatcoats on account of the season.

To re-equip his cavalry, he used saddles, harnesses, sabres, etc., recovered from the enemy. If there weren't any coat-bags, they were '*replaced with a sack*', and boots were taken from the Prussians, etc.

At any rate as far as clothing, equipment, etc., were concerned, soldiers could always be relied on to look after themselves and this started usually on the battlefield.

MISTAKES ABOUT JENA MADE BY THE PAINTERS

Painters and artists who were direct witnesses to the events are very precious, but there were also great painters who painted the principal battles without worrying too much about historical exactitude. The best example is Thévenin's painting in the Château of Grosbois, showing Napoleon acclaimed by his soldiers at Jena. It is reproduced everywhere.

These magnificently painted soldiers in their very beautiful uniforms are the Fusiliers of the Guard. Unfortunately, they had just been created and were not present; likewise the chasseurs à cheval of the Guard which can also be seen in the painting.

About his Fusiliers of the Guard, Napoleon wrote from Berlin on the 2nd November 1806 to General Dejean:

'*I understand that there is some sort of problem in Paris with my Guard, that they have not been paid, and that my regiment of Fusiliers has not been clothed properly. Kindly deal with these problems as I shall be needing my Guard shortly.*'

Even period paintings have discrepancies. In the painting which is reproduced on page 55 of this book, Rugendas depicts a dead Prussian hussar dressed in black in the foreground; his uniform is perfect… except that this regiment did not serve at Jena.

The great artists were not purists particularly, except those — like Adam in Russia — who followed the troops and jotted down scenes that they witnessed. We have added some engravings which give a real idea of what the French looked like just after Jena.

CONCLUSIONS

For a long time, strategists and historians have tried to analyse the causes of this disastrous defeat for the Prussians, who were so proud of their army. The old age of the Prussian generals has been compared to the youth of the French, the out-of-date tactics à la Frederick the Great with the suppleness of the French. The role of the skirmishers has been brought up, etc.

In fact at Jena, Hohenlohe didn't think he was going to be attacked. Knowing that the King's army was going on towards Magdeburg, he should have recalled the Duke of Weimar and Rüchel urgently, and not allowed the troops to be dispersed so stupidly. Holtzendorff left alone, with no possible reinforcements; the

The Prussian garrison of Stettin surrendering before Lasalle's hussars, engraving after the painting by Lalauze. (Author's Collection).

Saxons left on the Schnecke, where they did nothing, falling back on Weimar instead of rejoining the King; all these elements were a recipe for disaster. He had been beaten piecemeal, where he easily had a numerical advantage.

At Auerstaedt, Brunswick wanted not to fight, but to pass the Unstrut River at Freyburg and Laucha, covering Kösen on his right. Doubtless, he thought Davout was too weak, and started to engage his troops piecemeal, in the middle of the congestion of his marching army. He didn't know how to seize the advantage gained by his vast numerical superiority and proceeded to deploy too slowly in areas of secondary importance. Moving up Wartensleben's Division on the right on to a plateau devoid of enemy, with an accumulation of cavalry behind, was unthinkable when Scharnhorst sorely needed reinforcements on the left. If Wartensleben's Division had attacked Hassenhausen, Davout would not have had any reserves. Then the unsupported charges by this elite cavalry against Morand's squares, like those in the morning against Gudin's, were not at all as effective as they could have been.

So the commanders made mistakes.

The soldiers fought as well as they could, but their only experience was on the parade grounds of Potsdam; whereas Napoleon's troops had done a lot of mileage, including the Revolutionary wars and Austerlitz. The King of Prussia himself said after Saalfeld: '*These troops have gained their experience in fifteen years of fighting*'. They were agile, good shots; they knew how to make a bayonet charge when necessary. They were real professionals and they loved their commanders who more often than not had come up from the ranks and file like them. They supported the Emperor fanatically and they knew that they could reach any rank by their own merit. Their morale was unequalled.

In 1806, the symbiosis between Napoleon's genius and the quality of his soldiers was at its zenith.

The Emperor remained a brilliant strategist and organiser but, made over-confident by his victories, he gradually wore this ideal army down. First of all, there was the Spanish mistake where his best regiments in the hands of jealous Maréchals, just melted away into the impossible terrain. Then there was the Russian mistake. It was a campaign carried out with predominantly foreign troops. It was an army of Babel with Germans from the Confederation, from Bavaria, Saxony, Westphalia, Baden, Würtemberg, and Eugène's Italian 4th Corps. With regiments from Croatia, Switzerland, Spain, Portugal and a Prussian and an Austrian corps. In this huge army, there were, at most, 100,000 French soldiers and even then, among the Middle and Young Guard, there were conscripts from the newly acquired departements such as Hamburg and Piemont.

Apart from the Guard, only one corps remained firm. Guess which one… Davout's. In the difficult fighting, it was always this corps which was used. At Valoutina, Gudin was killed, having been sent on in front by the other Maréchals. At Borodino, three divisions were taken off Davout to plug the gaps elsewhere. In front of the Great Redoubt, Eugène had Morand's and ex-Gudin's Divisions, now rechristened Gérard's. Ney earned his Prince's title by leading Friant's Division. How and where did he lose his Würtembergers on the way?

Napoleon thus lost so many veterans, either dead or retired from wounds or from old age. He no longer possessed the right tool for victory. He thought that his own genius would see him through. The 1813 conscripts no longer had the same enthusiasm as the veterans. The Maréchals were too tired and too rich, Bernadotte had betrayed him, Jomini also; Moreau was helping the Allies against his old rival and morale had changed sides.

True, morale had gone over to the young Prussians and Austrians who were out for revenge; their leaders now understood Napoleon's methods and applied them to their new armies. It was they who had the volunteers, and the more or less reluctant and inexperienced conscripts were for the French.

Napoleon had forgotten the human factor; he thought and said that '*in war, men are nothing, it is one man who is everything.*' He also said that he could lose 100,000 men a year. Even a good pilot has to have a good machine.

The time for enthusiasm had passed. The prestigious commander deployed his prodigious activity but the machine didn't react as well as it did before, and despite the odd epic convulsion, defeat loomed... There were too many of them arriving from all sides and Napoleon hadn't been able to give up his conquests, thereby leaving good troops unused in German strongpoints, not recalling the army in Spain.

War schools enjoy strategic studies but the principles are very simple and take but a few lines.

You need a unique leader of great quality.

You need motivated men. Good colonels make good regiments, by setting the example and handing down their experience. Guderian and Rommel were always there, out front, moving. They had learnt the lessons of the Grande Armée.

An army has to be mobile. The myth of fortifications is stupid; as a German historian once said: '*the history of fortifications is mixed up with the history of capitulation*', the Maginot Line, the Atlantic Wall, Dien Bien Phu, etc.

Giap with his untiring and fanatical soldiers, followed by the coolies trotting along the camouflaged tracks pushing their bicycles, knew the value of mobility. Facing him were soldiers bogged down in a network of outposts, sacrificed by stupid generals. To be able to hold, go around and surround, you have to be mobile, just like Napoleon showed us at Jena.

Above all, strategy is trained, motivated men with good leaders up-front, setting the example. The good commander has to fashion and maintain this beautiful tool he is going to use.

As Patton once said:

'*In a war, the secret of victory lies in that living spark, unpalpable but as bright as light: the Soul of the Warrior.*'

A WORD ON FRENCH MILITARY TERMINOLOGY

In the many biographical notices to be found in this book (especially pp. 55 to 82 and pp. 101 to 111), the following rules have been adopted.

TRANSLATION OF RANKS

In order to avoid confusion, the French officers rank of '*Chef de bataillon*' (foot troops) or '*Chef d'escadron*' (cavalry) has been translated as 'Battalion commander' or 'Squadron commander' respectively. For the Napoleonic period, this rank could not be translated as 'Major' (in English), as there existed also a rank of '*Major*' (in French) immediately above it. When the rank 'Major' is used in this book, it always refers to the original French rank above Battalion commander and below Colonel – cf. plate p. 23).

- '*Général de brigade*' has been translated merely as 'General', or in some cases as 'Brigadier General' (only in the biographical notices).

- '*Général de division*' has been always translated as 'Major General' in the biographical notices.

- '*Lieutenant général*' (in the Royal French Army) has been translated as 'Lieutenant General'. This rank did not exist in the Army of Napoleon.

- '*Maréchal*' has been retained in French or translated in English as 'Marshall'.

- '*Maréchal de camp*' (in the Royal French army) has been retained in French. This rank did not exist in the Army of Napoleon.

ABBREVIATIONS USED FOR ORDERS AND DECORATIONS

LH : Légion d'honneur (*chevalier de la*).
OLH : officier de la Légion d'honneur.
CtLH : commandant de la Légion d'honneur.
CrLH : commandeur de la Légion d'honneur (*it replaced the* 'commandant' *mentioned above, on the 17th February 1815*).
GdCxLH : grand-croix de la Légion d'honneur (*it replaced the* 'grand-cordon' *on the 21th June 1814*).
GdOLH : grand-officier de la Légion d'honneur.
CrSL : croix de Saint-Louis (*chevalier de la*).
GdCxSL : grand-croix de Saint-Louis.

SOURCES FOR THE UNIFORM PLATES

L'ARMÉE FRANÇAISE, SERIE OF PLATES IN FRENCH BY LUCIEN ROUSSELOT
Officiers généraux, plate 71
État-major, aides de camp, plate 81
Infanterie de ligne, plates 3, 17, 62 and 89
Infanterie légère, plates 5 and 33
Chasseurs à pied de la garde, plate 58
Cuirassiers, plates 37, 46, 91 and 102
Dragons, plates 7, 20, 25 and 96
Hussards, plates 9, 22 and 54
4e hussards, plate 82
Chasseurs à cheval, plates 11, 49 and 97
Artillerie à cheval 1804-1815, plate 36
Artillerie à pied, plates 28 and 66
Train des équipages, plate 90
Train d'artillerie, plate 55

LE PLUMET, SERIES OF PLATES IN FRENCH BY RIGO
Infanterie légère, 9e régiment 1804-1808, plate U7
Infanterie de ligne, sapeurs, plates 155 et 239
Infanterie de ligne, tambours et tambours-major du 88e de ligne,
plates 148 and 170
Le 4e hussards, plate U2
Le 8e hussards, plate U24
Le 3e hussards, plate U10
Le 1er hussards, plate U1
Le 9e hussards, plate U25
Artillerie à cheval, 4e régiment, plate U22

ARTICLES IN THE FRENCH SPECIALIZED PRESS
Le chasseur d'infanterie légère, Michel Pétard in *Uniformes* n° 49
Le grenadier à pied de la vieille garde, Michel Pétard in *Uniformes* n° 38

Les chasseurs à cheval, Rigo in *Uniformes* n° 36
Les hussards 1805-1815, Rigo, in *Uniformes* n° 34
Le canonnier à cheval, Michel Pétard in *Uniformes* n° 43
Les généraux du Premier Empire, Alain Pigeard in *Tradition* n° 121
Les officiers d'ordonnance de l'Empereur, Alain Pigeard in *Tradition* n° 99
L'infanterie légère sous le Premier Empire, Rigo in *Tradition* n° 90/91
Les musiques d'infanterie, Alain Pigeard in *Tradition* n° 123
Le chasseur à pied de la garde, M.Pétard in *Tradition* n° 90/91
Les cuirassiers, Rigo in *Tradition* n° 54/55
Les hussards, Rigo in *Tradition* n° 74 et 77
Les artilleurs à pied, Rigo in *Tradition* n° 78/79
La musique du 3e de ligne, Rigo in *Tradition* n° 1

SPECIALIZED BOOKS IN FRENCH AND IN ENGLISH
L'uniforme et les armes des soldats du Premier Empire, L. & F. Funcken, Casterman 1968
L'équipement militaire de 1600 à 1870, Michel Pétard, volumes IV et V
Les uniformes du Premier Empire, Tome sur l'Infanterie, Cdt Bucquoy, Grancher 1979
Guide à l'usage des artistes et costumiers, H. Malibran, reprint by Olmes 1972
Les coiffures de l'armée française, J. Margerand, Leroy 1911
La cavalerie légère du Premier Empire, Rigo et Michel Pétard, Histoire & Collections
Napoleon's soldiers in Otto manuscript, G.C. Dempsey, Arms & Armour Press
Napoleonic Uniforms, J.R. Elting, Macmillan Publishing
La cavalerie au temps des chevaux, colonel Dugué Mac Carthy, EPA.

Editing by Denis GANDILHON
Design and lay-out by François VAUVILLIER revisited by Denis GANDILHON
© *Histoire & Collections 2005*

ISBN: 2-915239-76-2
Publisher's number: 2-915239
First Print
© *Histoire & Collections 1998*

© *Histoire & Collections 2005*

A book from
HISTOIRE & COLLECTIONS
SA au capital de 182 938, 82 €
5, avenue de la République
F-75541 Paris Cédex 11, France
Telephone (33-1) 40 21 18 20
Fax (33-1) 47 00 51 11
www.histoireetcollections.fr

This book has been designed, typed,
laid-out and processed by
Histoire & Collections
and 'le Studio Graphique A & C'
on fully integrated computer equipment.
Color separation by the *Studio A & C*
Printed by ZURE, Spain,
European Union
November 2005